Managed Care
What It Is and How It Works

Wendy Knight
President
Knight Communications and Consulting
Vergennes, Vermont

AN ASPEN PUBLICATION®
Aspen Publishers, Inc.
Gaithersburg, Maryland
1998

This publication is designed to provide accurate and authoritative information in regard to the Subject Matter covered. It is sold with the understanding that the publisher is not engaged in rendering legal, accounting, or other professional service. If legal advice or other expert assistance is required, the service of a competent professional person should be sought. (From a Declaration of Principles jointly adopted by a Committee of the American Bar Association and a Committee of Publishers and Associations.)

Library of Congress Cataloging-in-Publication Data

Knight, Wendy.
Managed care: what it is and how it works / Wendy Knight.
p. cm.
Includes bibliographical references and index.
ISBN 0-8342-1089-4
1. Managed care plans (Medical care)—United States. I. Title.
RA413.5.U5K655   1998
362.1'04258'0973—dc21
98-35906
CIP

Orders: (800) 638-8437
Customer Service: (800) 234-1660

About Aspen Publishers • For more than 35 years, Aspen has been a leading professional publisher in a variety of disciplines. Aspen's vast information resources are available in both print and electronic formats. We are committed to providing the highest quality information available in the most appropriate format for our customers. Visit Aspen's Internet site for more information resources, directories, articles, and a searchable version of Aspen's full catalog, including the most recent publications: **http://www.aspenpublishers.com**
Aspen Publishers, Inc. • The hallmark of quality in publishing
Member of the worldwide Wolters Kluwer group.

Editorial Services: Kathy Litzenberg
Library of Congress Catalog Card Number: 98-35906
ISBN: 0-8342-1089-4

Printed in the United States of America

1 2 3 4 5

To Eben, with love

TABLE OF CONTENTS

PREFACE

Managed Care: What It Is and How It Works is an introductory book on managed care for professionals unfamiliar with managed care. These include managers and clinicians recently joining managed care firms; professionals in other health care organizations, such as pharmaceutical companies, hospitals, medical groups, and health information firms; and professionals in non-health industries that are increasingly interfacing with managed care companies, including computer software, information technology, and publishing firms. The book intends to give such professionals a broad overview of managed care without excessive detail.

Because the book offers the reader a comprehensive and concise summary of managed care, it is also a useful textbook for students in undergraduate, graduate, post-doctorate, and professional development programs, as well as corporate training programs. To facilitate an interactive learning process, exercises and discussion questions are included throughout the text.

Although this book is authored by a health care professional who has worked in the managed care industry, it is written from an objective, third-party perspective. As the title implies, the book gives the reader descriptive information on managed care, including its basic structures, concepts, and practices. Dispersed throughout these factual discussions are the various criticisms and acclamations of managed care.

The book begins with the history and evolution of managed care, followed by chapters that explain the participants, structures, and operations of managed care arrangements. Separate chapters describe in more detail plan and provider interaction, the role of the purchasers, utilization management processes, and quality improvement initiatives. The book concludes with a chapter on the regulatory and legal framework of managed care.

As managed care—in its various stages and iterations—continues to assume a prominent role in our evolving health care system, it will be crucial for today's professionals relating to the industry—as well as future professionals—to increase their understanding of managed care. *Managed Care: What It Is and How It Works* aims to impart this important basic knowledge to its readers.

ACKNOWLEDGMENTS

As with most "solo" ventures, there were many people who participated in this project. I thank Jeanne Keller, MS, ARM, president of Keller and Fuller, Inc., for contributing Chapters 5 and 8. Without her knowledge, enthusiasm, and dedication, I would not have been able to complete the book I had envisioned.

I thank my colleagues who critiqued drafts of the manuscript or offered valuable insights about the managed care industry. They include Tracy Bahl, United HealthCare; Lillian Grillo, United HealthCare; Roberta Holtzman, consultant; David Koury, MedPartners; Joe O'Hara, Empire Blue Cross and Blue Shield; Herb Schultz, American Association of Health Plans; Lynn Shapiro Snyder, Epstein, Becker & Green, P.C.; and Karl Wichser, Aetna/U.S. Healthcare. Five anonymous reviewers provided very useful feedback on the scope, content, balance, and organization of the book, for which I am truly thankful.

My friend and colleague, Donovan Andrews, accommodated my desire to incorporate humorous illustrations in the book. As always, Erin Carlson, from the American Association of Health Plans, was extremely helpful in my research and fact-finding efforts. Jack Bruggeman, Sandy Cannon, Kalen Conerly, and Kathy Litzenberg combined the right blend of patience, encouragement, and prodding throughout the project, facilitating my completion of the manuscript. Having survived a previous book publication, my associate, Cindy Ringer, performed like a true veteran, handling the many administrative details of the book-writing process.

Most important, I am grateful to Alex and Eben, who give my life meaning.

CHAPTER 1

The Evolution of Managed Care

All progress has resulted from people who took unpopular positions.

Adlai Stevenson (1900–1965)

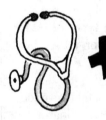 + =

Medicine   Business   Managed Care

Source: Drawings copyright © 1998, Donovan Andrews.

Learning Objectives

- Understand the factors influencing the development of initial managed care arrangements.
- Understand the obstacles facing early managed care pioneers.
- Understand the circumstances advancing the proliferation of managed care.
- Understand the characteristics of today's managed care market.

Key Terms

Health maintenance organization (HMO)—An entity that provides and manages the coverage of health services provided to plan members in return for a fixed, prepaid premium; the four types of HMO models are the group, independent practice association (IPA), network, and staff models.

Point-of-service (POS) plan—A managed care plan that provides flexibility for an enrollee to receive a service from a participating or non-participating provider, with corresponding benefit or "penalty" of co-pay depending upon the level of benefit selected, with the goal of encouraging the use of participating providers.

Prepaid medical care—Paying for medical care before services are rendered. Providers receive a set amount of money on a prospective basis to deliver prescribed health care services to certain individuals.

INTRODUCTION

The origins of managed care predate the passage of the HMO Act of 1973, a time we typically associate with the development of managed care. Managed care plans existed as early as the mid-1800s in the form of benevolent societies set up for working immigrants in urban and rural communities across the country. Plantation owners in Hawaii; lumber companies in Wisconsin, Michigan, and Washington; mining firms in

Minnesota and Pennsylvania; and railroad companies in the West recruited immigrants to work in these remote areas. To attract and retain workers, the companies set up health care arrangements that were precursors to managed care. Agreeing to provide medical care to their workers and families, these companies hired or contracted with local physicians, built hospitals and medical clinics, or contracted with local hospitals for a set number of beds.[1]

Contrary to today's managed care arrangements, the early examples were characterized by the voluntary participation of employers, workers, and physicians.[2] For the physician pioneers, involvement in prepaid medical care came with tremendous personal and professional sacrifice. Many were expelled from local medical societies and were threatened with license revocations. But they persevered because of a commitment to keeping patients healthy and an opportunity to start a practice in areas where few colleagues ventured.

ORIGINS OF PREPAID MEDICAL CARE

The group practice of medicine originated with the Mayo Clinic in the late 1880s.[3] However, the concept of prepaid medicine in group practices did not take hold until the industrial development of the 1920s and 1930s, perpetuated by railroad, lumber, and construction companies interested in attracting workers to remote areas of the West and Northwest. Fortunately, these practical and shrewd firms encountered entrepreneurial and gutsy physicians willing to accept prepayment for medical services provided to workers and dependents. There are numerous examples of early prepaid medical practices.

The Western Clinic in Tacoma, WA, was formed in 1916 as a traditional medical practice by two physicians, James Yocum, MD, and Thomas Curran, MD, who were interested in providing medical care to workers of the local mining and timber companies. Shortly thereafter, they entered into their first prepaid contract, agreeing to provide care to the local mill owners and their employees for a fixed monthly fee per worker. They also established a clinic in Seattle where they adopted the same practice approach. The King County Medical Society in Seattle refused to allow the physicians with Western Clinic admitting privileges at the hospitals where its members had privileges.[4]

Donald E. Ross, MD, a former railroad surgeon, and H. Clifford Loos, MD, of the Mayo Clinic, founded the first prepaid group practice in Los

Angeles, CA, in 1929. Originating as a traditional medical practice, the Ross-Loos Clinic began seeing patients on a prepaid basis when the water and power departments asked the clinic to provide medical coverage for the municipal workers for a set monthly price. Over the next two years, the Ross-Loos Clinic saw other municipal workers on a prepaid basis. Both physicians were eventually expelled from the Los Angeles County Medical Society because of its strong resistance to prepaid medicine. At the same time, the American Medical Association (AMA) issued a statement soundly opposing prepaid medical care.[5]

Michael Shadid, MD, a Syrian-born immigrant, perhaps can be considered the first trailblazer of managed care. His initial years of practicing in rural America left lasting impressions of poor people receiving inferior medical care, particularly deaths from unnecessary surgical procedures. In 1929, he embarked on a bold experiment—the first full-risk capitated contract. Seeing the financial ruin that illness could bring about during the Depression, he developed a concept that would protect people from such possibilities. In exchange for a $50 share per person to finance Community Hospital in Elk City, OK, Shadid promised that all medical care would be provided by the hospital and local physicians. In 1931, the Community Cooperative Hospital of Elk City was born. While supported by local residents, the physician–hospital cooperative met fierce opposition from the medical community. Shadid's membership in both the local and state medical societies was revoked and his fee-for-service colleagues threatened to revoke his medical license.[6]

Shadid traveled across the country championing the concept of prepaid group practice. At least two communities were influenced by his ideas and experiences in Oklahoma, Washington, DC, and Seattle, WA. The Home Owner's Loan Corporation in Washington, DC, organized a non-profit corporation, Group Health Association, in 1937, to provide prepaid medical care to mortgagees, since sizable medical expenses were a prime reason why people defaulted on their mortgages. Similar to other communities, the local medical society opposed the formation of Group Health Association, hampering Group Health's recruitment of physicians and restricting their access to hospitals; the insurance commissioner even prohibited the operation of Group Health. The protracted court battles that ensued garnered national publicity and the interest of other communities in prepaid group practice. Ultimately, the series of court rulings determined that prepaid group practice was not medical insurance and that the tactics of the local medical society constituted restraint of trade.[7]

In the 1930s, Sidney Garfield, MD, began his practice near the construction site of an aqueduct in Southern California. However, he saw few patients because the construction workers with serious injuries were sent to Los Angeles for treatment at the request of the insurance company. Garfield convinced Henry J. Kaiser and his son Edgar, the owners of the construction company, to pay him directly for certain medical care he would provide on-site to workers. Impressed by Garfield's boldness and ingenuity, the Kaisers later approached Garfield about starting a similar program for workers building the Grand Coullee Dam in Washington and for shipbuilders in the San Francisco Bay Area. The San Francisco project was important for two reasons: health care facilities were built and enrollment in the program was opened to the public.[8] This was the start of Kaiser Permanente.

The consumers who founded Group Health of Puget Sound in Seattle were inspired by a presentation Shadid made to the group in Renton, WA.[9] In 1945, 400 families agreed to contribute $100 each to form a medical clinic for their care. They subsequently bought assets of the Seattle Medical Securities Clinic (formerly the Western Clinic) and arranged for the physicians to deliver medical care. Once again, the local medical society opposed the formation of the cooperative and once again a legal fight developed: the prepaid practice was victorious. This particular court ruling outlined the rights of consumers in forming prepaid medical practices.[10]

Other Early Managed Care Arrangements

Traditional health insurance and the origins of the Blue Cross plans began in 1929 when Baylor Hospital in Texas agreed to provide hospital care to over 1,000 teachers for a set fee. The Depression created enormous financial uncertainty among individuals and institutions alike. Both the loss of income and high medical expenses associated with illnesses could cripple people financially. As hospitals could no longer rely on direct patient reimbursement, they needed a steady source of revenue. Agreeing to provide hospital care for teachers in exchange for paid premiums provided this.[11,12]

To compete with the success of prepaid practices, some physicians began to form foundations for medical care, where physicians practicing independently agreed to accept reimbursement according to a set fee schedule. Intrigued with the notion of prepaid medical care, labor organizations in the San Joaquin Valley attempted to establish a branch of Kaiser Permanente for their members. Rather than fight the idea through the court system, the local physicians responded by forming the San Joaquin Foundation for Medical Care, the first IPA-model HMO in the country.[13]

Southern California Edison developed the predecessor to the preferred provider organization (PPO) in 1934 when it contracted with local physicians, hospitals, and other health care professionals under a fixed fee arrangement to provide care to Southern California Edison workers.[14] While medical management techniques emerged in various settings during the 1970s, Blue Cross of Western Pennsylvania, in conjunction with the local medical and hospital societies, began to review hospital claims retrospectively in 1959 (after hospital care was rendered) to identify higher than normal hospitalizations.[15]

THE BIRTH OF HEALTH MAINTENANCE ORGANIZATIONS

A number of circumstances and perspectives converged in the late 1960s and early 1970s—including increasing distrust of physicians and hospitals, rising health care costs, and the realization that not all medical care was beneficial—that created the prospect for fundamental change in our nation's health care system. Discontentment on the part of consumers and some health care professionals prompted the government to review the merits and deficiencies of the system.

Fee-for-service medicine dominated the health care system of the 1950s and 1960s. Physicians treated patients and submitted bills to health insurance companies that paid them in full without regard to price or usefulness. Traditional health insurance shielded the patient and physician from understanding the true cost of medical care, creating incentives for physicians to perform more services and consumers to seek them. As a result, the cost of health care climbed.

After the enactment of Medicare and Medicaid in 1965, health care professionals received less money for treating the poor, elderly, and disabled patients covered under these programs. To compensate for lost income, many providers raised their private patient fees, further compounding the cost problem. By 1970, the annual growth of health care costs exceeded the overall Consumer Price Index (CPI).[16]

Physicians were becoming suspect in the eyes of consumers, seen as too greedy and self-interested. The number of malpractice suits increased. Many physicians were practicing without adequate information on the clinical efficacy of treatments. Public dissatisfaction with the American health care system was reflected in an editorial in a 1970 issue of *Fortune* magazine: "Much of U.S. medical care, particularly the everyday business of preventing and treating routine illnesses. . . .[is] inferior in quality, wastefully dispensed, and inequitably financed. [M]ost Americans are badly served by the obsolete, over-strained medical system. . . ."[17] The erosion of public trust in physicians and medical care was a decisive factor in the growth of managed care.

Paul Ellwood, MD

Paul Ellwood, MD, a pediatric neurologist and physiatrist from San Francisco, is widely acknowledged as the founding father of managed care as we know it today, particularly HMOs. In his role as executive director for the American Rehabilitation Institute in the 1960s and early 1970s, Ellwood saw that the existing fee-for-service system rewarded physicians only for treating illnesses, not for preventing or minimizing them. Dissatisfied by these inherent weaknesses in the traditional insurance system, and committed to the idea that physicians should be compensated to promote the health of their patients, he encouraged the federal government to embrace the prepaid medical practice approach that Kaiser and other groups were establishing across the country.[18] Hoping to avoid the negative connotations of the term "prepaid practice," he created the phrase "health maintenance organization."

In the early 1970s both Democrats and Republicans were jockeying to find a solution to the nation's health care crisis. As in recent legislative debates, the liberal politicians in Congress favored a government-run national health care system, while moderates and conservatives argued for a private-sector solution.[19] Ellwood's message was met favorably by key staff in the Nixon administration who were eager to adopt a formal health care policy and placate public concerns about growing health care costs and inferior care. Two key Nixon aides, Californians John Veneman and Lewis Butler, were well-acquainted with Kaiser Permanente and the San Joaquin Foundation for Medical Care and supportive of prepaid practice. Encouraged by these aides, Nixon embraced Ellwood's concept of health maintenance and in 1971, during his Health Message to Congress, he publicly supported HMOs, making them the cornerstone of his health policy platform.[20]

HMO Act of 1973

Pressured by the Nixon administration, Congress passed the HMO Act in 1973. The Act fostered the development of HMOs across the country by

- awarding two- and three-year grants and loans for the creation of HMOs
- superseding state laws restricting the formation of HMOs
- requiring employers to offer federally-qualified HMOs
- establishing a voluntary qualification process for HMOs

While federal certification was established as a voluntary process, there were many factors that motivated HMOs to pursue this option. First, government grants and loans were awarded to only federally-qualified HMOs. Second, by meeting the various standards outlined in the certification process, HMOs received a de facto "seal of approval" that the plan could point out to prospective clients and members. Another reason pertained to the requirement of employers to offer HMO options. The Act mandated employers with 25 or more employees already offering employees indemnity coverage to also offer at least two HMO options. This provision applied to only federally-qualified HMOs, however, as did the provision overriding restrictive state laws.[21]

When government funding for HMO development ended in 1980, $145 million had been spent on the creation and operation of HMOs and an additional $194 million in direct loans and loan guarantees had been given to HMOs.[22] At the same time, the private sector was investing millions into HMO development and expansion.

MANAGED CARE MATURES

By 1975, there were 183 HMOs, enrolling 6.85 million people; and close to 300 more HMOs were in developmental stages.[23] While HMOs were operational in 32 states, a disproportionate percentage of HMO membership was concentrated in California, particularly in Kaiser Foundation Health Plans. In 1978, nearly half of the country's HMO enrollment (3.5 million members) was in Kaiser plans. During this time, a few national networks of HMOs began to emerge, including those owned and operated by Kaiser, Prudential, Connecticut General (CIGNA), United HealthCare, Family Health Plan, and CNA Healthplans. While the six national HMOs represented a meager percentage of the total number of plans, they enrolled nearly half of the nation's HMO members, with Kaiser accounting for 94 percent of the total HMO enrollment.[24] The 1976 and 1978 Amendments to the HMO Act relaxed certain provisions, making it easier for HMOs to obtain federal qualification and increasing limits on funding for the initial development and operation of HMOs, further stimulating managed care growth.

Interest in managed care grew as the deficiencies of fee-for-service became more evident. By 1980, the inflation rate for health care was double that of the overall CPI, in part because of unchecked health costs associated with the fee-for-service payment mechanism of traditional insurance. Spiraling health care costs were prompting employers to seek out more cost-effective ways to provide health benefits to employees and their families. Employers began to encourage or require workers to join the offered managed care plans. At the same time, more people were becoming aware of the prevalence and danger of unnecessary medical care from which managed care claimed to offer protection. The 1982 President's Commission for the Study of Ethical Problems in Medical and Biological and Behavioral Research concluded that over one-third of high-tech hospital services were not necessary.[25]

HMOs experienced tremendous growth in the 1980s in terms of the number of HMOs and enrollees. The initial managed care experiences of employers demonstrated significant cost savings from previous indemnity plans, generating further interest in managed care programs. Also, network-model and IPA HMOs—which feature private-practice physicians— were becoming more widely available, making HMOs more attractive to a wider audience. From 1981 to 1985, the number of IPA-model HMOs doubled and the number of network-model HMOs quadrupled. During the mid-1980s, membership in HMOs grew by as much as 25 percent each year. In 1983, there were 323 HMOs in the United States enrolling 15 million people, and all but one of the nation's 38 major metropolitan areas was served by at least one HMO. By 1987, 662 HMOs enrolled over 29 million people and only two states were not served by an HMO.[26] Figure 1–1 illustrates the dramatic growth in HMO enrollment since 1980.

The public sector began to embrace managed care during the 1980s, as well. The Tax Equity and Fiscal Responsibility Act (TEFRA), passed in 1982, encouraged the enrollment of Medicare beneficiaries in HMOs by promoting the use of prospective risk contracts, which reflected the way HMOs were paid for commercial members. Arizona was the first state in the nation to enroll Medicaid recipients in managed care plans. Enrollment in Medicare risk contracts increased from 262,000 members in 1985 to 990,000 members in 1988. Additionally, the Omnibus Budget Reconciliation Act (OBRA) of 1981 afforded states more flexibility in contracting with HMOs for the Medicaid program, causing a rise in Medicaid HMO enrollment. From 1981 to 1986, the number of Medicaid recipients enrolled in HMOs increased from 187,000 to 802,000.[27]

The Results of Competition

The managed care market began to alter in the mid-to-late 1980s due to consumers' discontent with traditional HMOs. Consumers were express-

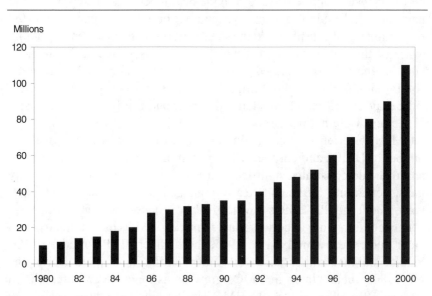

Figure 1–1 Historical and Projected HMO Enrollment, 1980–2000. *Source:* Reprinted with permission from *InterStudy Competitive Edge*, p. 31, © 1996, InterStudy.

ing dissatisfaction with the limited provider choices of staff- and group-model HMOs, which had historically dominated the market. As a result, HMOs began to develop hybrid products that incorporated broader physician networks and easier access to physicians. Twenty-three HMOs reported offering an "open-ended" product in 1987.[28] Today, roughly half of HMOs offer POS plans or open-ended HMOs, enrolling an additional 7.8 million people.

To compete with HMOs, insurance companies and other entities developed PPOs and hybrid HMO products that offered workers greater freedom to choose physicians for a slightly higher premium. By 1987, there were over 500 operational PPOs in the country, one-fifth of them based in California.[29] Specialty managed care programs (called "carve outs") spawned from competition for employer premiums dollars, as well.

Concurrently, to reduce administrative costs, employers sought to reduce the number of managed care organizations (MCOs) with which they contracted, but not at the expense of greater consumer choice. As a result, MCOs created multiple option products, affording workers a choice between two or more managed care plans from the same MCO. Typically, an MCO offers the employer an indemnity plan with a PPO option, an HMO, and a POS plan to replace all existing MCOs. Then employees select the plan most suitable to their personal needs.

To gain market share in highly competitive markets, MCOs have under-priced their products, setting prices below their costs. This price competition has reduced profit margins, weakening the financial stability of MCOs. Subsequently, stronger MCOs have been acquiring the less financially sound MCOs, while other MCOs have been merging. Such consolidations have resulted in fewer and larger MCOs, increasing their bargaining power with provider groups. Figure 1–2 shows the evolution of managed care models.

CURRENT MARKETPLACE

Managed care clearly dominates the current health care market. The American Association of Health Plans (AAHP), the national trade association representing managed care plans, estimates that there are over 153 million people enrolled in some type of managed care plan. On average, one in four Americans is enrolled in an HMO and millions more are enrolled in POS plans, PPOs, and other managed care products. According to KPMG

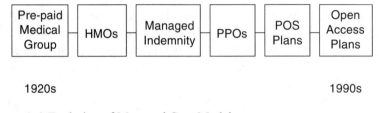

1920s   1990s

Figure 1–2 Evolution of Managed Care Models

Peat Marwick, an international consulting firm, 80 percent of employees with employer-based health coverage are enrolled in some type of managed care plan, compared to 29 percent in 1988 (Figure 1–3).

The continued proliferation of managed care is attributable to its own success, as well as the strong aversion to the alternative: a government-run,

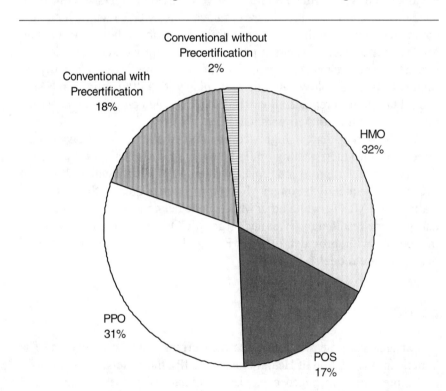

Figure 1–3 Managed Care Market Composition. Courtesy of KPMG Peat Marwick, LLP, Arlington, Virginia.

taxpayer-financed health care system. Managed care was thrust into the national spotlight during the early 1990s when the Clinton administration developed a health care bill seen by many as expanding the federal government's control and responsibility too much. Private-sector solutions were supported as the most efficient way to contain costs without stifling innovation or negatively impacting quality. Many proponents of managed care have pointed to the modest growth rate of health care as an example of its success. The annual growth of health care costs was just 2.5 percent from 1996 to 1997, up slightly from 2.1 percent the year before (Figure 1–4).

Despite its growing national presence, managed care is not consistent throughout the country, either in the structures and approaches of managed care firms or in how consumers, purchasers, and providers regard them. This is because managed care is market-driven, i.e., MCO business decisions are made based on the demands and preferences of its customers. As a result, the way MCOs structure their organizations, contract with and compensate providers, and develop and market their products varies substantially from region to region.

For example, an MCO may offer PPOs in rural areas relatively unfamiliar with managed care and HMOs in markets with higher managed care penetration. And a national MCO may operate an IPA-model HMO on the West Coast and a group-model in the Southeast to account for consumer preferences and provider organizational structures. In the West, HMOs are the dominant managed care plan. Sixty-four percent of enrollees in employer-sponsored plans are enrolled in HMOs or POS plans.[30] In the Northeast, POS plans are the favored managed care product, enrolling 38 percent of all health plan participants. Single-specialty networks created by groups of providers have emerged in the Northeast and Southeast as alternatives to traditional HMOs and PPOs and are growing steadily.

Intense price competition among MCOs has continued to curtail their profits. MCO operating (profit) margins have declined the past three years, in part because MCOs have kept their premiums artificially low to gain market share. (Operating margins reflect the percentage of the premium remaining after medical and administrative expenses.) Low profit margins also reflect the downswing of the underwriting cycle. In 1994, the industry-wide operating margin was 8 percent, followed by 7 percent in 1995, and 3 percent in 1996.[31] They are predicted to rise again after the three-year decline as MCOs begin to raise premiums.

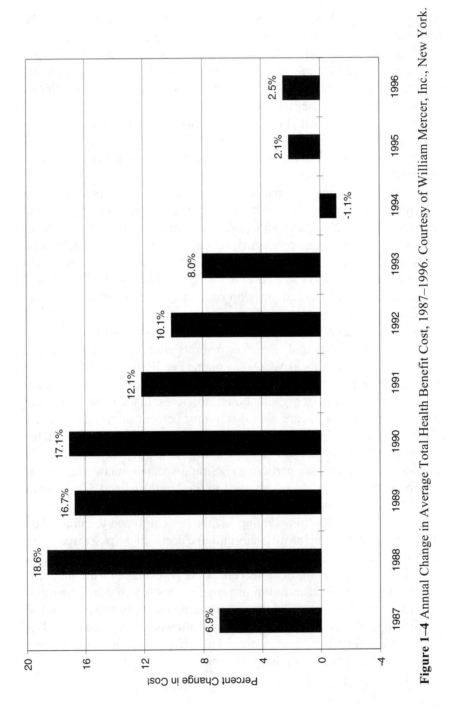

Figure 1–4 Annual Change in Average Total Health Benefit Cost, 1987–1996. Courtesy of William Mercer, Inc., New York.

CONCLUSION

Today's managed care market is characterized by constant transformation. To satisfy the ever-changing preferences and advancing sophistication of consumers, employers, and providers, MCOs are constantly developing innovative strategies and products. The managed care market will continue to evolve based on the demands of purchasers and consumers, and prompted by forward-thinking, entrepreneurial managed care executives. Just as progressive, risk-taking physicians, business leaders, and politicians fostered the development of early managed care arrangements, a new generation of professionals will lead the ever-transforming managed care market into the next century.

DISCUSSION QUESTIONS

1. What conditions existed that fostered the development of prepaid medical practices in the 1920s and 1930s?
2. Describe two early examples of prepaid medical care. What opportunities and challenges existed?
3. Describe the origins of Kaiser Permanente Health Plans.
4. What characteristics and developments of the 1960s and 1970s allowed HMOs to develop?
5. Why did the Nixon administration embrace Paul Ellwood's concept of "health maintenance"?
6. How did the HMO Act foster the development of HMOs?
7. What market conditions led to the emergence of hybrid managed care products in the 1980s?
8. What market changes did competition among MCOs generate in the 1980s and 1990s?
9. Why does managed care vary by region?
10. Describe some characteristics of the current managed care market.

REFERENCES

1. M. Friedman, "Capitation, Integration, and Managed Care," *Journal of the American Medical Association 275*, no. 12 (1996): 957.
2. Friedman, *Journal of the American Medical Association*, 961.
3. J. Nelson, "The History and Spirit of the HMO Movement," *HMO Practice 1*, no. 2 (1987): 75.

4. Friedman, *Journal of the American Medical Association,* 959.
5. T. Mayer and G. Mayer, "HMO Origins and Development," *The New England Journal of Medicine,* 28 February, 1985, 591.
6. Friedman, *Journal of the American Medical Association*, 959.
7. Mayer and Mayer, *The New England Journal of Medicine*, 591.
8. Mayer and Mayer, *The New England Journal of Medicine,* 592.
9. Friedman, *Journal of the American Medical Association,* 959.
10. Mayer and Mayer, *The New England Journal of Medicine,* 592.
11. Mayer and Mayer, *The New England Journal of Medicine,* 591.
12. P. Fox, "An Overview of Managed Care," in *The Managed Health Care Handbook*, 3d ed. (Gaithersburg, MD: Aspen Publishers, Inc., 1996), 4.
13. Mayer and Mayer, *The New England Journal of Medicine*, 593.
14. The Health Insurance Association of America, *Managed Care: A Health Strategy for Today and Tomorrow* (Washington, DC: 1993), 2.
15. Fox, *The Managed Health Care Handbook*, 8.
16. The Health Insurance Association of America, *The Fundamentals of Managed Care: Its History, Current Status, and Future* (Washington, DC: 1991), 4.
17. "It's Time to Operate," *Fortune*, January, 1970, 79.
18. Mayer and Mayer, *The New England Journal of Medicine,* 593.
19. M. Millenson, *Beyond the Managed Care Backlash: Medicine in the Information Age*, Health Priorities Project Policy Report No.1 (Washington, DC: Progressive Policy Institute, 1997), 6.
20. Mayer and Mayer, *The New England Journal of Medicine*, 593.
21. Friedman, *Journal of the American Medical Association,* 959.
22. Health Insurance Association of America, *Managed Care*, 3.
23. L. Gruber, M. Shadle, and C. Polich, "From Movement to Industry: The Growth of HMOs," *Health Affairs* 7.3 (Summer 1988), 198.
24. Gruber et al., *Health Affairs*, 200.
25. Millenson, *Beyond the Managed Care Backlash,* 6.
26. Mayer and Mayer, *The New England Journal of Medicine*, 594.
27. Gruber et al., *Health Affairs*, 203.
28. Gruber et al., *Health Affairs,* 206.
29. Gruber et al., *Health Affairs,* 206.
30. *The Mercer/Foster Higgins National Survey of Employer-Sponsored Health Plans* (New York, NY: Mercer/Foster Higgins, 1996), 27.
31. K. Abramowitz, "HMOs: Key Factors Crucial to Success," *Bernstein Research Weekly Notes*, November, 1996, Part II, 14.

SUGGESTED READING

Ellwood, P.M., Jr., "Health Maintenance Strategy," *Medical Care XI*, no. 3 (May/June, 1971).

CHAPTER 2

What Is Managed Care?

If there were only one truth, you couldn't paint a hundred canvases on the same theme.

Pablo Picasso (1881–1973)

"The new MSO handling the IPA in D.C. doesn't want to respond to the RFP for the POS contract because they might form a PSO that competes with our HMO, so I need your help ASAP, O.K.?"

Learning Objectives

- Understand the principal participants in managed care arrangements.
- Understand the basic models of managed care.
- Understand the different products and services offered by managed care organizations (MCOs).
- Understand how managed care differs from traditional insurance.

Key Terms

Gatekeeper—A physician who directs and coordinates the care of a member in a managed care plan. The gatekeeper is responsible for authorizing referrals to specialists and hospitalizations.

Member—An individual who is enrolled in or covered by a managed care plan.

Provider—A physician or other health care practitioner who delivers health care services to individuals in a managed care plan.

Provider-sponsored organization—A network of health care providers that forms for the purpose of contracting with purchasers and government entities to assume the risk of providing medical care to a group of individuals.

Purchaser—A public or private entity or organization that buys health coverage for workers, dependents, retirees, or other beneficiaries.

INTRODUCTION

Like beauty and truth, managed care has different connotations for different people, impeding all attempts to form its singular meaning. But as rational, thinking creatures, our impulse is to define in order to understand,

and so we search for concrete interpretations that perpetually elude us. Many see managed care as a response to a health care system that is expensive and fragmented, and not accountable for the medical care that is delivered. For others, managed care epitomizes shortsighted efforts to reduce health care costs with little regard to patients and physicians or the relationship between them.

An inherent assumption in managed care is that the right amount and type of health care is not always delivered by health care professionals who are sufficiently informed and in settings that are best suited to the patients or their medical conditions. Managed care attempts to rectify this by creating an organized system where care that is medically necessary is delivered by properly trained and educated health care professionals, in appropriate locations and facilities, and under practice guidelines that are likely to produce the best results for patients.

MCOs contract with individuals, employers, unions, and other purchasers to provide comprehensive health care services to people who enroll in the plan. This contract is known as the health insurance policy or subscriber agreement. The purchaser pays the MCO a fixed fee each month per individual or family. The enrolled individuals, who become known as "members" or "enrollees," may be responsible for paying all or a portion of the fixed fee, depending on whether they have purchased the policy themselves or whether it is offered by their employer or union as part of an employee benefits package. Based on employment or contractual arrangements with health care professionals, the MCO delivers or arranges for the delivery of health care services using various mechanisms to control the cost and use of health care services. Therefore, managed care is both a type of health insurance and a type of health care delivery system.

A variety of organizations offer managed care products to purchasers or incorporate managed care techniques into their existing insurance products. As the managed care industry evolves, the distinctions between the types of organizations offering managed care products and the products themselves are disappearing. Many health insurance companies offer limited traditional indemnity coverage and have re-engineered their business practices to focus exclusively on health maintenance organizations (HMOs) and other managed care products. To accommodate the evolving demands of customers for greater choice in providers, traditional staff models are developing point-of-service (POS) and administrative services only (ASO) plans that require traditional insurance experience, such as claims adjudication and financial management.

Managed care plans can be characterized by the following:

- arrangements with physicians, hospitals, and other health care professionals to provide a defined set of health care services to members
- criteria and processes for selecting and monitoring health care providers
- programs and systems to gather, monitor, and measure data on health services utilization, physician referral patterns, and other quality and performance measures
- incentives or requirements for members to use providers and procedures associated with the plan
- activities aimed at improving the health status of members
- incentives for providers to encourage the appropriate use of health care resources[1]

PRINCIPAL PARTICIPANTS

There are as many as five principal participants involved in any managed care arrangement: the MCO, the purchaser, the member, the health care professional, and sometimes, administrative organizations, such as a management services organization (MSO) or an independent practice association (IPA). In general, each has established roles and responsibilities, although the dynamics of the marketplace necessitate the convergence or exchange of some responsibilities. At an operational level, managed care is a series of contractual arrangements between the various participants that dictate the parties' interactions with each other. As with all contracts, there are numerous transactions, obligations, responsibilities, rights, and benefits between the parties.

Managed Care Organizations

According to the American Association of Health Plans (AAHP), MCOs are entities that offer an HMO, preferred provider organization (PPO), or POS plan, or any combination of these.[2] MCOs are organized in various ways. They can be owned by national managed care firms, physician groups, hospitals, commercial health insurers, Blue Cross and Blue Shield plans, community cooperatives, private investors, or other organizations. MCOs can be taxed as for-profit or non-profit entities and can serve clients nationally or in defined states or regions. They can operate as a single corporation or as a subsidiary of an insurance company or a third-party administrator. MCOs can offer comprehensive benefit packages or specific medical services, such as managed dental or vision care (also known as "carve outs"). By the end of 1995, there were an estimated 1,534 MCOs in the United States.

Originally, MCOs were structured as distinct entities with defining aspects, but as MCOs diversify and consolidate, the differences between managed care models are less pronounced. For example, many PPOs offer a gatekeeper product that requires members to select a primary care provider (PCP), a plan feature traditionally limited to HMOs. Even though the blurred distinctions of today's MCOs complicate the succinct description of managed care models, a summary of their basic similarities and differences is useful.

Health Maintenance Organizations

HMOs offer comprehensive health care services to members for a fixed monthly fee by contracting with or employing physicians, hospitals, and other health care professionals to provide medical care to enrollees. Half of the HMOs operating are owned by national managed care firms, and the remainder are divided among Blue Cross and Blue Shield and independent ownership. Roughly 10 to 12 percent of the nation's HMOs are owned by providers, including physician groups and hospitals. These provider-sponsored HMOs enroll more than five million people.

Historically, HMOs have differed from other managed care plans in many ways, including provider payments, benefits, and plan structure; however, as the market demands greater adaptability, HMOs are taking on characteristics of other managed care models. For example, HMOs have developed products with more flexibility for obtaining care from non-network providers. Although the differences between HMO models are fading, there remain four basic models.

1. Staff Model. Physicians and other health care providers are salaried employees and provide care exclusively to individuals enrolled in the HMO. Care is usually delivered at clinics owned by the HMO.

2. Group Model. The HMO contracts on an exclusive basis with a large physician practice to provide comprehensive benefits to the HMO's enrollees. While the HMO and the physician practice appear to be the same organization, they are distinct entities.
3. IPA Model. The HMO contracts with physicians or groups of independent physicians (known as IPAs) to provide care to HMO members in the physicians' own offices. These physicians are usually organized as solo practitioners or small group practices and see patients other than those enrolled in the HMO.
4. Network Model. The HMO contracts with several larger multi-specialty groups or IPAs, not individual physicians or small practices, who also see non-HMO members. An HMO that uses several contracting methods is often called a network-model HMO.

Preferred Provider Organizations

PPOs are networks of hospitals, physicians, and other health care professionals that provide medical care to individuals for a negotiated fee. PPOs are often sold as an option (also known as a rider) to a traditional insurance plan. In contrast with HMOs, PPOs do not assume the financial risk of arranging for health care benefits; risk is often assumed by the sponsoring organizations, such as an insurance company, third-party administrator, or self-insured employer. Consequently, PPOs do not perform many of the functions customary for HMOs and other risk-bearing MCOs, such as underwriting, utilization management, and quality assurance. Since the sponsoring organization determines what benefits are covered in the plan, PPOs are not in a position of making treatment decisions or denying claims; therefore, they have limited member service functions. Through a PPO, a sponsoring organization offers its beneficiaries access to a broad array of health care providers at discounted fees. Clients can also purchase utilization management services, such as case management and utilization review, as stand-alone products or as a compliment to the PPO network. While exact numbers on PPO enrollment are difficult to ascertain, the AAHP estimates that over 91 million people are covered through a PPO.

Provider-Sponsored Organizations

A provider-sponsored organization (PSO) is an MCO that is owned or controlled by health care providers. While many of the original HMOs were (and still are) provider-controlled, PSO is a recent term used to describe the emerging provider organizations that form for the purposes of directly contracting with purchasers to deliver care to beneficiaries. Unlike IPAs and other provider groups, PSOs are structured to assume the insurance risk of providing medical care to a set group of patients. As a result, many PSOs are licensed HMOs. PSOs are formed by IPAs, physician–hospital organizations (PHOs), integrated delivery systems (IDSs), and the like—sometimes as joint ventures with large provider organizations or MCOs.

Purchasers

Purchasers are employers, groups of employers, associations, unions, government agencies, and other entities that buy health coverage for their workers, dependents, retirees, or members. Health care benefits can be purchased directly by individuals (individual coverage) or by organizations on behalf of their employees or members (group coverage). The most common way people receive health coverage is from their own or a family members' workplace. According to KPMG Peat Marwick, a consulting firm, 148 million Americans and their families received health coverage through their place of employment.[3]

Group health coverage can be purchased by private firms (private-sector purchasers) or public agencies or programs (public-sector purchasers). Health coverage purchased on a fully-insured basis is when the MCO assumes financial risk for providing medical benefits outlined in the subscriber agreement by accepting the defined premiums per individual or family in exchange for providing care. When the purchaser reimburses the MCO for the direct medical costs incurred by workers and pays the plan a fee for handling the administrative duties of the contract, it is called self-insured coverage. Some of these self-insured employers (or groups of employers) develop their own managed care programs. Rather than purchase a managed care product from an existing MCO, they elect to create their own plan based on fundamental managed care features, such as a network of physicians and utilization management controls. These employers or coalitions may retain a benefits consulting firm or create an in-house unit to establish and manage the plan.

A purchaser may contract with several MCOs and administrative organizations to provide health benefits to its workers. Most large employers contract with numerous MCOs; small employers tend to offer fewer choices. Employers may "carve out" specific health benefits, such as treatment for mental health and substance abuse, or may use a company separate from the MCO to perform the utilization review functions. Since most HMOs and POS plans perform their own utilization review, the purchaser is more likely to use an outside utilization review organization (URO) in conjunction with an indemnity plan or a PPO.

Members

Members are individuals who are enrolled in the MCO. They are also referred to as enrollees, subscribers, or eligibles. They can be employees, dependents, or retirees of employers who have purchased health coverage from the plan; beneficiaries of government-financed programs, like Medicare or Medicaid; or individuals who have purchased health care themselves or through a membership association. The purchaser determines which individuals are eligible to receive health coverage and what benefits are covered or excluded. For example, not all employers elect to cover dependents or pay for certain medical services, like birth control pills.

Health Care Professionals and Facilities

MCOs structure relationships with health care professionals and facilities in various ways, including hiring physicians, purchasing hospitals, contracting with providers, or entering into strategic alliances with large provider groups. Depending on the organizational model of the MCO, health professionals can be employees of the plan (staff-model HMOs) or contracted workers (IPA-model HMOs and PPOs). Usually only IDSs and staff-model HMOs own hospitals and other facilities. The type of managed care product a plan offers will influence the number and types of providers with which it contracts (see Chapter 4 for a more detailed discussion).

Physicians

Private-practice physicians and other health care professionals work in various settings: solo practices, small group practices, multi-specialty medical groups or clinics, and hospital-based practices. The vast majority of physicians operate in solo or small practices. According to the American Medical Association (AMA), half of the nonfederal physicians were in group practices of two to eight physicians and another 40 percent were in solo practice.[4] For the purposes of contracting with MCOs, physicians also affiliate or contract with IPAs, single-specialty networks, and other provider organizations (see Chapter 4 for a more detailed discussion). The percentage of physicians participating in managed care contracts has grown steadily. In 1996, 88 percent of physicians had at least one managed care contract, up from 61 percent in 1990 (Table 2–1).

In light of managed care's emphasis on primary and preventive care, PCPs are the backbone of many managed care plans. PCPs are valued because of their ability to diagnosis and treat a broad range of medical conditions. Additionally, because they are familiar with all the health care conditions and circumstances of their patients, PCPs are often better able than specialists to ascertain what type of specialty care a member might need. This is one reason some MCOs require members to select a personal physician (known as a gatekeeper) to manage and coordinate care. By keeping track of the treatments patients receive from multiple providers, the PCP ensures that duplicate, contradictory, or unnecessary care is not provided and that routine care is not overlooked.

Primary care specialties include internal medicine, pediatrics, family practice, and general practice. In response to growing consumer and employer requests, more gatekeeper-model MCOs are allowing female enrollees to select obstetricians and gynecologists (OB/GYNs) as their PCPs. Aside from OB/GYNs, most MCOs frown upon specialists functioning as PCPs. Therefore, PCPs with subspecialties are often not permit-

---

Table 2–1 Proportion of Physicians with Managed Care Contract

	1990	1991	1992	1993	1994	1995	1996
IPA	19	20	21	27	32	39	50
HMO	36	37	42	49	55	64	72
PPO	49	54	58	66	64	69	75
Any managed care contract	61	65	70	76	77	83	88

Source: Reprinted with permission from *Socioeconomic Characteristics of Medical Practice*, American Medical Association, copyright © 1996.

ted to participate as specialty care providers. Exceptions are made, of course, in markets where there are few providers or the demand exceeds the supply for certain specialties.

To deliver comprehensive health care benefits to members, MCOs contract with an array of specialists, including those in the following specialties:

- cardiology
- cardiovascular surgery
- dermatology
- ear, nose, and throat (ENT)
- gastroenterology
- general surgery
- nephrology
- neurology
- OB/GYN
- oncology/hematology
- orthopedics
- plastic surgery
- urology

While PCPs continue to play an essential role in a managed care plan, MCOs are recognizing the value of the specialists' expertise and experience in caring for specific patients. For example, some MCOs are discovering that patients suffering from moderate-to-severe asthma respond better when treated by an allergist rather than a PCP, so they are reconfiguring how care is delivered to asthmatics and making the specialist the primary care manager. Oxford Health Plans has created specialty-led health care teams for asthma and other medical conditions.

In better understanding asthma and other chronic diseases, including what treatments work best and at what stage certain clinical interventions should be used, some MCOs are creating specialty-based advisory panels. Sharing their collective years of clinical expertise, these panels of specialists assist MCOs in assessing the adequacy of care delivered, developing practice guidelines, and implementing other clinical and administrative changes that improve the care for patients with chronic conditions.

Independent Practice Associations

An IPA is a group of physicians who form a legal entity to deliver medical care through contractual arrangements with MCOs or purchasers, usually on a capitated basis. Physicians are generally required to contribute dues or in-kind donations as a condition of participation in the IPA, or are offered stock in the IPA and become its shareholders. Hospitals are involved in the development of many IPAs and provide initial capital for start-up expenses, donate office space, and make financial loans. Like any corporation, an IPA will create a board of directors and various committees to oversee the operations of the organization.

According to the AMA, 39 percent of physicians had a contract with an IPA in 1995.[5] In markets where IPAs are the dominant physician structure, like California and other parts of the West, IPAs yield great power and influence in managed care arrangements. In these markets, managed care firms contract with IPAs under exclusive capitated arrangements, not directly with physicians, and therefore, interact mostly with the IPA on contract negotiations, implementation of plan policies and procedures, and other administrative matters.

Hospitals and Health Systems

MCOs contract with community hospitals, tertiary care facilities, teaching hospitals, academic health centers, and health systems, depending on availability and market needs. As with MCOs, hospitals are structured as for-profit or non-profit entities and can be owned by local or state governments, religious organizations, national corporations, academic health centers, or private investors. The number of hospitals participating in managed care networks is increasing. In 1996, 58 percent of the 5,134 community hospitals in the United States had a contract with an HMO, and 68 percent had a contract with a PPO, up from 49.6 percent and 60.6 percent respectively in 1994, according to hospital statistics compiled by the American Hospital Association.

Just as physicians are creating larger organizations to increase their negotiating power relative to managed care firms, many hospitals are forming PHOs, MSOs, and other joint ventures with physicians to gain better leverage with managed care plans.

Integrated Delivery Systems

IDSs are groups of hospitals, physicians, and other health care professionals and facilities that provide the full spectrum of health care services under one legal structure. Because of their ability to assume risk directly from the purchaser, IDSs can function both as a participating provider in a managed care network or as a direct competitor of plans. In fact, many IDSs that are formed by academic medical centers or larger hospital systems, such as Tufts Associated Health Plan, have obtained HMO licenses to compete directly with other managed care plans. IDSs tend to own the hospitals and facilities in the system and employ the affiliated physicians, although some IDSs are joint ventures created to gain greater leverage in highly-penetrated managed care markets.

Physician–Hospital Organizations

A PHO is a legal entity formed by a hospital and physicians to contract with managed care plans and employers. PHOs are composed of one or more hospitals and their medical staff, and other community physicians and health care professionals who become members or shareholders of the PHO. The majority of PHOs are separate business entities, not hospital divisions.

The PHO assumes responsibility for the contracting, administrative, and marketing functions of its members. PHOs enter into full- or partial-risk arrangements with MCOs. Most PHOs were formed by hospitals in response to the growing dominance of managed care plans in their market and are still perceived as hospital-controlled, even though the majority of them have equitable hospital and physician ownership and board representation. In 1995, 67 percent of PHOs surveyed indicated that they were equally owned by physicians and hospitals.[6]

Other Health Professionals and Facilities

To offer a full complement of medical care to members, MCOs contract with many ancillary providers including physical, occupational, and speech therapists; podiatrists; radiologists; anesthesiologists; pathologists; chiropractors; and complementary medicine providers, like acupuncturists and massage therapists. Other facilities and organizations that are part of managed care networks include

- sub-acute care facilities
- rehabilitation centers
- outpatient surgical centers
- ambulatory care centers
- skilled nursing facilities
- home health care agencies
- outpatient substance abuse facilities
- diagnostic imaging centers
- ambulance companies

Administrative Organizations

Rather than provide all of the administrative functions necessary to deliver patient care, some MCOs and provider groups work in conjunction with third-party administrators (TPAs), UROs, and other administrative organizations and intermediaries.

Third-Party Administrators

Typically, a TPA provides claims processing, enrollment, and other administrative functions for self-funded employers, PPOs, and small or emerging MCOs. Some TPAs assume broader responsibilities, such as utilization review, actuarial analysis, and network development. Most do not assume insurance risk, however.

Utilization Review Organizations

A URO (also known as a utilization management organization) is a separate organization that performs utilization review services for MCOs or self-funded groups. UROs can be independently owned or wholly-owned subsidiaries of insurance companies. Some UROs offer services beyond medical reviews of hospital claims, such as case management and disease management.

Preferred Provider Organization Intermediaries

PPO intermediaries negotiate and manage managed care contracts on behalf of individual physicians. These organizations can represent a handful or numerous providers, in multiple or single specialties, and in wide or confined geographic areas. They also vary in their scope of services offered. Some PPO intermediaries assume all responsibility for building and managing PPO networks, in turn leasing them to insurance companies or self-funded employers. Others contract on behalf of a small group of physicians within a single county.

Management Services Organizations

MSOs provide contracting and administrative services for provider organizations, usually those under full-risk arrangements with MCOs. Such services range from handling the finances of the group to managing all aspects of the practice. MSOs can be wholly-owned subsidiaries of hospitals, joint ventures between physicians and hospitals, or physician-owned. Physicians can maintain their own practices and contract with the MSO to provide administrative support or can sell their practices to the MSO. Depending on the structure of the MSO and state laws, the MCO may contract directly with physicians and hospitals represented by the MSO or with the MSO.[7,8]

Physician Practice Management Companies

Like MSOs, physician practice management companies (PPMCs) provide administrative support to providers, including billing, contracting, and practice management; however, PPMCs usually limit their services to physicians. PPMCs can own or manage physician practices, medical groups, or IPAs in a broad range of specialties (multi-specialty) or within one specialty (single specialty), like cardiology. Relationships between PPMCs and physicians vary. Some PPMCs buy physician practices or a sizable portion of the practices' assets and sign multi-year contracts with the physicians to provide care. Other PPMCs offer physicians equity and a governance role in the PPMC.[9]

MANAGED CARE PRODUCTS

Managed care products are the different programs that MCOs market and sell to purchasers. Traditionally, the organizational structures and products of managed care were used interchangeably since the product sold reflected its sponsoring organization, i.e., HMOs only sold HMO products. However, since market forces have fostered flexibility and innovation, MCOs of all types offer different managed care products and services.

Plan design, utilization management controls, breadth of provider networks, rating methodologies, and populations covered are characteristics that define managed care products. For example, plans that contract with the federal government to cover Medicare beneficiaries will create a Medicare risk product, and plans that offer an HMO to self-insured employers will create a self-funded or ASO product. Table 2–2 compares the different managed care products.

Closed-Panel HMO

A closed-panel HMO refers to the traditional HMO that does not provide members with financial coverage when they use non-panel providers or when they seek care directly from network specialists. HMOs require members to select a PCP who will coordinate and oversee any necessary specialty care and to obtain authorizations before obtaining diagnostic or hospital care. In a traditional HMO, the member pays a small co-payment for office visits, usually $5 to $15. While the majority of HMOs cover hospitalizations and other services in full, one-third of HMOs now require a co-payment or deductible for these services.

Since individuals enroll in HMOs, these plans have defined populations to whom they are responsible for providing care. As a result, they usually have tighter utilization management controls and a more rigorous selection process for providers than PPOs.

Exclusive Provider Organization

The exclusive provider organization (EPO) is a closed-panel product similar to an HMO in that it does not provide coverage for enrollees who

Table 2–2 Managed Care Product Comparisons

	Role of PCP	Patient Cost Sharing	Access to Specialists	Out-of-Network Coverage
Closed-panel HMO	Member required to select a PCP; PCP functions as a gatekeeper, managing and coordinating care and authorizing visits to specialists	Minimal co-payment for office visit; 100% hospital coverage	Must have referral from PCP for coverage	No
EPO	Member not required to select a PCP; PCP does not function as a gatekeeper	Minimal co-payment for office visit; 100% hospital coverage	Permits direct access to network providers	No
Open-access HMO	Member required to select a PCP; PCP functions as a gatekeeper, managing and coordinating care and authorizing visits to specialists	Higher co-payment when self-referring to a specialist	Permits self-referral to network specialists with higher co-payment	No
POS plan	Member required to select a PCP; PCP functions as a gatekeeper, managing and coordinating	Minimal co-payment for in-network care; higher co-payment and deductible for out-of-	Must have referral from PCP for in-network coverage; permits direct access to	Yes

continues

Table 2–2 continued

	Role of PCP	Patient Cost Sharing	Access to Specialists	Out-of-Network Coverage
	care and authorizing visits for in-network coverage	network coverage	network providers with higher co-payment	
Open-access HMO	Member not required to select a PCP; PCP does not function as a gatekeeper	Minimal co-payment in network; coinsurance and deductible for out-of-network coverage	Permits direct access to network providers	Yes

seek treatment from non-affiliated health care professionals. Like a PPO, an EPO offers members access to all affiliated health care professionals without first seeing, or receiving authorization from, a PCP. Many EPOs are sponsored by employers or managed by independently owned PPOs.

Open-Access HMO

For an additional co-payment, open-access plans allow members to see specialists in the provider network without seeing their PCP first. The self-referral option can be exercised at the time the member seeks medical treatment. Unlike POS plans, open-access HMOs do not provide members with coverage if they elect to receive care from providers not in the HMO network.

Open-access plans were developed in response to HMO member dissatisfaction with the ability to access care, specifically the role of the PCP and plan in limiting or delaying access to specialty care. These products give the member flexibility to see specialists directly, while enabling the plan to manage the care since the access is to physicians within the network.

Point-of-Service Plan

POS plans are the fasted growing managed care model. Over 60 percent of all HMOs offer a POS product.[10] POS plans include features of HMOs and indemnity insurance. The "in-network" component of the POS plan is similar to an HMO, where the member has greater coverage when using network providers in accordance with the plan's utilization management protocols. The member selects a PCP who authorizes and coordinates all necessary medical care the member receives within the network. To encourage members to use network providers rather than non-network providers, the plan charges members a minimal co-payment for in-network office visits. In-network hospitalizations are generally covered in full, although some plans may include a deductible or co-insurance for certain services where utilization has been particularly high.

Unlike an HMO member, the member in a POS plan has coverage when seeking medical care from non-network providers or when being seen by a specialist without a referral from the PCP, but at less coverage. The out-of-network feature of the POS plan functions like a traditional insurance plan. The member must pay a portion of the medical expenses before coverage begins. The "deductible," as it is called, ranges from $100 to $300 per individual or $300 to $1,000 per family. After the deductible is satisfied, the member will pay a co-insurance, or percentage of each bill. This is usually 20 to 30 percent, but can be higher for certain services like treatment for mental health and substance abuse.

POS plans are also called open-ended HMOs, POS HMOs, or gatekeeper PPOs. A gatekeeper PPO may differ slightly from a POS plan offered by an HMO in its utilization management and quality assurance requirements since these managed care processes tend to reflect those of its sponsoring organization.

Open-Access PPO

An open-access PPO is the conventional benefit design of a PPO. Members have health coverage when using network and non-network providers. They usually are responsible for a co-payment when obtaining care from a participating provider and a deductible and co-insurance if seeing providers outside the network. Under an open-access PPO, members do not need to see or receive authorization from a PCP prior to seeking specialty care (hence, the term open-access). However, they may need to contact the MCO for prior authorization of hospital or diagnostic treatment.

Unlike individuals in HMOs, individuals enrolled in a PPO have coverage when they seek care from health care providers not affiliated with the network or when they see a specialist directly without obtaining a referral from their PCP (also known as "self-referring"). People enrolled in PPOs are not required to select a PCP or obtain authorization to receive specialty care when using the in-network feature of the plan, except for those enrolled in gatekeeper PPOs.

Specialty Carve Out

Unlike their traditional counterparts, specialty carve outs (also called specialty or single-service networks) offer specialized health care services to enrollees. Specialty networks can be purchased as a supplement to a comprehensive plan that does not provide these specific services or as a separate or "stand-alone" product. Prescription drugs and dental, mental health, substance abuse, and vision care are often packaged and marketed as specialty HMOs or PPOs. In recent years, a greater array of health care services is being organized and marketed as specialty networks, particularly those centered on specific specialties, like cardiology and radiology, and those involving a subset of services, such as complementary medicine.

Centers of Excellence

Several MCOs have developed "centers of excellence," or networks of tertiary care facilities that provide very specialized and complex medical procedures, such as organ transplants or cancer therapies. The MCO will contract with a select number of facilities throughout the country to perform a majority of the specialized treatments needed by members. Medical centers and hospitals chosen for participation in the network are generally regarded as among the best facilities in the country, if not the world, for that particular treatment. In addition to reputation, MCOs select facilities based on patient health outcomes, experience in performing the procedure, affiliated physicians, location, and cost.

A centers of excellence network gives the member with a catastrophic or terminal illness convenient and personalized access to highly specialized treatment centers. The managed care plan usually covers all expenses related to the treatment, including physician visits before and after the treatment; travel and lodging expenses during the treatment; and rehabilitation, home care, and other follow-up care.

Other Products and Services

MCOs and other organizations have developed a variety of managed care products and services to address the unique needs of particular market segments. For example, traditional health insurance companies entered the managed care market by purchasing or creating PPOs and offering indemnity products with medical management features (called "managed indemnity") for clients not interested in the emerging forms of prepaid medical care. To capitalize on the strong interest in managed care techniques, many companies have created a continuum of utilization management services, such as utilization review, case management, and disease management, as well as distinct products such as managed workers' compensation programs and alternative care networks.

Exercise: You are a human resources manager at a mid-size construction company in New Jersey, and you are responsible for recommending health benefit options to the president. You are asked to make an oral presentation to the executive committee on managed care products and which one(s) might be best suited to the employees in the firm. Make any assumptions about the firm that you wish in your presentation.

MANAGED CARE VERSUS TRADITIONAL INSURANCE

To understand the essence of managed care, it is often useful to contrast it to traditional insurance programs. Although this may seem meaningless given the permeation of managed care features into most traditional insurance plans, such a comparison engenders a good comprehension of managed care.

From a financial perspective, health care is a transaction between two or more parties involving a medical treatment: one who seeks it (patient), one who provides it (health care professional), and one who pays for it (insurer and employer). Sometimes more than one role is occupied by the same entity or individual. For example, the person who pays for a medical procedure on his or her own is seeking and paying for medical care. Other times, multiple organizations will fulfill a single role, as with the employer and insurer who share the cost of health coverage.

Managed care introduces a new role to the equation: one who arranges for medical care. Network-based MCOs will arrange for health care professionals to deliver medical care within certain cost and utilization parameters. Some MCOs employ health care professionals to provide care, as well. As such, managed care plans are positioned to provide, arrange, and pay for medical care, depending on their organizational structure. Traditional health insurance companies, on the other hand, only pay for the health care services incurred by individuals.

Total Patient Health

A managed care system differs from traditional indemnity insurance in many ways, most significantly in how it regards the individuals for whom it is contractually obligated to provide medical care. Unlike indemnity insurance policies that pay the medical bills of patients who develop particular illness or medical conditions, a managed care plan has responsibility for providing the full spectrum of medical care to individuals enrolled in the plan. This includes medical services that

- keep patients in good health (e.g., annual physical exams)
- detect illnesses or conditions (e.g., cancer screenings)
- treat acute illnesses (e.g., hospitalizations, surgical procedures)
- minimize complications from chronic ailments (e.g., home care, medical equipment)

Managed care, then, regards each individual as a total patient and not the sum of individual body parts that need repair on occasion. This perspective is fundamentally different from that of traditional insurers, which take no ownership for a person's health status. By agreeing to provide a broad range of health care services to an enrollee for a fixed fee, a managed care plan, one could argue, has implicitly accepted the challenge to keep that person healthy. Conversely, one can assert (as many opponents of managed care do) that accepting a fixed fee for a patient encourages MCOs to enroll only the healthiest individuals and to deny necessary medical care to members to keep costs down.

A managed care plan will provide a continuum of care adapted to the particular health needs of patients and designed to maintain or improve patient health. Such an approach necessitates processes and functions not required in traditional insurance plans, including health education literature, wellness programs, and disease management programs.

Benefit Coverage

Generally, traditional insurance plans cover basic medical and surgical procedures and hospitalizations, while MCOs cover the full range of health care services, including preventive care services, physician visits, hospitalizations, home care, and various outpatient treatments and services. There is usually greater patient cost sharing in traditional plans in the form of higher co-insurance amounts. MCOs require deductibles and co-insurance for certain procedures or products, particularly those with high utilization. The majority of them charge patients a small fee per visit, or co-payment, for most services.

Access to Health Professionals

The most common way people differentiate managed care from traditional insurance is the mechanism for seeing health care professionals. Managed care plans create "networks" of health care professionals they direct members to use. Complete or maximum payment for medical services is predicated on the member using these providers. Depending on the type of managed care product, the plan may require the member to see his or her designated PCP (also called a gatekeeper) to obtain authorization from the plan before receiving specialty care. With many MCOs, the member typically needs to receive authorization for hospitalizations, outpatient procedures, and diagnostic services. The frequency of services or treatments may be limited to a certain number of visits or days. While most traditional insurance plans have incorporated medical management techniques of managed care (e.g., pre-certification for hospitalizations), they usually allow unrestricted access to specialty care providers.

Provider Payment

In a traditional insurance arrangement, health care professionals are paid a certain fee for each procedure they perform, i.e., fee-for-service. This fee-for-service payment mechanism creates incentives for physicians to perform services for financial gain, not necessarily because the procedures may be effective or appropriate in treating a patient. As a result, total health care expenditures continue to escalate without a clear sense of improved patient care. The payment policies of managed care plans are designed to make providers more accountable for the services they perform. This is done by limiting the frequency of unnecessary medical procedures, reducing the per unit cost of services, compensating physicians for total treatments or cases, or prepaying physicians for the partial or total medical care of a patient, i.e., capitation. While capitation is not the only way MCOs pay physicians, it is the one payment mechanism that is most closely associated with managed care, particularly managed care's negative attributes. Many insist that capitation payment systems encourage physicians to withhold necessary medical care solely for profit and to eschew patients who consume greater health care resources.

Population-Based Health Management

Because individuals are enrolled in the managed care plan, MCOs have the opportunity to understand the unique medical experiences of each patient. Using computers and other information systems, MCOs can collect patient information from medical records, claims, enrollment data, patient surveys, and other sources to develop programs to treat and manage patient care. Such information includes past and current medical conditions and illnesses, historical use of specific health care services, and lifestyle behaviors that affect the health of individual patients and within specific categories, such as gender and age. The collection and analysis of this information enables the MCOs to first identify the prevalent risk factors and incidence of diseases among their membership and then to develop target programs to best care for their membership. Population-based health care management, as this is called, is an element of health care management unique to managed care, although such initiatives are still in their infancy.

Exhibit 2–1 identifies the principal differences between managed care and traditional insurance programs.

Exhibit 2–1 Managed Care versus Traditional Insurance

Managed Care	Traditional Insurance
• Network of credentialed health care professionals provide care	• Any health care professional provides care
• Restricted access to speciality providers	• Unlimited access to specialty providers
• Coverage for primary and preventive care	• Coverage for acute illness or injury only
• PCP usually designated to manage and coordinate all patient care	• Multiple providers deliver care without knowledge of total patient health
• Extensive relationship with providers, giving them practice management tools and incentives to manage care	• Relationship limited to reimbursing providers for care rendered
• Financial controls of care	• Limited financial controls of care
• Programs to encourage patients to maintain good health	• No health promotion programs
• Tracking and analysis of data on costs, utilization, and quality	• Collection of claims data only
• Some transfer of risk to providers	• Assumption of all financial risk
• Prospective review of treatment	• Retrospective audit of claims

> **Exercise: Describe other ways managed care differs from traditional insurance programs based on what you've read or heard or from personal experiences.**

CONCLUSION

It is difficult to define managed care given its continuous modification and contradictory perceptions of it. Because managed care is shaped by fluid market forces, its structure and focus change frequently and swiftly, sometimes faster than one can absorb. Such rapid mutations do not permit easy comprehension. Moreover, the various perceptions of managed care mold the understanding of it among its key audiences. Consequently, clear definitions of managed care are elusive and are outdated almost as soon as they are formulated. Continuous change in the managed care market is inevitable as purchasers, consumers, providers, and others grapple with how best to deliver quality health care with finite economic resources.

DISCUSSION QUESTIONS

1. Who are the five principal participants in a managed care arrangement?
2. How does an HMO differ from a PPO?
3. Describe the four basic HMO models.
4. What is the difference between fully-insured and self-insured health coverage?
5. Why are PCPs valued in managed care plans?
6. Describe two types of provider organizations, including their similarities and differences.
7. How does a PPMC differ from an MSO?
8. What are some features that define a managed care product?
9. How does an open-access HMO differ from a POS plan?
10. Describe two primary ways in which MCOs and traditional insurance programs differ.

REFERENCES

1. W. Knight, "Understanding Managed Care Contracting," in *Managed Care Contracting* (Gaithersburg, MD: Aspen Publishers, Inc., 1997), 2–3.
2. American Association of Health Plans, *National Directory of MCOs and Utilization Organization Review* (Washington, DC: 1997), i.
3. KPMG Peat Marwick, LLP, *Health Benefits in 1997 Executive Summary* (Newark, NJ: 1997), 2.
4. American Medical Association, *Physician Marketplace Statistics* (Chicago: 1996), 170.
5. American Medical Association, *Socioeconomic Characteristics of Medical Practice* (Chicago: 1996), 16.
6. American Association of Physician–Hospital Organizations/Integrated Delivery Systems, Inc. and Tyler Company, *1995/1996 Profile of Physician–Hospital Organizations and PHO Executives* (Glen Allen, VA), 3.
7. D. Blanco, M. Alper, and R. Gold, "Exploring Issues for Group Contracting," in *Managed Care Contracting* (Gaithersburg, MD: Aspen Publishers, Inc., 1997), 135.
8. P. Kongstvedt and D. Plocher, "Integrated Health Care Delivery Systems," in *The Managed Health Care Handbook,* 3d ed. (Gaithersburg, MD: Aspen Publishers, Inc., 1996), 47.
9. Kongstvedt and Plocher, *The Managed Health Care Handbook,* 49.
10. *Russ Coiles's Health Trends* 8, no. 10 (1996), 3.

SUGGESTED READING

Fox, P.D. "An Overview of Managed Care," in *The Managed Health Care Handbook*, 3d ed. (Gaithersburg, MD: Aspen Publishers, Inc., 1996).

CHAPTER 3

The Infrastructure of Managed Care

Good counselors lack no clients.

William Shakespeare (1564–1616)

Source: Drawings copyright © 1998, Donovan Andrews.

Learning Objectives

- Understand the basic infrastructure of managed care organizations (MCOs).
- Understand how MCOs provide services to customers and members.
- Understand how MCOs price, market, and sell their products.
- Understand the operational functions of MCOs.

Key Terms

Demand management—Techniques and programs MCOs use to reduce member demand for health care services and to encourage members to maintain good health.

Information management—The process of collecting, analyzing, manipulating, and storing the clinical and financial information that is generated by and exchanged among MCOs, providers, purchasers, and members.

Member services—The department or function of an MCO that provides customer service, including member education and problem resolution.

Premium rate—The amount MCOs charge purchasers to provide health coverage for beneficiaries. Premium rates (also called "premiums" or "rates") are usually based on a per employee, per couple, or per family amount.

Request for proposal—A questionnaire purchasers use to seek bids from prospective MCOs to provide health coverage for the purchasers' workers and dependents. In the request for proposal (RFP), purchasers request detailed information about the MCOs' operations, financial stability, and other characteristics and specify the parameters for provider networks and quality initiatives.

Underwriting—The process MCOs use to assess the risk of providing health insurance coverage to specific populations and to adjust the premium rates accordingly.

INTRODUCTION

The basic governance and management structure of an MCO is like any business: a board of directors provides oversight and strategic direction, an executive management team defines and modifies the company's strategic goals and provides the leadership and vision to achieve them, and directors and managers oversee departments that perform the key business functions of the organization. Figures 3–1 and 3–2 depict sample organizational charts of a health maintenance organization (HMO) and preferred provider organization (PPO), respectively. The sample organizational chart in Figure 3–1 illustrates the departments most unique to HMOs. HMOs and other MCOs also have functions, such as human resources, accounting, and corporate communications that are universal to most businesses. This chapter focuses on those functional areas and roles specific to MCOs, particularly HMOs and other risk-bearing plans.

MCOs have three principal customers: purchasers, members, and providers. The departments with principal responsibility for interfacing with these customers are Marketing and Sales, Member Services, Provider Relations, and Health Services. These can be referred to as external departments, since employees in these departments are mostly communicating with individuals outside the company—chiefly customers—on a regular basis. Other divisions like Claims, Information Management, and Underwriting offer vital support to the work of the external departments and can be known as internal departments, since these departments primarily interact with individuals from within the company. The organization of this chapter allows the reader to become acquainted with the specific departments that have the most direct interaction with customers before reading about the details of MCO operations.

MARKETING AND SALES

The marketing and sales area of an MCO is responsible for identifying customers (both purchasers and members) and their preferences, developing products or services they will buy, selling these products and services at competitive prices, retaining customers, and maintaining customer satisfaction. Some plans combine the marketing, sales, and service functions in one department, while others create separate units dedicated to each, as illustrated in Figure 3–1. Sales staff can be organized by product

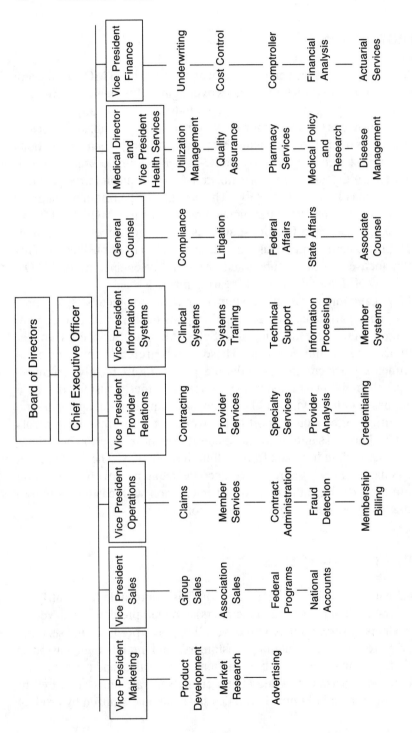

Figure 3–1 Sample HMO Organizational Chart

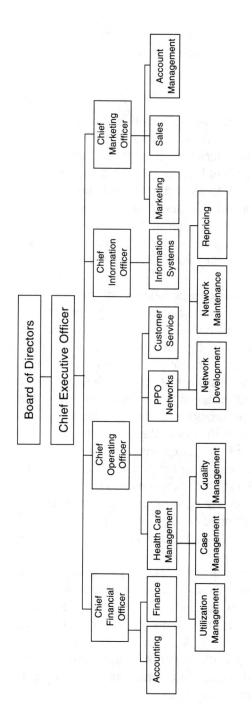

Figure 3–2 Sample PPO Organizational Chart. *Source:* Copyright © 1998, Roberta Holtzman.

(i.e., Medicaid HMO, commercial HMO) or by distribution channel (i.e., small firms, associations, and government purchasers).

Market Research

Before entering a new market or establishing operations, it is prudent for an MCO to conduct a thorough market assessment to ascertain the plan's opportunities and challenges in that particular market. The information contained in the market assessment will help the MCO create, price, and market its products successfully and develop effective network development, medical management, and operational strategies. Although an MCO should conduct market assessments when entering new markets, expanding its existing service area, or offering a new product, many do not. As a result, they operate in markets where they have limited understanding of the market dynamics.

Key components of a market assessment include the following:[1]

Market overview. A summary of the market captures the general characteristics of the health care market. This includes population, age/sex/race/ethnicity distribution, expected population growth or decline, total health care expenditures, percentage of population uninsured or insured through government programs, managed care market maturity (i.e., how long have MCOs existed in the market), and managed care penetration (i.e., what proportion of the market is covered through managed care plans).

Economic profile. This component illustrates the general health of the local economy. The unemployment rate, employment growth rate, and average per capita income are indicators of the economic health of the community. The MCO should also know the composition of the business community and the dominant and emerging companies or industries.

Competitive analysis. An evaluation of competing MCOs is an essential component of a market assessment. Such an analysis includes knowing about competitors' premium rates, clients, enrollment and annual growth rates, size and composition of provider networks, marketing approaches, provider contracting strategies, and medical management techniques.

Business community profile. Knowledge of its existing customer base is important for an MCO. This includes the composition of current clients, member retention rate, and market share. Additionally, an evaluation of the business community will reveal the benefits, patient cost sharing, funding, and other plan features that appeal to employers, as well as their receptivity to and experiences with managed care.

Provider assessment. MCOs evaluate the provider community by gathering information on the numbers, types, and distribution of providers, as well as their credentials, receptivity to managed care, level of integration, referral patterns, and managed care contracting experiences.

Legislative and regulatory analysis. Finally, a plan needs to understand the legislative and regulatory environment of the market, for example, the licensing and other regulatory requirements, the focus of current legislative activity, and the existence of any willing provider (AWP) and mandated coverage laws.

Product Development

The product development function of an MCO varies widely in its scope and structure. Plans with advanced product development activities will designate product managers to oversee the design, management, enhancement, and profitability of each product in the plan's portfolio. National MCOs are more likely to have distinct product development areas given the variety and geographic coverage of their products. Plans with limited resources or scope of products might confine their product development activities to producing product collateral materials, handling product-specific inquiries, and providing other basic sales support services.

Before a plan introduces a product to the market or enhances an existing product, it conducts research to determine the customer preferences and the competitor activity related to the product. Through industry, competitive, and consumer research, the plan attempts to ascertain

- the national and local penetration and growth rate of the product
- which plans are offering the product
- competitors' strategies for designing, implementing, and pricing the product
- the age and sex of customers currently buying the product
- how these customers make their MCO decisions

Product Teams

Cross-functional product teams comprising staff from operations, systems, medical management, members services, marketing, and provider relations will convene to brainstorm about the plan's ability to design, manage, implement, rate, and position the product. By critiquing the various competitor product designs and strategies and assessing their relevance to the capabilities and characteristics of the plan, the product teams can determine what makes the most sense for the plan. A plan contemplating the development of a Medicare product will need to determine the additional training, staffing, workflow processes, and information systems the product will require for successful operation. In examining the marketing strategies of competitors vis à vis its current marketing operations, the MCO can determine whether to hire or subcontract telemarketing representatives, for example.

Product Testing and Implementation

After the product team has created a narrow list of possibilities for the product's design and operation, the MCO will conduct focus groups of potential customers and health benefit decision makers, such as employers, brokers, consultants, and consumers, to test the working concepts. To assess the general interest of the participants, the plan will ask questions about the concept of the product, its basic features, and benefits. The MCO determines the magnitude of interest by tying a dollar value to certain decisions. For example, it will ask the participants if they would consider buying the product if it cost them $10 more each month. Plans may also conduct a written or telephonic quantitative survey of the same benefit-decision makers. Based on the results of the focus groups and survey, the MCO will make final decisions about the product, including how the product will be designed, which benefits will be covered, how it will be marketed, and how the network will be modified. The product team often oversees the implementation of the product, assigning specific responsibilities to the appropriate departments (e.g., the marketing department will develop the collateral materials).

Marketing

MCO marketing activities include monitoring the competitive environment, positioning the product in the market, developing company-wide and product-specific communication and marketing strategies, and supporting the sales staff through advertising and sales promotion activities. MCO marketing can be divided into brand, image, and product marketing.

Brand marketing. Branding is building consumer recognition for that particular brand of MCO. Potential and existing customers differentiate the brand (i.e., plan) from its competitors by recognizing the plan's logo and slogan. Brand marketing is becoming increasingly important as health care becomes more focused on the individual customer (or end-user) and more employers offer multiple MCO options.

Image/message marketing. Once customers recognize the brand, the marketing efforts emphasize the customer perceptions of the brand. Customers may be familiar with the plan, but how do they perceive it? Through message marketing, MCOs create and send images and messages they want customers to associate with the plan. For example, an MCO might project an image of a fast-growing, innovative plan and would tailor messages accordingly.

Product marketing. These marketing efforts focus on differentiating specific products from similar products offered by competitors and from the plan's other products. In many MCOs, product managers assume responsibility for positioning and marketing the product.

Advertising

Advertising and communications are the primary marketing techniques of MCOs. Plans use radio, television, print, and outdoor (e.g., billboards, buses) advertising and will vary their advertising strategies depending on the market, product, and customer. The lack of public transportation in rural markets precludes MCOs from advertising on buses and trains, and expensive television advertising in urban markets can force plans to advertise in print media instead. MCOs with primarily commercial (i.e., employer-based) business do very little product advertising. Instead, they focus on building brand loyalty and positive images among their customer base. However, a plan releasing a new direct-pay product may pursue a limited product advertising campaign.

Market Communications

Plans see each interaction and communication with employers and members as an opportunity to convey brand and image messages. For instance, the plan's logo and slogan will appear on sales collateral materials like brochures, pamphlets, plan designs, provider directories, member handbooks, and health education materials. And promotional gifts such as T-shirts and keychains, written materials, and pre-recorded messages on member services telephone lines may include the plan's logo or slogan.

Cooperative Marketing

A new approach for MCOs is cooperative marketing. Using this strategy, an MCO would align with a company that is not a competitor but is attempting to reach the same customers, for the purposes of jointly marketing each company's respective products. For example, a plan developing an alternative medicine product might market its product and those of a vitamin supplement company, and vice versa.

The Sales Process

MCO staff usually establish a strong network of professional relationships, as developing prospects through professional networks is far more effective than contacting prospective clients without a reference or introduction (i.e., cold calling). Brokers, consultants, existing clients, purchasing alliances, and business organizations are excellent sources of referrals. Sales representatives also rely on referrals from colleagues, family members, friends, and personal acquaintances to generate leads. After identifying prospects, the sales representative will determine who at the company makes the organization's health benefit decisions. Depending on the size and structure of the company, this person could be the national benefit manager, the regional human resource director, the president, or the chief financial officer. If the sales representative is successful in piquing interest of the prospective company in the plan's products, he or she will develop a sales presentation and work with underwriting to quote the group a set of premium rates. The interaction between the sales and underwriting departments is critical to the proper pricing of the account, as illustrated in Exhibit 3–1.

Requests for Proposal

Many large purchasers will use a formal process to obtain and compare information on MCOs and their products. Through an RFP process,

Exhibit 3–1 Steps in the Sales and Underwriting Process

Step 1: Sales and underwriting personnel collaborate on identifying and targeting key employers, industries, and/or employer characteristics for use by the sales force.

Step 2: Sales personnel contact targeted groups and collect data, prequalifying the employer group using checklists or criteria supplied by underwriting.

Step 3: Sales personnel prepare and submit a request for a quotation to underwriting.

Step 4: Underwriter reviews the request, qualifies the employer group, and identifies any additional questions that sales is requested to pursue.

Step 5: A clerk prepares an analysis of basic group characteristics and runs the initial pricing of the requested benefit plan(s) and contract effective date(s).

Step 6: An underwriter reviews the case materials, including updated data from sales, and determines whether the case should be declined or quoted.

Step 7: Through an iterative process, the underwriter develops the benefit plans, pricing, conditions, and/or options that the MCO will tentatively offer to the employer group.

Step 8: Sales reviews the underwriting proposal, and any questions or differences between sales and underwriting are resolved.

Step 9: Sales presents the MCO proposal to the targeted group, closes the sale, and assists the employer group throughout the enrollment process.

Step 10: Underwriting reviews the actual group enrollment and identifies any major variations from the assumptions made during the sales/underwriting process.

Source: Reprinted from G.J. Lippe, Operational Underwriting in Managed Care Organizations, in *The Managed Health Care Handbook*, 3rd ed., P.R. Kongstvedt, ed., p. 684, © 1996, Aspen Publishers, Inc.

employers solicit bids from various MCOs to provide health coverage to their employees and dependents. Often the employer will retain a broker or consulting firm to manage the RFP process. The consultant will develop the RFP, send it to selected MCOs, review the completed RFPs, and recommend plans for final consideration by the employer. The RFP requests a range of information about the plan, including its organization, products, pricing, network size, existing membership, profitability, service standards, performance guarantees, and extent of quality assurance programs. A request for information (RFI) is frequently used in the RFP process to pre-screen potential plans or by small firms as an informal method for soliciting MCO information (see Chapter 5 for a sample RFP).

Member Enrollment

Unless the sale is a total replacement account (i.e., the plan's product replaces all other MCO offerings), the plan must also make the sale to employees during the member enrollment (also called open enrollment) period. Since many employers offer workers multiple health benefit options, most MCOs are in the position of encouraging workers to enroll in their plan. The plan will use collateral materials to identify the product's specialty access features, cost-sharing obligations, benefits, network providers, and other points of distinction with its competitors. PPOs offered as an option to indemnity insurance plans do not "enroll" members but may distribute information to beneficiaries describing the benefits of using the PPO "option."

Account Management

Because it is more costly to attract a new member than it is to retain an existing one, member retention is of critical importance to MCOs. MCOs continue to use brand and image advertising to enhance or solidify positive customer recognition and perceptions of the plan. Additionally, customer service strategies are used to maintain loyalty and satisfaction. Account managers are usually responsible for servicing existing accounts. Serving as a client's principal contact person, the account manager will field questions and inquiries from employees and benefit managers, replenish the account's supply of collateral materials and provider directories, facilitate the resolution of issues, and ensure the smooth interaction between plan and client staff. The account manager works closely with the sales representative, claims manager, and member service representative assigned to the particular group.

MEMBER SERVICES

An MCO's member services department is the equivalent of a traditional customer service unit in most businesses, ensuring that its customers are satisfied with the products and services offered by the organization. For some MCOs, particularly PPOs and smaller plans, the account management and customer service functions are combined. Because most PPOs do not enroll members or determine benefits to cover, their customer service function is limited. For HMOs and other plans, the myriad administrative rules and underlying focus on patient wellness distinguish their customer service functions from those of the typical corporate customer service department. The member services department, also called consumer affairs or member affairs, is responsible for

- educating members about the plan
- resolving and tracking member issues with the plan or participating providers
- handling member grievances
- monitoring member satisfaction with the plan
- facilitating members' access to health care services
- encouraging members to better understand and manage their own health care

Many MCOs organize their member services department into dedicated service units responsible for certain accounts or products. This enables the representatives to become very knowledgeable about the unique issues of a particular group or product, improving member satisfaction and staff efficiency. For example, plans with a Medicare HMO might create a separate unit to handle telephone calls from Medicare beneficiaries who have unique health care concerns and needs. Member service departments field calls from employers and providers, as well.

Member Education

A principal function of the member services department is to educate members about the plan, including affiliated providers, emergency care policies, hospitalization procedures, covered benefits, and cost-sharing obligations. Employers often play a significant role in educating employees about health benefit programs, as well. Because member education is an important and ongoing process, MCOs have developed diverse ways to educate and inform members.

Audio-videotape libraries. These resources range from 10-minute videos on how the plan works, to shared–decision making videos that involve patients in making appropriate treatment decisions.

Member newsletters and magazines. These are usually sent to members monthly or quarterly and include general information about plan procedures, tips on maintaining good health, and news about provider network changes.

Computers in staff clinics, public areas, or client worksites. Computers equipped with interactive software programs allow employees to access plan provider directories, read about specific medical conditions, or take personal health assessments. Convenient, public access of plan information helps MCOs better inform members.

Telephone consultative services. Member services and nurse-based toll-free telephone lines are examples of how plans make themselves available to members. More active telephone services involve plan staff contacting members to encourage them to schedule necessary preventive and primary care appointments.

Company websites. While in their infancy, company home pages on the Internet can greatly improve a plan's accessibility to its members through convenient and timely communication. A multitude of information can be found on an MCO's website including physician directories, plan and product information, personal health assessments, health education information, and plan member newsletters or magazines.

Once enrolled in the MCO, the member receives an identification card, a provider directory, instructions on accessing care, and other information about the plan. Initially, members may contact the member services department to select a primary care physician (PCP) or understand their benefits. At open enrollment periods, the member services department is also likely to communicate with the member about updated eligibility requirements or changes in coverage or co-payments. The continuous education of members is vital to the MCO's success since it minimizes member complaints and the inappropriate use of health care services, and improves member understanding of and satisfaction with the plan.

Demand Management

Demand management programs (also known as personal health management and wellness programs) are designed to help members make better-informed health decisions. The goal is for members to keep themselves healthy by understanding their medical conditions better, monitoring symptoms to avoid complications, seeking treatment early on, maintaining healthy lifestyles, and self-treating minor ailments. Components of demand management programs may include

- health education classes and seminars
- self-care books and other written materials
- personal health assessments
- shared–decision making videos or software programs
- triage call centers or nurse hotlines
- targeted member outreach programs

Member services departments often take the lead in launching member outreach programs that encourage members to obtain necessary preventive care services, such as immunizations and cancer screenings. By analyzing their claims and utilization records, MCOs can identify members who have not yet received particular cancer screenings and develop initiatives to bring them in for needed care. For example, some plans discover that many of their female members over the age of 50 have not received an annual mammogram as is recommended by established guidelines. The MCO will send a reminder notice to the member encouraging her to make an appointment with her PCP for screening. The MCO sends a notice to the member's PCP so he or she can follow up with the member, as well.

Outreach programs also strive to inform members with particular medical conditions on ways to minimize complications associated with the disease. For example, an asthma patient not taking medications properly may receive health education materials on how to avoid asthma triggers, assess breathing levels, and manage asthma attacks. Member outreach is an essential component of disease management programs that target members with chronic illnesses (see Chapter 7 for a detailed discussion on disease management).

TRIAGE CALL CENTERS

Triage call centers (also known as nurse telephone hotlines) attempt to reduce unnecessary use of health care services and increase the use of necessary services. Call center staff guide members in obtaining health care services suitable to their symptoms, conduct risk assessments of members to identify members at risk for developing specific diseases, encourage members to comply with treatment plans and prescription regimens, and promote members' good health through disease awareness and self-care treatments. In some instances, MCOs use the call center as a substitute for the PCP-authorized referral. If the call center staff determines that the member's condition warrants a visit to a specialist, this judgment replaces the PCP's authorization for the specialty visit. Call centers often include pre-recorded health messages for members to improve their understanding of specific health issues.

Members can reach the call centers through a toll-free telephone line that is staffed by registered nurses and other clinicians 24 hours a day. Using established medical protocols and decision-making software, these specially-trained nurses guide patients through possible conditions and treatments based on the member's symptoms and help patients choose the appropriate course of treatment. For example, members can be instructed to seek immediate medical care, visit an urgent care center the next day, schedule an office visit with the PCP, or pursue a self-care regimen.

Problem Resolution

Resolving member problems represents a sizable share of the member service representative's time. To ensure customer satisfaction, issues or difficulties members have with the plan must be resolved promptly and professionally. MCOs track the volume and nature of member calls to identify trends in member complaints or issues, support member grievance procedures, assess member satisfaction, and give employers and providers specific feedback. The information from the member services tracking system allows the plan to improve customer service by

- re-designing plan workflow procedures or member interfaces
- targeting problem providers for appropriate follow-up action, i.e., education or discipline
- informing employers of miscommunications about plan procedures
- developing new products based on member feedback

The most frequent inquiries employees have about their health benefit programs relate to cost (how much will this service cost me personally?), coverage (will my plan pay for this service?), and access (how do I get this service?).[2] However, the type of member questions and complaints range from non-payment of claims and denials of specialty referrals, to rude office staff and unclean physician offices. Exhibit 3–2 gives examples of the types of member calls.

Exhibit 3–2 Examples of Member Calls

Administrative—"My identification card has the wrong name." "Can I receive another copy of the provider directory?" "Where do I send this claim?" "I need to add my new baby on the plan."

Plan procedure—"Do I need a referral from my PCP to see my OB/GYN?" "I thought my physician was responsible for contacting the plan for authorization for my outpatient surgery, not me?" "I took my son to the emergency room last night without contacting his PCP first. Will this be paid?"

Benefits—"Does the plan cover medical equipment?" "How many outpatient mental health visits does my plan cover?" "Does the plan pay for out-of-network physical therapy?"

Claims—"I received a bill from the hospital for my maternity stay even though it was pre-approved." "Why didn't the plan pay for my recent chiropractic visit?" "I submitted a bill for Dr. Stone last month. Has it been paid yet?"

Provider network— "My PCP is not participating in the plan anymore; can you recommend a new PCP?" "My PCP is never available when I need him. Can I switch PCPs?" "The receptionist in Dr. Cliff's office was rude to me yesterday." "I usually have to wait two weeks before I can get my daughter in to see her PCP."

Quality—"It has taken me months to be scheduled for my surgery." "My PCP won't refer me to a dermatologist." "Dr. Martin does not return my calls."

Increasingly, MCOs are using computer and information technology to automatically track and record member calls. Automated and integrated member services tracking systems enable MCOs to improve the productivity of customer service representatives, increase customer satisfaction through prompt and effective response, and decrease administrative costs. Additionally, consumer information technology can improve the access to and comprehensiveness of health information.[3]

For example, automated call distribution (ACD) systems track incoming calls and route them to the next available member services representative. If no telephone lines are available, the ACD system places callers in a queue. The system allows the plan to monitor call volume and staff productivity, generating reports that summarize the number of calls, the average time a caller is on hold, and the average time it takes for a call to be routed to a representative.[4]

An integrated voice/data system allows information from multiple sources to be integrated and easily accessed by the customer service representative at the time of a member call. It enables the customer service department to exchange information with other departments and with external entities, such as employers and providers.

Member Grievances

Grievances are formal complaints from members about some interaction with the MCO or its participating provider. They usually stem from the plan's inability to satisfactorily resolve a member's informal complaint. State and federal regulations require HMOs and sometimes point-of-service (POS) plans to establish specific procedures for handling member grievances, such as time parameters for submitting and responding to grievances and responsibilities for reviewing grievances. A member grievance procedure usually proceeds according to the following steps:

1. *Submission.* Member sends plan a written grievance within X days of the incident.
2. *Investigation.* Plan conducts interviews with family, member, providers, and other parties and responds to member with its proposed resolution within a specified time period.
3. *Appeal.* If the member is not satisfied with the plan's resolution of the formal complaint, he or she can appeal the decision within a specified time period.

4. *Formal hearing.* The plan must offer the member a formal hearing to present his or her case to a panel of impartial individuals. This panel might be an outside review agency or comprising senior management, board members, or providers. Based on the member's presentation, the investigation, and further consideration, the panel makes a decision to support the initial plan resolution or develop an alternate one.
5. *Arbitration/government agency.* If the member is still not satisfied with the outcome of the formal hearing, he or she can appeal to an arbitration panel if arbitration is allowed in that particular state or to the applicable government agency, i.e., state insurance department or Health Care Financing Administration.

Exercise: You are recently hired as the member service director of an MCO that has a reputation for poor customer service. Apparently, the MCO has had significant difficulty responding to member inquiries and disseminating information to members. You are asked to develop a plan for improving customer service. Assuming you know nothing about the programs and efforts the MCO has historically used, what strategies would you use and why?

PROVIDER RELATIONS

The principal role of the provider relations department is to develop and manage the provider network. Some MCOs segregate the functions of network development and management into two separate divisions under one central provider relations department. With this structure, the individuals who are responsible for contracting with providers and facilities do not manage the relations once the contracts are finalized. These individuals, called contract specialists or contract managers, are responsible for contracting with new providers and renegotiating existing contracts. Other plans create provider relations positions that encompass both contracting and management duties requiring the individual to negotiate contracts and maintain the relationships with affiliated providers.

The key functions of provider contracting include

- selecting, recruiting, and credentialing providers
- negotiating and re-negotiating provider contracts
- terminating providers
- amending provider contracts

The primary responsibilities of managing the provider network include

- re-credentialing providers
- resolving provider issues
- educating physicians and office staff
- updating and maintaining provider information
- creating provider profiles
- implementing new administrative procedures or policies

(See Chapter 4 for a detailed discussion of provider relations.)

CLINICAL MANAGEMENT

The fundamental pursuit of an MCO is to monitor and manage the use of health care services among its members (known as clinical management, medical management, and utilization management). Initially, managing the utilization of health care resources was instituted solely as cost-containment strategy. Increasingly, however, as plans assume a greater responsibility for improving the quality of care members receive, their clinical management activities have become more comprehensive. Primitive efforts to ensure a basic quality standard are replaced with more sophisticated initiatives to actually improve the care delivered to members. Plans employ various techniques to manage health care utilization, including the following:

Referral authorizations. Requiring members to obtain an authorization from the MCO or PCP before seeking care from specialists.

Pre-certification. Requiring the member to obtain authorization from the MCO before being admitted to the hospital or undergoing certain diagnostic or surgical procedures.

Concurrent review. Assessing the appropriateness of the hospitalization.

Case management. Identifying the appropriate treatment plan (including type, duration, and location of treatment) for particular medical cases, usually patients with expensive, complicated, or lengthy care.

Clinical management activities are handled by a department commonly known as health services, utilization management, or medical affairs. Sometimes, MCOs will divide the basic medical management and quality improvement functions into two separate departments or subdivisions within one department. Staffed by nurses and other health care professionals, the medical management department is the interface between the plan and affiliated providers on all clinical matters. The plan's medical director has oversight of the clinical management department and is responsible for developing the plan's medical policy (see Chapter 6 for more information on utilization management and Chapter 7 for more information on quality of care).

RATING AND UNDERWRITING

Rating

Rating, also known as pricing, is the process plans use to develop premiums (also known as prices or rates) for their products. A premium is the price a purchaser pays for health coverage for each employee. Premiums are usually structured as per member per month (PMPM) figures. MCOs use different rating methods to develop prices depending on the particular market, size and type of employer, regulatory requirements, and other factors. The rating methods include community rating, experience rating, and no rating (i.e., self-funding).

Since most PPOs do not assume risk for providing health coverage (i.e., are not at financial risk for paying health care claims), they develop prices for their products not based on prior claim experience, but on their costs of providing administrative services and ultimately, on what the market will pay for such services. For example, rates for access to a PPO network are based on the cost of building and maintaining a provider network (sometimes called a "network access fee").

Community Rating

Standard community rating sets the same rates for all groups, regardless of the industry, enrolled population, size of group, or other factor. For a given plan design, there is a standard set of rates. Because this rating methodology places HMOs at a disadvantage vis à vis other products that can adjust their rates based on the risk factors of the group (e.g., managed indemnity plans), states have developed variations of community rating that account for certain risk factors. Under community rating by class (CRC), states allow plans to modify the standard community rates for particular groups based on classes of business or categories of risk, e.g., industry, average employer size, age, and gender. Adjusted community rating (ACR) allows the community rates to be further adjusted based on the specific claims experience of the group.

Experience Rating

Using an experience rating method, plans look at actual or anticipated experience of the employer based on claims history, utilization experience, and age and sex of the population, and develop a specific rate unique to the customer. Each account is assigned some level of statistical credibility depending on the size of the group. The larger the group, the more credible prior claims experience is in predicting future claims experience. For example, employer groups with 2 to 100 employees may have zero credibility for experience rating and groups with 1,000 employees may have a 100 percent credibility factor. Because the actual medical costs of larger groups (those with over 1,000 employees) are deemed to be credible, they are more likely to be experience rated.

Self-Funding

Self-funding is when an employer opts to assume the financial risk of paying for the medical claims incurred by employees and dependents. Rather than contract with the plan so that the plan assumes all financial risk for providing medical services (i.e., fully-insured basis), the employer will enter into an administrative services only (ASO) contract with the plan. Under an ASO contract, the plan handles the enrollment, claims payment, and other administrative functions. Traditionally, self-funded employers have selected third-party administrators (TPAs), or indemnity plans with

PPO options, to administer their health benefit plans. More MCOs are developing HMO and POS options for self-funded employers as the self-insured segment of the market expands.

MCOs use different rating approaches depending on the product, market, client, and applicable regulations. Many states have passed legislation requiring MCOs to offer community rates to small groups (those with 25 or fewer employees). Therefore, in a market dominated by small businesses, plans would have little need to offer experience-rated products.

Premium Rate Development

The first step in developing a set of premium rates is to establish a PMPM target premium revenue (also called book rate). This is the amount of PMPM premium revenue the plan should collect to cover its medical and administrative expenses. MCOs develop the PMPM target premium revenue by totaling the projected medical costs, administrative expenses, taxes, and profit. Table 3–1 shows an actuarial cost model.

Because the target revenue is developed prospectively, plans must make assumptions about future costs and utilization. For example, in a given year (1997), a plan will adjust the actual data from the previous year (1996) by certain cost and utilization projections to compute the premium rates for the following year (1998). The plan will consider any changes in (1) provider reimbursement arrangements, (2) demographic characteristics of the membership, (3) plan design, or (4) benefits when developing the premium rates. Plans will break down the components of medical costs into service categories, such as

- capitated physician services (if applicable)
- fee-for-service physician services
- inpatient hospital
- outpatient hospital
- pharmacy services
- home health care services

The level of detail will depend on the plan's claims and information management systems and financial arrangements with providers. The plan's actual medical costs are trended forward, i.e., adjusted by the projected rate at which medical costs will increase each year. Administra-

Table 3–1 Actuarial Cost Model: Required Revenue for Calendar Year 19xx

	1	2	3	4	5	6	7
Benefit	Utilization per 1,000	Allowed Average Charge	Per Capita Monthly Claim Cost	Frequency of Co-pay	Co-pay	Per Capita Monthly Cost-Sharing Value	Per Capita Monthly Net Claim Costs
Hospital inpatient							
Medical-surgical	247 days	$1,276.76	$26.28				$26.28
Psychiatric/ substance abuse	67 days	657.31	3.67				$3.67
Extended care	5 days	250.00	0.10				0.10
Total hospital inpatient	319 days	$1,130.56	$30.05				$30.05
Hospital outpatient							
Emergency department	261 visits	$159.99	$3.48	196	$25.00	$0.41	$3.07
Surgery	85 visits	1,172.46	8.30				8.30
Other outpatient services	512 visits	149.53	6.38				6.38
Total hospital outpatient			$18.16			$0.41	$17.75

continues

Table 3–1 continued

Benefit	1 Utilization per 1,000	2 Allowed Average Charge	3 Per Capita Monthly Claim Cost	4 Frequency of Co-pay	5 Co-pay	6 Per Capita Monthly Cost-Sharing Value	7 Per Capita Monthly Net Claim Costs
Physician							
Primary care capitated							
Office and inpatient visits	2,152 visits	$42.77	$7.67	2,035	$10.00	$1.70	5.97
Immunizations and injections	154 procedures	17.14	0.22			—	0.22
Total primary care capitated			$7.89			$1.70	$6.19
Fee for service							
Surgery	374 procedures	$266.63	$8.31				$8.31
Anesthesia	78 procedures	575.38	3.74				3.74
Office and inpatient visits	1,025 visits	45.78	3.91	944	$10.00	$0.78	3.13
Total fee for service			$36.44			$0.78	$35.66
Total physician			$44.33			$2.48	$41.85

continues

Table 3–1 continued

Benefit	1 Utilization per 1,000	2 Allowed Average Charge	3 Per Capita Monthly Claim Cost	4 Frequency of Co-pay	5 Co-pay	6 Per Capita Monthly Cost-Sharing Value	7 Per Capita Monthly Net Claim Costs
Other							
Precription drugs	5,209 scripts	$36.00	$15.63	5,209	$5.00	$2.17	$13.46
Home health care	29 visits	228.21	$0.55				0.55
Ambulance	15 runs	322.43	$0.40				0.40
Durable medical equipment/ prosthetics	32 units	269.54	0.72				0.72
Total other			$17.30			$2.17	$15.13
Total medical costs			$109.84			$5.06	$104.78
Administration							18.00
Coordination of benefits							4.19
Net cost of reinsurance							1.41
PMPM revenue required							$120.00

Source: Reprinted from S.M. Cigich, Rating and Underwriting, in The Managed Health Care Handbook, 3rd ed., P.R. Kongstvedt, ed., p. 670, © 1996, Aspen Publishers, Inc.

tive costs (e.g., advertising, salaries, taxes, overhead) are also adjusted for expected annual increases.

The PMPM targeted premium rate is translated into case-specific premium rates based on the size of the employee contract (i.e., employee, employee and spouse) and the experience of the group (see "Underwriting"). Premium rates by size of the employee contract are generally reflected in tiers. For example, a plan may offer a prospective employer a different rate for an employee, an employee with one dependent, and an employee with a family. Employers request rates based on two, three, four, or more tiers. Table 3–2 is an example of a four-tier premium rate.

Underwriting

Underwriting is the process plans use to assess the risk of specific employers and adjust the premium rates based on this risk. Because the volume of medical resources the group will consume is not known, the plan uses actuarial assumptions (i.e., assumptions that have statistical meaning) to predict the expected experience of the group. Some of the factors known

Table 3–2 Four-Tier Premium Rate Development

	1	2	3	4	5
Contract Type	Contract Distribution (%)	Members per Contract	Premium Loading Factor	PMPM Target Revenue Requirement	Target Premium Rate ($)
Employee	41	1.0	1.19	120.00	142.80
Employee with spouse	15	2.0	3.08	120.00	369.60
Employee with child(ren)	10	2.5	2.04	120.00	244.80
Employee with spouse and child(ren)	34	4.0	3.42	120.00	410.40
Composite	100	2.32	2.32	120.00	278.40

Source: Reprinted from S.M. Cigich, Rating and Underwriting, in *The Managed Health Care Handbook*, 3rd ed., P.R. Kongstvedt, ed., p. 675, © 1996, Aspen Publishers, Inc.

to influence future medical cost and utilization include the age, gender, industry, and prior medical costs and utilization. In developing case-specific premium rates, the plan will also consider plan design (i.e., out-of-network usage, patient cost sharing); previous health benefit options of employer (i.e., indemnity or managed care); and type of offering (i.e., multiple product offering or total replacement). Table 3–3 shows how a plan adjusts its target premium revenue based on the previous claims experience of the group.

OPERATIONS

The operations department of an MCO is the nuts and bolts of the plan. While other departments publicly represent the plan with its principal clients, the operations department is responsible for implementing workable and efficient processes to fulfill the contractual obligations of the plan. As a support department, it relies on direction and input from internal departments, like marketing and provider relations. The work processes of

---

Table 3–3 Claim Cost Experience Rating Example

Step A: Group-Specific Experience

Category	Year* t	Year* $t-1$
1. Paid claims	$68.00	$50.00
2. Incurred claims	$82.00	$65.00
3. Pooling charge	$8.00	$7.00
4. Pooled claims	($10.00)	($2.00)
5. Claims charged (2+3+4)	$80.00	$70.00
6. Employer expected claims	$75.00	$60.00
7. Experience ratio (5/6)	$1.07	$1.17
8. Credibility	60%	20%

Step B: Plan expected PMPM revenue target = $120

Step C: Group experience rating development

PMPM revenue target = $120 x [(1.07)(60%) + (1.17)(20%) +

(1.00)(20%)] = $129.12

*t, most recent year; t–1, next most recent year

Source: Reprinted from S.M. Cigich, Rating and Underwriting, in *The Managed Health Care Handbook*, 3rd ed., P.R. Kongstvedt, ed., p. 675, © 1996, Aspen Publishers, Inc.

the operations department have the most impact on administrative costs; as such, they are constantly being scrutinized and revamped for maximum efficiency and client satisfaction.

Member Enrollment and Eligibility

Since only "members" of MCOs are provided health benefits, the process for receiving and maintaining accurate and timely membership information is important. The sponsors of health coverage send plans lists of eligible members, i.e., employees, beneficiaries, retirees, and dependents, on a regular basis by paper copies, magnetic tape, computer disk, or via an electronic data interchange (EDI) network, i.e., computer to computer. The plan generates and sends an identification card and membership material to new members, and maintains the membership database. To ensure that plan–purchaser and plan–provider transactions function smoothly (premiums are collected and providers are paid), member information must be continuously updated.

To streamline the enrollment and eligibility process, some MCOs are implementing electronic eligibility systems and other consumer information technology. Electronic eligibility systems allow members to enroll in plans and make enrollment changes electronically, from desktop personal computers, kiosks in the workplace, and plan websites. Through EDI networks, eligibility lists can be transmitted electronically among employer and plan and affiliated providers. This eliminates the re-entering of member data, reduces the lag time and administrative expenses associated with printing and mailing hard copies or downloading computer files, and provides real-time information.[5] Automated voice response systems give providers immediate telephonic access to up-to-date member eligibility information, eliminating the need to verify eligibility directly from an MCO representative.

Premium Collection and Distribution

Since employer premiums and provider capitation payments are calculated on a per member basis, the collection and distribution of the premiums is based on the member eligibility lists. The monthly premium check the employer sends the plan is based on the eligible members for that month adjusted by any additions and deletions from previous months. This is also the case for the monthly capitation checks the plan distributes to providers who receive capitation payments (see Chapter 4 for more information on capitation). Eligibility lists may accompany the checks depending on whether the employer, MCO, or provider has electronic capability. If eligibility rosters are exchanged electronically, but payments are made manually, they will be sent separately. Automated banking arrangements between plan and purchasers are often established for administrative services or large accounts. For any given month, an MCO needs to ensure that the premium revenues it collects exceed the medical expenses (i.e., provider payments). Given the delays in the enrollment and eligibility processes, the timing of collecting and distributing premiums is particularly important to MCOs.

THE CASE OF MR. WOODSON

Assume that Mr. Woodson was eligible for benefits on October 1, but his eligibility information was not entered into the plan's system until November 15 because of delays by his employer. The plan would not collect a premium for Mr. Woodson until the December 1 bill, which would reflect two months' worth of premiums for Mr. Woodson (October and November). Likewise, Mr. Woodson's PCP, Dr. Blake, would not receive a capitation payment for Mr. Woodson until the December capitation check, which would also reflect two months' worth of retroactive capitation payments for Mr. Woodson. However, if Mr. Woodson saw Dr. Blake on October 10, both the plan and Dr. Blake would have incurred a medical expense for which they had not yet received payment.

Claims Adjudication and Payment

The principal goal of the claims department is to pay members' health care claims accurately and on time, and in accordance with the terms of the contracts the plan establishes with both employers and providers. The claims department must translate the terms of the subscriber and provider agreements into workable processes and procedures. For example, covered benefits need to be entered into the claims system as specific procedure codes (CPT-4 codes), and provider compensation arrangements need to be translated into explicit reimbursement instructions.

Many MCOs are beginning to see their claims systems as data repositories, giving them a wealth of information on aggregate and employer-specific health care costs, utilization trends of members, practice and billing patterns of providers, and the incidence of certain disease or risk factors among their population. Plans can collect, analyze, and manipulate this information in their fraud and abuse detection efforts, case management programs, member outreach activities, and quality improvement initiatives. As fraudulent billing practices become more prevalent, many MCOs are creating special units, sometimes within the claims department, to identify fraud committed against the plan by providers and members.

The claims department usually has responsibility for

- processing and paying claims
- handling claim inquiries from members, providers, and employers
- correcting claims payment errors
- collecting reimbursement from third parties
- identifying fraudulent and inappropriate billing practices
- analyzing and tracking data

Claims units can be organized by product line, account, provider type, or claim function. For example, a plan may have a group of claims adjusters only re-process and pay claims that were previously paid erroneously, or it may designate special units to process claims for a large account or for its PPO claims.

Claim Adjudication

Claims are submitted to the MCO by providers or members manually or electronically. Paper claims are manually sorted into batches by dates of service (and by account or provider depending on the organizational structure of the claims department) and then entered into the claim system. Electronic claims are automatically sorted and entered. Claims adjudication (also known as claims processing) is the process by which a claims adjuster determines that the claim contains the necessary information and meets the plan's requirements for payment. Before paying a claim, the claims adjusters must consider several factors related to the subscriber agreement and provider contracts.

- Is the member eligible on this date of service?
- Is this a covered benefit?
- Was the service authorized?
- What is the member's co-insurance obligation?
- Is this a participating provider?
- Is this an in-network or out-of-network claim?
- What is the provider's contracted rate?

The claims system usually contains all the pertinent information, such as benefit coverage, provider rates, and member eligibility, so the claim adjuster can process the claim. Exhibit 3–3 outlines the information typically contained in an MCO claims system. As is evident in Exhibit 3–3, the information in the claims system comes from other departments. So while the claims department supports the fundamental role of the provider relations, member services, and marketing departments, it is also quite reliant on these departments to successfully perform their functions correctly and promptly (i.e., update their databases on provider reimbursements, customer benefits, and member eligibility).

Claims are either paid, denied, or pended for further review. Many MCOs have explicit guidelines for paying claims and will build automatic edits into the system to flag claims that do not fall within the parameters for payment, e.g., the procedure does not match the age or gender of the patient or the standard frequency for the service. The following list identifies the data that plans need to process claims:

1. member name and address
2. member sex and date of birth
3. member identification numbers
4. date(s) of service
5. provider name and address
6. provider tax identification number
7. procedure code(s), i.e., CPT-4 codes
8. diagnosis or nature of injury/illness, i.e., International Classification of Diseases, Ninth Edition, Clinical Modification (ICD-9-CM)

9. name of attending physician
10. name of PCP
11. other health insurance coverage

Generally, plans can pay claims with complete information within 30 days of receiving them. However, incomplete or questionable claims may take considerably longer. There are numerous reasons why a claim is pended or further denied, e.g., the member is not eligible, the provider is not found in system or approved for the procedure, or there is no record of an authorization. The type of managed care product also influences how much time is involved in claims adjudication. For example, POS plans have different payment rules depending on whether the service was delivered within or outside the network. Specialty care services rendered to members through the in-network component require a referral from the PCP, while those rendered through the out-of-network feature do not. Also, the member's financial responsibility for an in-network office visit

Exhibit 3–3 Claims System Information

Type	*Elements*
Group record	Account and subaccount identifiers, benefit plans purchased by accounts and subaccounts, eligibility period, premium payment status, eligibility rules (e.g., pre-existing conditions, waiting periods, student age limitations)
Member record	Member identifiers, alternate carrier information, re-lationship to subscriber, group affiliation, PCP selection, member benefit accounting, eligibility period
Benefit record	Description of covered services and procedures, benefit limitations and maximums, benefit exclusions and benefit cost sharing at the CPT-4, HCPCS, and ICD-9-CM procedure code levels
Provider record	Contracted and credentialed network providers, reimbursement methodologies, eligible services, tax identifier, payment location, practice relationships and network affiliations, contract period, payment status, covering physicians, risk-sharing mechanisms

continues

Exhibit 3–3 continued

Price	A series of reimbursement tables: capitation (procedure specific), planwide fee schedules (procedure specific), provider-specific fee schedules (case rates, procedure-specific rates, per diems, percentage of charge, percentage of fee schedule), other plan- and/or provider-specific tables (resource-based relative value scale, relative value units, ambulatory patient groups, diagnosis-related groups), location-specific tables at the procedure level
Authorization record	Medical management parameters to define preapproved procedures, provider, number of services and time frame, case management identifier and to identify third-party liability (TPL) potential
Code files	Place of service, type of service, procedure codes with modifiers, diagnosis codes (identify TPL potential), remittance and explanation of benefits codes (denials, limitations, reductions, cost sharing, etc.), pend reasons, adjustment reasons, processor codes
Claim rules	A series of tables that define benefit coverage issues, including medical necessity and appropriateness, validity and consistency edits (gender-procedure, age-procedure, place-procedure, provider/specialty-procedure, type-procedure, diagnosis-procedure, lifetime-procedure, etc.), rebunding rules, reinsurance amounts, duplicate parameters, processor limitations, claim to authorization record matching parameters, table of procedures that allow assistants
Accounts payable information	A table mapping procedure codes or ranges and/or type of service codes to financial revenue codes
Vendor record	A record that identifies the payee, including tax and discount information

Source: Reprinted from R.S. Eichler and R.L. McElfatrick, Claims and Benefits Administration, in *The Managed Health Care Handbook*, 3rd ed., P.R. Kongstvedt, ed., p. 521, © 1996, Aspen Publishers, Inc.

might be a $5 co-payment, compared to a $150 deductible and 20 percent co-insurance for an out-of-network office visit. Therefore, the claims adjuster receiving a claim from a network specialist will need to determine if the member sought the treatment using the in-network or out-of-network component and then pay the claim accordingly.

Encounter Data

Compiling and tracking encounter data is crucial to MCOs that have entered into numerous full-risk arrangements with providers. (Encounters are claims generated for services that are capitated, not paid according to a fee schedule.) To achieve a complete record of utilization, encounters are entered into the claims system like actual claims. Without encounter data, plans are unaware of the volume and types of services capitated providers render to members and have incomplete information from which to price products, establish capitation rates, ascertain overall utilization trends, and assess quality of care.

Claims Payment Performance

The ability to pay claims accurately and on time is usually a good measure of a plan's efficient operations, financial stability, and strong management. Because the payment of medical claims affects members, providers, and employers alike, it is regarded as a high priority within the organization. An MCO's efficiency at paying claims contributes to low administrative expenses and high member satisfaction. Claim reports show management the number and percentage of claims that have been received, pended, paid, and denied for a given month or week. To determine the productivity of the department, the reports will also indicate the oldest claim being processed and the dates of service of the current workload.

Other Party Liability

Under some circumstances, a party other than the MCO is responsible for the medical bills of the member. Other party liability includes coordination of benefits (COB) and third-party liability, such as auto insurance. COB refers to the process by which a patient's primary and secondary insurers coordinate the payment for medical services so that the total

Table 3–4 Sample Claims Triangle

		Incurred Claims								
		Dec-95	Jan-96	Feb-96	Mar-96	Apr-96	May-96	Jun-96	Jul-96	Aug-96
	Dec-95	6,635	0	0	0	0	0	0	0	0
	Jan-96	13,060	6,359	0	0	0	0	0	0	0
	Feb-96	7,716	15,050	5,693	0	0	0	0	0	0
	Mar-96	3,877	13,142	12,166	7,106	0	0	0	0	0
Paid	Apr-96	1,937	1,766	17,407	27,084	6,767	0	0	0	0
Claims	May-96	593	1,167	944	32,712	16,849	10,990	0	0	0
	Jun-96	567	0	1,212	4,095	5,157	18,768	4,013	0	0
	Jul-96	148	1,802	730	435	4,095	5,029	20,206	6,502	0
	Aug-96	593	78	4	25,152	72	1,303	11,307	15,930	5,275
	Sep-96	2,011	26	176	26	1,514	178	9,501	8,793	17,585
	Oct-96	35	6	0	94	3,106	441	5,631	3,663	14,113
	Nov-96	236	0	0	2,088	205	927	2,045	217	943
	Dec-96	0	0	0	22	0	0	3	388	366
	Jan-97	0	0	0	0	0	468	0	0	548
	Feb-97	0	0	0	0	0	222	90	278	304
	Mar-97	0	49	373	0	137	26	312	419	227
	Apr-97	0	0	0	0	0	0	0	0	125
	May-97	0	0	0	0	0	0	0	0	0

continues

payment does not exceed the amount allowed under the member's insurance policies. Because of the prevalence of working couples who each have health coverage through their respective employers, many people have duplicate or overlapping coverage: primary coverage through their employer and secondary coverage through their spouse's employer. Medicare beneficiaries can also be covered by Medicare and an employer-sponsored retiree health plan or supplemental insurance policy. Third-party liability (also known as subrogation) is when the plan seeks reimbursement from a third party that is legally responsible for medical claims resulting from a negligent act or omission, such as an accident or medical malpractice. In these instances, the third party (e.g., a medical malpractice or auto liability insurer) has principal liability for the claim, and the MCO can request reimbursement for payments made to providers.

Claim Reserves

Incurred but not reported (IBNR) claims are health care services that are rendered but not yet reported to the plan. Because of the delay between when a service is rendered to a member and when the plan receives the bill (called a lag time), IBNR claims represent unknown medical expenses.

Table 3–4 continued

				Incurred Claims					
Sep-96	Oct-96	Nov-96	Dec-96	Jan-97	Feb-97	Mar-97	Apr-97	May-97	Total
0	0	0	0	0	0	0	0	0	6,635
0	0	0	0	0	0	0	0	0	19,419
0	0	0	0	0	0	0	0	0	28,459
0	0	0	0	0	0	0	0	0	36,291
0	0	0	0	0	0	0	0	0	54,961
0	0	0	0	0	0	0	0	0	63,255
0	0	0	0	0	0	0	0	0	33,812
0	0	0	0	0	0	0	0	0	38,947
0	0	0	0	0	0	0	0	0	59,714
4,994	0	0	0	0	0	0	0	0	44,804
23,146	6,034	0	0	0	0	0	0	0	56,269
3,564	31,402	10,410	0	0	0	0	0	0	52,037
920	2,477	19,309	6,406	0	0	0	0	0	29,891
446	2,152	23,398	16,769	4,779	0	0	0	0	48,560
48	359	1,195	8,035	10,785	5,222	0	0	0	26,538
365	768	330	3,528	6,175	22,924	8,239	0	0	43,872
447	69	22	883	120	9,860	6,968	5,879	0	24,373
0	350	146	172	1,169	20,081	19,551	11,032	5,153	57,654

(The use of EDI, of course, eliminates this lag time.) Since the MCO has no way of knowing the amount of such claims, it must estimate the amount based on historical claims patterns. The plan must accrue monies to pay these claims once they are submitted. These monies are known as claim reserves. To properly balance revenue and cost, an MCO will evaluate its IBNR and adjust its claim reserves monthly. If a plan forcasted that its IBNR claims would be higher than they actually turned out to be, its financial statements would reflect inflated expenses and it would not recognize all of its profit. If the IBNR estimates are lower than actual, the plan will not have adequate reserves to pay claims. A common method plans use to estimate IBNR claims is a claims triangle, illustrated in Table 3–4.

INFORMATION MANAGEMENT

Management information systems (MIS) and information technology allow MCOs to collect, transmit, manipulate, and store a variety of information electronically, which is central to the successful operation of an MCO. Meaningful data on costs and utilization support every aspect of the plan's operations, including financial planning, pricing and underwriting, provider capitation and profiling, quality measurement, and medical management. By using information technology rather than manual processes, plans can reduce administrative costs, improve plan efficiency, eliminate time lags, and enhance quality measurement.

Plans can electronically exchange the following data with members, provider, and employers:

- enrollment information
- eligibility lists
- claims and claims payments
- referrals
- hospital authorizations
- capitation checks and payments
- premium statements and payments
- medical records
- member education materials

Most MCOs have multiple systems that handle different functions. For example, accounting systems collect and distribute premiums, claims systems process claims, utilization management systems record the use of health care services, and provider systems store provider information. Moreover, employers and providers use various financial, clinical, and administrative systems to operate their respective businesses and practices. To be meaningful, the multiple information systems must allow the exchange of information among departments, between plan and provider, and between plan and employer. EDI allows plans to exchange information with customers in a standard way. Without EDI, plans need interface applications that link abundant data from disparate information systems.

CONCLUSION

While the basic infrastructure of MCOs, like that of most businesses, will remain relatively constant, their organization will undoubtedly be molded to accommodate emerging areas of focus. Increased attention to customer service may force MCOs to equip customer service units with the latest information technology to respond to inquiries more accurately and efficiently. Clearly, information technology will continue to have an enormous impact on MCOs. While the use of technology greatly improves plan efficiency, the continued progression into the information age requires significant financial resources and the acquisition of computer-literate individuals, and raises concerns about the confidentiality of medical information. Already, MCOs have designated chief information officers to oversee complex and growing information management systems. Additionally, the continued role of MCOs in influencing how participating providers practice has caused MCOs to hire more medical personnel, especially physicians and nurses. Health care practitioners on staff give MCOs credibility with participating providers. They also share their clinical expertise with non-clinical managers, creating an MCO more capable of successfully managing patient care.

DISCUSSION QUESTIONS

1. Describe the principal rating methods MCOs use to price their products.
2. What factors do MCOs consider in developing premium rates?
3. List the key components of a market assessment and describe how each contributes to the MCO's ability to operate in that market.
4. Why do some MCOs create product development teams?
5. Describe how MCOs position their company and the products they offer.
6. List four responsibilities of a member services department.
7. Describe why MCOs sometimes contact members.
8. How has computer technology improved the ability of MCOs to respond to customers?
9. Describe the key operational functions of an MCO.
10. Why is it important for MCOs to collect and store accurate claims and utilization data?

REFERENCES

1. W. Knight, "Understanding Managed Care Contracting," in *Managed Care Contracting: A Guide for Health Care Professionals* (Gaithersburg, MD: Aspen Publishers, Inc., 1997), 13–14.

2. Watson Wyatt Worldwide, *Getting What You Pay For: Quality, Access, and Value* (Bethesda, MD: 1997), 11.
3. J. Nobel and J. Brody, "Telecomputing as a Tool To Increase Consumer Participation in Managed Care," *The American Journal of Managed Care*, November/December, 1996.
4. Health Insurance Association of America, *Managed Care: Integrating the Delivery and Financing of Health Care, Part B* (Washington, DC: 1996).
5. B. Hansen, "Electronic Eligibility Rosters Put 'Managed' Into Managed Health Care," *Managed Healthcare*, March, 1996.

SUGGESTED READING

Brosgol, F. "Data Integration: Blue Skies Ahead for Network Management," *Medical Interface*, January, 1996.

Jossi, F. "A New Way to Choose a Personal Physician," *Healthplan Magazine*, March/April, 1996.

Kongstvedt, P. *The Managed Health Care Handbook*, 3d ed. (Gaithersburg, MD: Aspen Publishers, Inc., 1996).

Prescott, M. "A Friendly Voice in the Night," *Healthplan Magazine*, March/April, 1996.

CHAPTER 4

Provider Networks

The management of a balance of power is a permanent undertaking, not an exertion that has a foreseeable end.

Henry A. Kissinger (1979)

"Sorry, Jeff. I'd pick you for my team but you don't meet the criteria: must have a .400 batting average, must have pitched at least 10 no hitters, must have averaged 100 RBIs . . ."

Learning Objectives

- Understand why and how managed care organizations (MCOs) create provider networks.
- Understand the essential elements of the contract negotiation process between MCOs and providers.
- Understand the principal reimbursement methods MCOs use to compensate physicians.
- Understand the structure and implications of a capitation reimbursement model.

Key Terms

Capitation—A prospective reimbursement based on the historical cost and expected use of health care services for the average member. In exchange for providing a defined set of health care services for members, providers receive a monthly capitation rate (that usually varies depending on the age and sex of the individual) for each member enrolled in their practice.

Contract negotiation—The process of agreeing to the financial and administrative terms of a managed care contract between network-based MCOs and providers.

Credentialing—The process MCOs use to confirm the qualifications of providers. MCOs verify that providers have the necessary credentials to practice medicine and meet the standards of care established by the plan.

Provider profiling—The collection and analysis of various information (including medical claims, utilization data, member satisfaction surveys, patients' medical records, and hospital admissions records) to assess the practice patterns, quality, service, and cost-efficiency of participating providers.

Risk-sharing contracts—Agreements between MCOs and providers that shift all or some portion of the financial risk of managing the care of members to the providers. Such risk-sharing can take the form of capitated payments (i.e., fixed dollar amounts per member) and bonus arrangements that reward providers for achieving expected cost and utilization targets.

INTRODUCTION

MCOs create provider networks by hiring, purchasing, or contracting with physicians, hospitals, and other health care professionals and facilities. Traditionally, MCOs have primarily pursued a single network development strategy. For instance, staff-model health maintenance organizations (HMOs) have primarily hired physicians to work exclusively for the plan, while network-based plans have contracted with physicians and hospitals to provide health care services to members. The dynamics of the market have required greater flexibility in developing provider networks, prompting MCOs to use multiple contracting approaches. This chapter focuses on the development of provider networks through contractual relationships between MCOs and providers.

The selection of specific health care professionals for participation in a provider network is a defining feature of managed care. Formation of a network based on a select number of providers is predicated on the ability of the MCO to enroll large volumes of members. In exchange for channeling members to selected physicians, the MCO receives a commitment from the physician to accept reduced reimbursement rates and abide by the procedures of the managed care program. Consequently, MCOs seek to contract with the optimum number of physicians needed to provide care to the plans' members. Too many physicians in the network prevent the plan from directing a sufficient volume of patients to each physician to warrant the desired reductions in payments.

The size of the provider network will depend on the managed care product, current and projected membership, availability of providers, and scope of service area. Preferred provider organization (PPO) networks, particularly those of open-access PPOs, tend to be broader than HMO networks because their basic design prevents PPOs from directing patients to specific providers. This expanded provider panel is also a chief reason why PPOs appeal to clients, giving PPOs incentive to maintain large networks. Plans with few members will require small networks, at least initially, and plans in rural areas may have relatively smaller networks reflecting the corresponding availability of providers in these areas. Employers are often attracted to a particular MCO for the size and scope of its provider network, with a larger network often viewed more favorably because of the greater choice of providers. MCOs must balance the marketing advantage of a large network with the administrative and financial inefficiencies such large networks create.

MCOs create or modify provider networks when entering a new market, expanding into a new service area, introducing a new product to an existing market, or reconfiguring the network to accommodate changes in compensation, contracting strategy, or enrollment. This is done through a process known as network development or provider contracting. An analysis of the provider network or medical community is the first step in developing or altering a network.

NETWORK ANALYSIS

Whether building a new provider network or modifying an existing one, some MCOs will conduct an analysis of the provider community or its existing provider network to prepare a suitable contracting strategy. A thorough analysis will enable the MCO to (1) determine a sufficient network size and composition, (2) develop realistic compensation methodologies, and (3) identify and target specific providers for contracting or re-contracting.

In conducting an analysis for a new network, the MCO will assess the available providers in the community to determine their numbers, distribution, organization, fees, credentials, referral patterns, admitting privileges, experiences with managed care, and other characteristics. In addition, the plan will ascertain the provider preferences of clients and members, the number and distribution of current and prospective members, existing managed care models in the market, and any legislation affecting provider contracting. This information can be obtained from the provider and competitive profiles of the market assessment or from informal feedback from existing or prospective clients, providers, and competitors.

An evaluation of an existing network requires similar information. Depending on the goals of its re-contracting effort, the MCO will examine the existing provider network to determine the sufficiency of provider coverage, physician referral and prescribing patterns, utilization trends, costs, patient satisfaction, patient volume, and provider familiarity with capitation and other risk-sharing arrangements. For example, in seeking to expand its existing network to accommodate an increase in enrollment, a plan will need to understand if the current providers can handle the additional patient load. Conversely, if an MCO is creating a new product requiring a subset of the existing provider network, it may review the patient satisfaction, utilization trends, and costs of participating physicians to select the high-performing physicians.

Network Adequacy

To determine the adequacy of a network, some MCOs use member-to-physician ratios (i.e., X members for every one physician) by comparing the numbers of members to physicians in specific geographic areas, as defined by county borders or ZIP codes. This is done manually or with computerized software programs that map the locations of members and providers. In determining acceptable member-to-physician ratios, the plan can ensure that the network includes a sufficient number of physicians in each specialty. Ideal ratios for primary care physicians (PCPs) range from 250 to 500, i.e., one PCP can serve 250 to 500 members; accepted ratios for specialists are 2,500 or more.[1] Using employee information from prospective or current clients, MCOs can generate member-to-physician ratios by client, which are useful for network expansions that occur because of client-specific membership growth.

Purchasers, including many Medicaid programs, impose provider access standards on MCOs based on geography or time. For example, plans must ensure that each member has access to at least one PCP within 15 miles or 30 minutes of his or her residence or job site. Geographical standards are usually less restrictive in rural areas to account for the dispersion and scarcity of health care practitioners. The degree to which MCOs evaluate their provider networks varies significantly, depending on the staffing resources available to the plan and the need to be selective in recruiting physicians.

THE CONTRACTING PROCESS

The basis for the relationship between a network-based plan and its participating providers is a contract, a legal document that binds the parties to perform certain duties. Once the MCO has completed its network development strategy, it will embark on the process of contracting with health care professionals and facilities. Depending on the contracting model, the plan's network development process may involve sending prospective physicians an application, submitting or requesting proposals, and negotiating the provider contract.

The Provider Contract

MCOs prepare standard legal agreements for use in contracting with health care providers and facilities. Some plans create standard contracts for distinct types of providers to reflect their differing responsibilities in a managed care environment. For example, an MCO might use separate contracts depending on whether it is contracting with a PCP, specialist, ancillary care provider, hospital, independent practice association (IPA), physician–hospital organization (PHO), or integrated delivery system (IDS). Separate contracts also can be used for each type of product the MCO offers. For instance, a plan may prepare standard contracts for its PPO, HMO, and Medicare products, reflecting the different requirements of each product. Generally, standard provider contracts do not differ considerably from plan to plan (a sample provider contract is found in Appendix 4–A). Provider contracts include the following sections:

Purpose. States the purpose and intent of the parties to establish a contractual relationship. Also defines the parties in the contract.

Definitions. Defines the terms used throughout the agreement, such as medical necessity, covered services, and referral.

Obligations of parties. Identifies the obligations of the MCO and provider, including responsibilities for following administrative procedures, verifying member eligibility, obtaining pre-authorizations for hospital admissions and specialty care referrals, submitting reports, and reimbursing providers.

Term and termination. Outlines the effective date and duration of the contract. Also specifies the renewal and termination provisions, whether the contract renews automatically, and how and under what circumstances the parties can terminate the agreement.

Miscellaneous. Includes provisions related to amending the contract, assigning the duties of the contract to other parties, using the respective names of the parties, and not disclosing proprietary information.

Provider Recruitment

When MCOs contract with individual providers rather than larger provider organizations—as PPOs, some network-model HMOs, and plans in rural areas do—the contracting process rarely involves the actual negotiation of contracts. Exceptions are when the plan is recruiting sought-after specialists, like anesthesiologists at a premier hospital, or a physician in an under-supplied specialty, such as the only general surgeon in a rural community. Generally, the terms for participation are standard, do not deviate dramatically from one provider to the next, and are non-negotiable.[2]

MCOs recruit providers through mailings, personal meetings, or both. Initially, the MCO will send prospective providers a recruitment packet that includes an application, standard contract, provider directory, sample benefit plans, a partial list of clients, and the plan's service area. Because the compensation arrangements and utilization review requirements for HMOs and point-of-service (POS) plans are more involved than those for PPOs, MCOs recruiting for HMO and POS networks will usually schedule a follow-up meeting with physicians to review the recruitment materials. PPOs, on the other hand, recruit providers by mail and telephone almost exclusively.

Through the application process, MCOs request basic information from the provider, such as specialty, degree, office location(s), office hours, hospital affiliations, and medical training. If the provider is interested in participating in the network, he or she will complete and submit the application, including documentation of board certification status, licensure, and other credentialing information (see below for a more detailed discussion of credentialing).

Upon receipt of a completed application, the MCO will ensure that all documentation and requested information have been submitted and that the contract has been signed where appropriate. If there is missing information or questions about the administrative aspects of the application, the provider relations department will follow up with the provider. Completed applications are forwarded by the provider relations department to the plan's medical director, peer review committee, or credentialing committee for final approval or to address potential quality issues identified in the initial review. Before the contract is executed, a representative from the provider relations or health services departments may conduct a site visit to ensure that the office is clean and accessible. The health services staff may also conduct a medical chart review to verify that the practice properly completes and maintains patient medical records. Because of the less stringent regulations governing PPOs, site visits and medical chart reviews are usually not performed for these networks.

Providers that are accepted in the network are usually notified in writing within 90 days of submitting an application. They receive a signed provider contract and an operations manual or other instructions on network participation. A provider relations representative will usually conduct an orientation session at the same time, or shortly thereafter, to review the policies and procedures of the plan. For most PPOs and some POS plans, this education is typically handled through written materials and periodic telephone consultations.

Credentialing

MCOs select providers based on their ability to meet certain quality standards and practice cost-efficiently. The credentialing process helps the plan determine if the physician is qualified to practice medicine. Additionally, to obtain accreditation from the National Committee for Quality Assurance (NCQA), or other private accrediting bodies, MCOs must meet or exceed the credentialing guidelines established by the organization. The plan requests information in the form of written documentation from providers on the following:

- board certification status
- hospital admitting privileges
- medical licensure status

- malpractice history and coverage
- existence of Medicare or Medicaid sanctions
- medical education and training
- drug dispensing licensure

After reviewing the materials submitted, the MCO verifies the accuracy of the information by contacting the sources directly, called "primary source verification." For example, MCOs contact each residency program identified by the physician to ensure that the programs were completed successfully, and they contact the state medical licensing board to determine if the physician's license is current and unrestricted. Plans also access the National Practitioner Data Bank to determine if the physician has had incidents reported by other states or plans. Based on the results of the verification process, site visits, and medical chart reviews, the medical director or credentialing committee determines whether the physician meets the quality standards for participation in the network.

Some MCOs choose to hire credential verification organizations (CVOs) to perform this verification function. Because they work with multiple clients, CVOs have amassed extensive files on many providers across the country. With electronic access to provider databases, including the American Board of Medical Specialties, Medicare sanction files, and the National Practitioner Data Bank, these organizations can be more efficient at verifying credentialing information than individual MCOs.

If the MCO contracts with a large provider organization that has an extensive physician database and a credentialing process in place, it may choose to delegate the credentialing responsibilities for providers affiliated with the provider organization to the organization itself. While this may be more efficient, the MCO must be sure to retain proper oversight of these activities as a poorly managed delegated credentialing process can negatively impact a plan's accreditation status.

Submitting or Requesting Proposals

When contracting with large provider organizations, the MCO will often prepare a detailed contract proposal for the provider group to review and consider. The basis for the proposal will be a provider contract that may incorporate specific financial proposals and other suggested terms. As an initial proposal, some MCOs prefer to send the provider group a standard contract and use a separate document to outline its proposed financial arrangements. Because negotiating a provider contract can be lengthy and arduous, the parties frequently want to ensure that they are in agreement on the financial aspects of the contract before pursuing a thorough review of the contract. Basic elements of a plan contract proposal include the following:

Plan organization and administration. The model, size, tax status, service area, management, and organizational structure of the MCO. May include an organizational chart, administrative office address, contact name and number.

Affiliated providers. A listing of the physicians, hospitals, and other health care professionals and facilities participating in the network.

Products. The types of managed care products offered by the MCO.

Marketing goals. Current enrollment by product line, existing and prospective clients, expected enrollment growth rate, targeted markets, and marketing strategies.

Financial proposal. The proposed compensation arrangements, including payment terms, assumptions, and expectations.

Utilization management procedures. The providers' responsibilities for obtaining authorizations for hospitalizations and specialty referrals and following "medically necessary" guidelines.

Distinguishing provider programs. Programs or processes that would appeal to providers including electronic data exchange capabilities, on-line eligibility verification, ongoing education, group purchasing, disease management programs, and non-gatekeeper plans.

If the MCO is modifying its network, establishing a specific contracting program, or creating a smaller network of providers within its existing provider network, it may prefer to receive written proposals from provider groups to evaluate, rather than make the initial proposal itself. For example, MCOs creating a capitation program for certain medical services, such as laboratory or radiology, or establishing a small network of high

---

Exercise: You are a provider relations director of an MCO. Prepare a contract proposal for a large medical group to consider. Be as specific and creative as possible.

performers usually request proposals from interested providers. This is done through a formal request for proposal (RFP) process.

Contract Negotiation

Unlike provider recruitment, contracting with large provider organizations usually involves a negotiation of the contract. Contract negotiations can be protracted, depending on the strengths, weaknesses, flexibility, and leverage of the parties, and the complexity and scope of the proposed contractual relationship. Increasingly, MCOs are shifting financial risk to providers, delegating utilization management and administrative functions to providers, and negotiating exclusive and long-term contracts with providers—all of which involve lengthy discussions. Contract negotiations usually encompass the following phases:

1. initial meeting
2. follow-up meetings/discussions
3. letter of intent/understanding
4. contract agreement
5. contract execution

Depending on the MCO's size and staffing levels, relative importance of the provider group, and complexity of the proposed relationship, the plan may designate a provider relations coordinator, contract manager, or executive director as the lead negotiator with the provider organization. Throughout the contract negotiation, both the MCO and provider organization may seek advice and counsel from various internal and external sources, including lawyers, actuarial consultants, physicians and other clinicians, and information systems experts. To prevent the negotiation of infeasible or expensive contract terms and to avoid unnecessary delays in the contracting process, the MCO will often establish contracting guidelines for the lead negotiator.[3]

Often the parties will sign a letter of intent (or letter of understanding) specifying their mutual interest in a contractual relationship and their intention to finalize an agreement within a certain time period. This enables the provider to begin seeing the MCO's members while the parties complete the details of the arrangement.

Exhibit 4–1 identifies the steps an MCO may take in contracting with a group. The contracting checklist helps the plan's contracting staff navigate the details of provider contracting and documents the contracting steps needed for NCQA accreditation.

Hospital Contracting

For many MCOs, the construction of a provider network begins with identifying the principal hospitals in the service area with which to contract, and then recruiting a portion of the hospital's affiliated physicians or entering into contract negotiations with the primary medical groups or IPAs that admit to the facility. Because of the proliferation of risk arrangements (where the plan and provider share in the risk of providing medical care to members), more hospital contracting these days is done in conjunction with provider group contracting (a detailed discussion of risk arrangements is below).

The primary issue in hospital contracting is the volume of patients the MCO can direct to the prospective hospital. To ensure that the actual volume of patients channeled to the hospital meets the MCO's expectation or promise, some hospitals will seek an exclusive arrangement with the plan within a defined service area or contractual volume guarantees. Volume guarantees state that the negotiated rate will be in effect as long as the volume of patients (as defined by bed day per 1,000 or number of admissions) the MCO directs to the hospital meets or exceeds a certain level. If the level is not met, an alternative payment schedule (e.g., billed charges) will apply. MCOs are more willing to grant such volume assurances when contracting for specific tertiary care services that they can realistically funnel to selected hospitals, such as neonatal care or cardiac procedures.

The relative negotiating leverage of the MCO and hospital will depend on the numbers and distribution of the hospitals in the market, the overall managed care penetration, the relative size and importance of the MCO, the perceived value of the hospital, and other characteristics of both parties. For example, an MCO new to a market with minimal managed care enrollment is likely to have difficulty securing substantial discounts from any of the hospitals it targets. Conversely, a national MCO with sizable national accounts might be successful in convincing a hospital in an oversupplied market to grant it competitive per diem rates. MCOs select

Exhibit 4–1 Contracting Checklist

PR/contracts coordinator: _____

Provider organization:_____

Contract Steps	Date
1. Send or present initial proposal to provider. Include overview of plan, summary of products, sample benefit plans, provider directory, sample contract, rate proposal (if appropriate), and provider application.	_____
2. Receive completed application and credentialing information from provider.	_____
3. Arrange provider site visit. Provider relations and/or health services representatives visit office to review physical location, administrative procedures, clinical protocols, and medical records.	_____
4. Review results of site visit and completed questionnaire with appropriate management.	_____
5. Execute letter of intent. Outline financial terms under letter of intent.	_____
6. Negotiate contract. This includes reaching conclusion on all financial, administrative, and contract language issues.	_____
7. Prepare final contract for review by appropriate management. All language changes and deviations from the standard contract must be approved in writing by management before sending to provider for signature.	_____
8. Send provider two copies of the agreement for signature.	_____
9. Receive both signed copies of the agreement for management signature.	_____
10. Bring the provider to operational status. This includes assigning provider codes, entering provider information in the provider database, creating a provider file, and notifying appropriate departments of the new provider.	_____
11. Send one copy of executed agreement to provider and retain one for the provider's file.	_____
12. Conduct a provider orientation.	_____

Source: Reprinted from W. Knight, Understanding Managed Care Contracting, in *Managed Care Contracting: A Guide for Health Care Professionals*, W. Knight, ed., p. 19, © 1997, Aspen Publishers, Inc.

hospitals based on reputation, affiliated physicians, scope of services offered, location, rates, morbidity and mortality statistics, accreditation status, costs, and willingness to accept discounted fees. Some plans are beginning to use quality measures, like patient outcomes, as a principal criteria for selecting or re-contracting with hospitals.

HOSPITAL CONTRACTING BASED ON QUALITY MEASURES

An analysis of hospital data by Anthem Blue Cross and Blue Shield in Ohio revealed significant disparities in the treatments and related outcomes of cardiac care among the participating hospitals. The review revealed that hospitals performing fewer coronary artery by-pass graft surgeries had the highest mortality rates. As a result, the plan embarked on an ambitious hospital contracting strategy using strict quality standards as the basis for selection in the network.

Hospitals and their affiliated physicians selected for participation in the plan's Coronary Services Network must meet rigorous standards for coronary care, including low mortality rates, complication rates, and lengths of stay. Ensuring the quality of care delivered by these facilities is an ongoing process; hospital, physicians, and plan representatives meet regularly to share best and worst practices and discuss ways to improve service.

Mortality rates for bypass surgery and other surgical procedures performed by the hospitals in the Coronary Services Network are well below national averages. The rate of heart attack within 24 hours after surgery and surgical complication rates declined, as well. Significantly, each hospital applying for participation in the program has shown some improvements in quality indicators, suggesting that the Coronary Services Network has impacted the overall quality of cardiac care in the community.

Courtesy of Blue Cross and Blue Shield Association, Washington, D.C.

Sole-Source Contracting

For certain ancillary services, such as laboratory, radiology, physical therapy, and home care, a plan may negotiate a contract with one company to provide specified services to members. These arrangements, which are generally structured as capitated agreements, can be national or regional depending on the service area of the plan. MCOs develop sole-source contracts with ancillary providers to

- achieve predictable costs
- reduce the administrative expense of processing claims
- share financial risk with providers
- obtain more complete and uniform utilization data
- develop targeted disease management and other patient care programs[4]

There are many issues that need to be understood by both parties in sole-source contracts. Since the plan is usually eliminating other providers from the network when entering into such an arrangement, the ability of the selected provider organization to meet the many obligations of the contract (and the plan to provide the necessary support) will be critical. Exhibit 4–2 outlines some questions MCOs need to address and providers need to consider when negotiating sole-source contracts.

COMPENSATION

Various reimbursement methodologies exist for the different types of providers (Table 4–1). For example, hospitals are usually paid discounted fee-for-service, per diem rates, case rates, diagnosis-related groups (DRGs), or capitation, while home health care agencies are usually paid according to a per hour or per visit fee schedule. Some compensation arrangements are limited to certain types of providers while others have universal use. For instance, DRGs are used exclusively for hospitals, while others, like discount fee-for-service, can apply to all providers. Most MCOs will use several different reimbursement methods within a given market, reflecting

Exhibit 4–2 Questions To Consider in Negotiating Sole-Source Contracts

---

1. What scope of services is included? Are ancillary services included?
2. What parameters exist for subcontractual arrangements?
3. Who is responsible for network development and provider relations?
4. What if the vendor doesn't service all the MCO markets?
5. How does the contract address future MCO expansions into new markets?
6. Does the contract cover all product lines?
7. How will payments for out-of-network benefits be handled?
8. Will some services be reimbursed fee-for-service? Are these defined in the contract?
9. Who has responsibility to minimize out-of-network leakage? What are the penalties or incentives to reduce leakage?
10. Who has responsibility for managing client and member relations, including staffing member services telephone lines and developing member education materials?
11. How will the contract be administered in each market? What additional administration and management is necessary?
12. Is there an administrative fee for managing the network?
13. What utilization assumptions were used in developing the capitation rate? Do these mirror existing utilization rates for the services or are they lower than present utilization rates?
14. Does the contract include utilization (or risk) corridors?
15. What utilization and medical management reports will be provided and expected?

Source: Reprinted from W. Knight and L.A. Sansone, Ambulatory and Ancillary Care Contracting, in *Managed Care Contracting: A Guide for Health Care Professionals*, W. Knight, ed., p. 221, © 1997, Aspen Publishers, Inc.

---

the relative preferences and leverage of the providers and plan. For example, a start-up MCO in a mature market may be limited to negotiating discount fee-for-service arrangements with providers.

Discounted Fee-for-Service

Under a discounted fee-for-service arrangement, MCOs pay providers a percentage of the provider's usual fee schedule or billed charges. Despite its connection with traditional insurance, discounted fee-for-service is still widely used by MCOs. PPOs, for example, use discounted fee-for-service arrangements almost exclusively. As illustrated in Table 4–1, 70 percent of

Table 4-1 Methods of Provider Reimbursement (*n* = 266)

Method of Reimbursement	Number of HMOs	Percentage of HMOs
Hospitals		
Fees or discounted fee schedules	187	70.6%
Per diem rates	239	89.8%
DRGs	128	48.9%
Capitation	94	35.6%
Primary care physicians		
Multi-specialty group settings		
Fees or discounted fee schedules	114	48.5%
Relative value scales	63	23.7%
Capitation	165	70.2%
Salary*	26	11.1%
Solo or single specialty practices		
Fees or discounted fee schedules	153	60.7%
Relative value scales	82	32.5%
Capitation	178	70.6%
Salary	12	4.8%
Specialty care physicians		
Multi-specialty group settings		
Fees or discounted fee schedules	154	66.7%
Relative value scales	76	32.9%
Capitation	108	46.7%
Salary*	18	7.8%
Solo or single specialty practices		
Fees or discounted fee schedules	187	75.7%
Relative value scales	93	37.6%
Capitation	96	38.9%
Salary	8	3.2%

*Respondents may have reported how the physician was paid by a group practice rather than how the HMO pays the multispecialty group.

Source: Reprinted with permission from *HMO Industry Report 7.1*, p. 60, © 1997, InterStudy.

HMOs reported using discounted fee schedules with hospitals and more than 60 percent of HMOs reported using such arrangements with specialists in solo or single specialty practice.

The discount can be a flat percentage for all procedures, known as a straight discount, or can vary by service. For example, a plan may contract with a hospital for a 25 percent discount off inpatient charges, 30 percent discount off outpatient diagnostic services, and 15 percent discount off charges for emergency room services. To ensure that the volume of services directed at the provider or institution warrants a certain discount, such arrangements can be modified by volume of services, also known as sliding scale discounts. For example, an ambulatory surgical center may give a plan a 20 percent discount off charges for surgical procedures but will increase the discount to 30 percent once the volume exceeds 1,000 surgeries per year.

Discounted arrangements can also include a fee maximum that is applied to the claim before the negotiated discount is taken. Fee maximums are usually set between the 40th and the 80th percentile of a community's average charge, saving the MCOs from paying more for a procedure than is customary in an area. For example, a discount of 25 percent for emergency room procedures might be limited to a $300 payment; that is, no more than $300 would be paid on an emergency room claim even if the bill exceeded $300.

Relative Value–Based Fee Schedules

Relative value–based fee schedules are payments based on the relative value of medical and surgical procedures. Unit values are assigned to each procedure identified by CPT-4 codes based on their relative values. A procedure with a unit value of two has twice as much value as another procedure with a unit value of one. The MCO determines the dollar amount, called a conversion factor, that will be multiplied by the unit value to produce a fee for each procedure, and thus a fee schedule. For example, if the plan used a $35 conversion factor, a procedure worth two unit values would be paid $70. Relative value fee schedules are used to pay physicians and other health professionals that organize and bill services according to CPT-4 codes. Separate conversion factors can exist for different services, such as medical and surgical procedures. There are three principal versions of unit values used to create a fee schedule: the McGraw-Hill Unit Value System, the Resource-Based Relative Value System (RBRVS), and the unit values published by the American Society of Anesthesiologists for anesthesia procedures.

McGraw-Hill Unit Value System

Used for commercial business only, the McGraw-Hill Unit Value System, published by McGraw-Hill, Inc., is used broadly throughout the country. It has established unit values for all procedures (CPT-4 codes), except anesthesia. The procedures are grouped into four major categories—surgery, medicine, radiology, and pathology—with varying conversion factors. While the unit values for procedures within each category, like medicine, have relative relationships, there is not a relative relationship among categories.[5]

Resource-Based Relative Value System

Originally developed by the Health Care Financing Administration (HCFA) for Medicare reimbursement, the RBRVS is a unit value fee schedule now used widely by many plans for non-Medicare populations. RBRVS unit values are composed of three components—work expense, practice expense, and malpractice expense—and are adjusted by a geographic factor to consider variations in health care costs throughout the country. To create a fee schedule, the total unit value for each procedure is multiplied by the applicable conversion factor established by the plan. Using one conversion factor (as was the original intent of the RBRVS system) generates disproportionate fees across physician specialties, with many of the specialists seeing a sharp reduction in their compensation vis à vis primary care specialties. To account for the realities of physician recruiting, many plans create multiple conversion factors—for example, primary care, surgical, and non-surgical services—to generate fees acceptable to most specialists.

Commercial RBRVS fee schedules are often presented as a percentage of the Medicare RBRVS fee schedule by specific CPT-4 medical services (Table 4–2). Another way plans adjust for the disparities in fees among physician groupings is by applying different percentages of the Medicare RBRVS schedule to specific CPT-4 groupings of medical services, such as general surgery and orthopaedics. While this tactic negates the intent of the RBRVS payment system, it enables MCOs to recruit specialists without negotiating special reimbursement arrangements.

Using the base relative value unit of 2.415 in the example illustrated in Exhibit 4–3, procedure code 99202 (office visit) is valued at 1.2. If the plan has a non-surgical conversion of $32.00, the fee for an office visit would be $38.40.

Exhibit 4–3 Calculating an RBRVS Fee Schedule

Relative value unit adjusted by geographic factors	
Work:	.950
Practice:	.965
Malpractice:	.500
Total:	2.415
Conversion factors	
Surgical:	$35.00
Non-surgical:	$32.00
Sample fees by CPT-4 codes	
99202 office visit, RVU 1.2:	$38.40
58260 hysterectomy, RVU 20.3:	$710.50

American Society of Anesthesiologists

The American Society of Anesthesiologists (ASA) publishes a relative value unit system for all anesthesia procedures—the only generally recognized system for anesthesia procedures. Fees for anesthesia services are determined by multiplying a conversion factor by the base unit value plus the time unit value of each procedure. Each procedure's base unit value includes the time preparing for a surgical procedure. Time unit values, measured in 12- or 15-minute intervals, are for the actual time elapsed during the procedure. Since the ASA relative value system only encompasses anesthesia services, it is used in combination with other relative value systems or reimbursement arrangements.[6]

Case Rates

A case rate is the total reimbursement for a particular treatment or service that usually has a defined duration, referred to as a "case." An outpatient surgery, maternity delivery, and organ transplant are examples of treatments that lend themselves to case rate reimbursement. As a result, this reimbursement methodology is most often used with hospitals and other facilities. Case rates (also called flat rates) cover all services and procedures associated with the treatment. For instance, a case rate of $20,000 for a heart bypass operation would include the surgery and any

Table 4–2 Sample RBRVS Fee Schedule

Specialty	CPT-4 Codes	Percent of Medicare
Surgery:		
Dermatology	10040–17999	140
General surgery	19000–60699	190
Orthopaedic	20000–29909	185
Ear, nose, and throat (ENT)	30000–69979	180
Cardio/thoracic	31600–37799	185
Urology	50010–55899	180
Gynecology	56300–58999	155
Obstetrics	59000–59899	155
Neurosurgery	61000–64999	175
Ophthalmology	65091–68899	140
Medicine:		
Office visits and consults	90701–99499	120
Ophthalmology	92002–92499	130
ENT	92551–92599	130
Cardiology	92950–93799	140
Pulmonology	94010–94799	135
Allergy	95000–95199	135
Neurology	95805–95999	140
Chemotherapy	96400–96549	135
Physical therapy	97010–98929	140
Radiology	70010–79999	145
Pathology	80002–89399	130

pre- and post-operative care in the hospital or physician's office. Depending on whether the contract is with a hospital, physician group, or organization that encompasses both, case rates can be global (i.e., professional and facility charges), professional only, or facility only (also called "technical"). For example, a case rate for an obstetrician would include the prenatal and postnatal care rendered and the professional component of the delivery, while an ambulatory surgery case rate with a PHO would include both the professional and technical services of the surgery and the pre-operative and follow-up care.

Per Hour or Per Visit Payments

Flat rates also refer to per hour or per visit (usually defined as two hours) payments for home care services, including nursing care, infusion therapy, and physical therapy. Flat rates can vary based on the level or category of care. For example, a home care visit by a registered nurse might be $60 while a visit by a licensed practical nurse would be $50. Home care services requiring more than two hours are paid according to a per diem rate schedule (see below).

Per Diems

"Per diem" is a Latin term meaning per day. As such, per diem reimbursements are used for services that consume all or most of a day. The provider receives one payment to cover all facility charges (not professional charges) for each day of service. For example, if the negotiated rate is $800 per day and the service requires five days, the facility receives $4,000 ($800 × 5 = $4,000). Plans negotiate per diem rates with hospitals and facilities for both inpatient and outpatient services. Nearly 90 percent of HMOs use per diem rates as a method of reimbursing hospitals (see Table 4–1).

Although seldom used, the most basic per diem rate is flat rate for all services—$900 for all inpatient services, for example. Per diem rates usually vary by level of care. For example, a skilled nursing facility can be reimbursed at $110 per day for skilled nursing care and $250 per day for subacute care. Likewise, a plan can negotiate different per diems with a hospital based on whether the patient was in the intensive care unit (e.g., $1,200 per day) or medical ward (e.g., $1,000 per day). More intensive services are reimbursed at higher per diem levels.

MCOs establish per diem rates that fluctuate based on the total length of the inpatient stay, as well. For example, a plan might negotiate a sliding scale arrangement with a hospital for a normal vaginal delivery as follows: the payment for a one-day delivery would be $1,100 per day; the payment for a two-day delivery would be $900 per day (or a total of $1,800); and the payment for a three-day delivery would be $700 per day (or a total of $2,100). Per diem rate arrangements can vary for each day of the hospital stay. For example, the first day of a normal vaginal delivery might be reimbursed at $900 per day, while subsequent days would be paid at $650 per day.

Diagnosis-Related Groups

DRGs are case rate reimbursements made to hospitals based on the primary diagnosis of the admission. The method was developed by HCFA as a reimbursement method for the Medicare program and is being used by MCOs for their commercial population. HCFA determines the relative values and the acceptable length of stay for each diagnosis. Fees for each diagnosis are calculated by multiplying the relative values of the diagnoses by the conversion factor negotiated between the plan and hospital. For example, if the negotiated conversion factor is $5,000 and the value for DRG 106 (coronary bypass) is 5.66, the fee for the procedure would be $28,300 ($5,000 × 5.66 = $28,300). To account for the severity of some cases, plans may negotiate per diem rates for the days that exceed the accepted case length of stay. However, because the length of stays are based on the Medicare population (who have longer hospital stays than the under-65 population), the use of per diem outliers should be monitored carefully. Conversely, since hospitals will gain financially by managing a case within the accepted length of stay, the MCO must ensure that the hospital is not inappropriately discharging patients early.

Capitation

A capitation payment is a fixed monthly amount a provider receives for each member enrolled or assigned to his or her practice or facility. Instead of being compensated for specific services delivered, the provider receives a prepayment designed to cover all the medical care (as defined by the contract) a member might need regardless of the actual services provided. A capitation method of payment requires a sufficient member base to generate enough funds to endure the risk of high cost or utilization of a select few. Capitation rates are used predominantly by HMOs, although some POS plans compensate some physicians according to a capitation schedule. Because PPOs are not risk-bearing entities, they are not assuming any financial risk of managing care that they can "shift" to providers.

Capitation rates are usually structured as fixed dollar amounts per member per month (PMPM) and are adjusted by the age and sex of the member to better reflect the actual costs and utilization of services by people within certain age and sex categories. Table 4–3 illustrates a sample set of age/sex factors for primary care capitation.

Capitation rates can also be based on a percentage of the premium rate that the MCO receives from the purchaser. Percentage of premium contracts are negotiated with hospitals and integrated provider groups, not individual physicians. These arrangements can seem appealing to provid-

Table 4-3 Age/Sex Factors for Primary Care Capitation

	Age/Sex Band	Age/Sex Factors
Male		
	0–1	2.775
	2–6	0.992
	7–18	0.623
	19–24	0.502
	25–29	0.644
	30–34	0.651
	35–39	0.714
	40–44	0.822
	45–49	0.932
	50–54	1.094
	55–59	1.368
	60–64	1.565
	65+	1.585
Female		
	0–1	2.660
	2–6	0.936
	7–18	0.548
	19–24	0.771
	25–29	1.101
	30–34	1.151
	35–39	1.243
	40–44	1.317
	45–49	1.334
	50–54	1.441
	55–59	1.585
	60–64	1.668
	65+	1.812

Source: Reprinted from N.L. Reaven and K.S. Patterson, Analyzing Financial Arrangement, in *Managed Care Contracting: A Guide for Health Care Professionals*, W. Knight, ed., p. 103 © 1997, Aspen Publishers, Inc.

ers because they eliminate the uncertainty of how much of the premium dollar is funneled to them. However, they can leave the provider with a financial deficit if the plan's premium rates do not generate ample funds to cover the costs of services the practitioner must provide. This can happen if the MCO does not perform underwriting properly or deliberately lowers premiums to gain market share. Under these scenarios, the proportion of the premium allocated to the provider will diminish, but the actual cost of providing services will not.[7] In accepting a percentage of the premium from the plan, providers can negotiate a flat dollar amount—or "floor"—to ensure that they receive a minimum dollar value for the services they are expected to provide.[8]

Capitation is a controversial method of compensating providers. Because a capitation rate results in a set dollar amount for each patient, regardless of the health care services the patient actually uses, many contend that this form of reimbursement encourages physicians to withhold necessary treatment to gain financially. This contention supposes an untrustworthy physician population and raises questions about the impact of capitation on the frequency of health care services delivered. Under fee-for-service reimbursement, patients represent sources of revenue for physicians; however, under capitation, patients become expenses. Does this change the way physicians treat patients? This is a question being addressed in studies analyzing the impact of managed care on physician practice.

The utilization of health care services is expected to decline under a capitation model, proponents argue, because care will be managed more efficiently when providers receive capitation. But this assumes that the expectations of future utilization are credible, and that the patients the physicians actually see mirror the demographic populations on which the capitation rates are based. Many people challenge the assumptions and methods on which capitation rates are constructed, arguing that current methodologies do not account for the vast differences in health care utilization by specific demographic populations.

Primary Care Capitation

Primary care capitation is the most prevalent type of capitation. Over 70 percent of HMOs pay PCPs a capitation rate (see Table 4–1). Services that are included in the capitation payment are defined in the contract, which may be negotiable depending on the plan and the leverage of the physician. Providers not capable of delivering all contracted health care services may be required to subcontract with or reimburse another provider to perform the services. Services excluded from the capitation rate are usually reimbursed according to a fee schedule.

In addition to the basic capitation rate, some MCOs reimburse PCPs a patient management allowance (also known as an administrative fee) for managing and coordinating the care of members. For example, a PCP might receive $10 PMPM plus an administrative fee of $1.50 PMPM. This usually occurs only in markets where PCPs or their administrative agents have significant negotiating leverage.

Specialty Care Capitation

Capitation of specialty care services is increasing among some MCOs, as they seek to control rising medical costs related to specialty care. MCOs are more likely to capitate specialists practicing in multi-speciality groups than those in solo or single specialty practice. From the plan's perspective, the capitation of specialists is most successful in specialties that generate sufficient medical costs to justify the administrative expense of configuring the capitated program. MCOs pursue specialty care capitation for several reasons.

- to reduce medical costs of high-cost specialties
- to gain an advantage in the market through competitive premium rates and profitability
- to create new products for price-sensitive market segments, such as Medicare and small businesses
- to build strong strategic alliances with specialty care providers
- to develop clinical practice guidelines that will improve the process and outcomes of care
- to eliminate the administrative costs associated with multiple specialty contracting arrangements, claims processing, and fraudulent and abusive billing practices
- to form a downsized and workable specialty network to better manage specialty costs and utilization[9]

The number of members that can be directed to the physician must be sufficient to offset the risk of high utilization. Specialties with low frequency of services and high average cost per service, such as neurosurgery and cardiothoracic surgery, would require much larger member panels to justify capitation, while specialists with a high frequency of services and a low average cost per service, such as specialists in radiology and pathology, require fewer members. Because members in a managed care program do not select specialists, as they do PCPs, it is more challenging for plans to structure specialty care capitation. Key issues in specialty capitation include aligning members to capitated specialists, understanding and managing referrals to specialists, and addressing exclusions from the capitation payment.

Aligning members to capitated specialists. Since capitation payments are based on the number of members assigned or directed to a practice, plans capitating specialists must develop a mechanism for aligning members (and thus payments) to the specialist. If the plan is capitating individual specialists (rather than one large specialty group for all MCO members) the MCO must tie members to the specialists by assigning PCP offices to certain capitated specialists. In this way, the specialist is paid a capitation rate for members who are enrolled in the PCP practice that is now tied to the specialty practice. This can be done by geographic region (i.e., all PCPs in certain ZIP codes are assigned to the capitated specialist in that region) or PCP choice, where the PCP selects the specialist he or she will use exclusively.[10]

Understanding and managing referrals to specialists. Since specialists rely on PCPs and other specialties to send them patients, they have limited control over the utilization of their services, at least initial consultations. The plan must ensure that PCPs and other specialists do not unnecessarily shift care to the capitated specialist—for example, by routinely sending the specialist patients with ailments the PCP should be able to treat, referred to as "dumping."[11] Moreover, a capitation specialty program always involves downsizing the specialty network. Consequently, the MCO must understand how the capitation of specialists will disrupt the existing referral patterns. The MCO will need to instruct PCPs on any new referral requirements and establish a mechanism to handle referrals sent to non-capitated or non-designated specialists.

Addressing exclusions from the capitation payment. Some services may be excluded from the capitation rate because the plan provides for them another way, the specialists cannot provide all services within the defined specialty, or the specialists will not provide the service within the scope of the capitation rate. The MCO can opt to (1) exclude these services directly from the capitation payment, reimbursing them separately, according to a fee schedule; (2) allow the physician to subcontract with another specialist to provide the service; or (3) pay the excluded services on a fee-for-service basis and deduct these services from the specialist's capitation payment.

> **Exercise: You are a cardiologist in a group practice. What questions do you have for the MCO before you agree to the capitation rate it has proposed to your group?**

Multi-Specialty Capitation

MCOs often pay IPAs and multi-specialty groups according to a capitation schedule. Under this arrangement, the provider group receives a payment to provide all primary and specialty care physician services to members who are assigned to, or choose, the group. If the group cannot provide a particular service, it usually makes arrangements with another provider to deliver the care and pays that provider directly. To retain the influence of provider groups in hospital utilization, many MCOs will structure a hospital bonus arrangement with capitated multi-specialty groups (see the discussion of risk-sharing arrangements below).

Hospital Capitation

Occasionally, MCOs pay hospitals a capitation rate, although this usually occurs in the context of a broader risk-sharing arrangement with physicians, given their role in admitting patients. One-third of HMOs reported paying hospitals according to a capitation schedule (see Table 4–1). Without incentives for physicians to control hospital utilization, a hospital capitation contract can result in significant losses for the institution. The capitation rate the hospital receives is based on the number of members assigned to PCPs or medical groups who admit exclusively to the hospital. As with all capitation contracts, the issue of exclusions must be addressed. Will the plan "carve out" from the capitation services the hospital cannot provide, like neonatal care or magnetic resonance imaging, or will the hospital need to subcontract with other facilities to provide these services? Hospital capitation rates can be based on straight PMPM rates, age/sex-adjusted PMPM rates, or a percentage of premium. The MCO should attempt to establish a capitation rate based on the historic performance of the hospital risk pool and prevailing capitation rates in the market.

Risk Pools or Bonus Arrangements

In addition to the regular compensation it pays providers, the plan may structure a risk pool (also known as a bonus arrangement) to further encourage the providers to appropriately manage the care of members. Nearly 40 percent of HMOs reported having a risk pool in place for PCPs, and one in four reported having a risk pool for specialty care physicians.[12] Risk pools enable providers to share with the plan the financial loss (i.e., risk) or gain (i.e., reward) of managing care for members, especially inpatient care.

While there are many variations in risk pool and bonus arrangements, such as who participates in the pool, how the pool is funded, what services are included in the pool, and how the surplus/deficits are distributed, they share a similar concept and structure. First, services that are to be covered under the risk pool are determined. The projected costs of paying for these services are allocated to the risk pool. (A portion of any capitation payments for other services is usually also allocated to the risk pool.) When claims for the services covered under the risk pool are submitted to the MCO, they are deducted from the pool. This leaves a surplus or deficit depending on the utilization of services and dollar amount of medical claims. A surplus in the pool is distributed to the providers and the MCO according to the negotiated arrangement (a deficit is funded by the providers and the MCO, as well). This is usually handled at a year-end reconciliation of the contract. Since the hospital receives fee-for-service payments and does not share in the risk pool, it has little incentive to conserve the funds in the pool. Full-risk (or global) capitation contracts, on the other hand, align the incentives of the physicians and hospitals (see below).

HOW A RISK-SHARING ARRANGEMENT WORKS

Great Doctors Medical Group (GDMG) and Savvy Health Plan (SHP) have entered into a risk-sharing arrangement where any surplus or deficit of the hospital risk pool is shared equally. SHP pays GDMG $40 PMPM for professional services and allocates $40 PMPM for hospital services. Ten percent ($4 PMPM) of GDMG's monthly professional capitation payment is withheld (known as a withhold) to help fund the hospital risk pool. Assuming 5,000 of SHP's members are enrolled in GDMG throughout the year, the annual withhold would be $240,000

(5,000 × $4 × 12). In addition, the $40 PMPM reserved for hospital services is allocated to the risk pool, equaling $2,400,000 (5,000×$40 × 12). The total amount of the risk pool is $2,640,000 ($240,000 + $2,400,000). Payments for hospital services are paid from the risk pool. If the hospital claims exceed the amount in the pool, the group loses its withhold and shares in the loss with the MCO. For instance, if the annual hospital claims generated by GDMG total $3,000,000, the group forfeits its withhold and must reimburse the MCO $180,000 ($3,000,000 − $2,640,000 divided by 2). If the actual hospital claims are less than the amount in the pool, the withhold and a share of the surplus are returned to group. For example, if GDMG's hospital claims amounted to $2,200,000, then the group would receive its $240,000 withhold plus half of the surplus, or $100,000 ($2,400,000 − $2,200,000 divided by 2).

The most common type of risk arrangement is when an MCO pays a provider group a capitation rate for professional services and establishes a risk pool for hospital and other services. This is illustrated in Figure 4–1.

Full-Risk Capitation

In a full-risk (also known as global) capitation model, the provider organization, usually a PHO, IPA, or IDS, receives a capitation rate for all

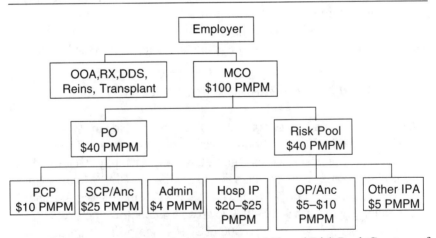

Figure 4–1 Provider Organization Capitation and Shared-Risk Pool. Courtesy of Meridian Health Care Management, Thousand Oaks, California.

professional and institutional services for a defined membership. A full-risk capitation contract gives the hospital and physicians equal incentive to control all medical utilization.

If the organization does not provide the services directly, it is usually required to make arrangements with other providers to deliver the care. Because it is responsible for providing all medical care for members, the group involved in a full-risk capitation arrangement will need to track and monitor member eligibility and coverage information, authorize and track referrals to specialists, process claims, and submit financial and utilization reports to the plan. Administering full-risk arrangements places sizable financial demands on the provider group to acquire or lease information and financial management systems to perform these functions.

Figure 4–2 illustrates the full-risk capitation model.

Stop Loss Coverage

Stop loss is a form of reinsurance that offers MCOs and providers financial protection when medical expenses exceed a certain dollar limit or percentage of risk pool funds. There are two types of stop loss coverage: specific and aggregate. Specific stop loss pertains to a particular case or individual. Under specific stop loss coverage, the provider group is responsible for all medical claims up to a specific dollar amount, called a

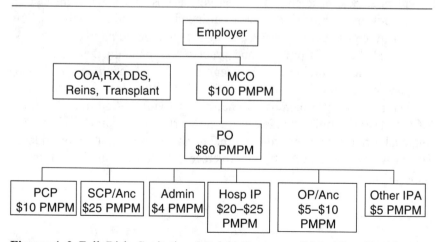

Figure 4–2 Full Risk Capitation Model. Courtesy of Meridian Health Care Management, Thousand Oaks, California.

deductible or threshold. For physician groups, the threshold amount is usually $5,000 per case or individual. Once the medical claims of that individual exceed the threshold, the reinsurer assumes responsibility for paying the majority of the individual's medical claims, usually 80 or 90 percent. The provider group must share in the remaining 10 or 20 percent of the individual's medical claims.

Primarily used in risk arrangements, aggregate stop loss coverage protects providers against excessive medical claims in total, not just those for one individual. As with specific reinsurance, the provider with aggregate stop loss coverage is responsible for all medical claims up to a certain threshold, defined as a percentage of the expected claims or risk pool. Once the total medical claims for a defined period (usually one year) exceed the threshold, the reinsurer pays all remaining medical bills for the provider. For instance, suppose Provider Group One has an aggregate stop loss policy with Plan Two to protect its risk pool arrangement. The threshold is set at 120 percent of the group's hospital risk pool. If the total medical claims of the plan's members assigned to the group exceed 120 percent of the risk pool, the reinsurance policy covers the rest of the medical claims for that year.

NETWORK MANAGEMENT

Once a network has been created, the provider relations staff is responsible for ensuring that the administrative interactions between the plan and providers work as efficiently and positively as possible, and that the health care practitioners abide by the terms outlined in the provider contracts. For example, the provider relations staff ensures that participating physicians understand the plan's policies and procedures, maintain their qualifications to practice medicine, receive accurate and timely payments, maintain adequate office hours, comply with the plan's standards for access and availability, and refer members to network providers. Additionally, most MCOs make periodic changes to the network, such as introducing new financial arrangements or reducing the number of participating providers. The provider relations staff will oversee the implementation of these changes, as well.

Re-Credentialing

Most MCOs re-credential network providers periodically to ensure that their qualifications are still valid. Because NCQA requires MCOs to re-credential providers once every two years, most HMOs have adopted this as standard practice. A re-credentialing effort involves the same steps as the initial credentialing process. Based on the physician's participation in the network, the plan may have additional information from which to evaluate providers, including total claims costs, costs per member or costs per procedure, number of hospital admissions and average length of stay, and number of non-network referrals and number of referrals by specialty.

Additionally, the plan will use the results of member satisfaction surveys and any reported incidents to the member services department when considering the renewal of the provider contract.

Handling Provider Issues

The provider relations staff is the liaison between the MCO and participating providers, responsible for communicating the policies and procedures of the plan and addressing any concerns providers and their office staff encounter with the program. Examples of issues providers might have include non-compliant or disruptive members, late claim payments, inaccurate capitation checks/statements, and difficulties accessing member eligibility systems. While addressing provider issues often entails the involvement of other departments, such as claims or members services, the provider relations department is usually held accountable for their successful resolution.

Implementing Network Changes

To remain competitive in the dynamic managed care market, MCOs frequently revise their network strategies by modifying financial arrangements, expanding or reducing network size, and changing referral patterns. Many contemplated changes to the network require modifications to the provider contracts first. For example, if a plan introduces a new open access product to a market, it may need to amend the existing provider contracts to reflect the different referral and authorization requirements of this product. Likewise, if a plan initiates a capitated home care program, it may need to terminate contracts with home care providers not selected for participation in the new program. The provider relations department oversees the re-contracting effort, ensuring that contracts are terminated according to the contract provisions. Other network changes are made that do not require an amendment to existing provider contracts. For example, most provider contracts include provisions that allow the MCO to update fee schedules annually and implement certain policy changes without the prior approval of the provider.

Educating Physicians and Office Staff

Educating providers and their office staff about the plan is an ongoing responsibility of MCOs. Once a provider has been recruited into the network, the plan will conduct an initial orientation of the respective roles and obligations of the parties under the contract. MCOs sometimes schedule separate orientation sessions for physicians and their office staff. Orientations for providers should be scheduled around practice hours— early morning, noon, and late afternoon—and need to be brief. For hospitals, larger provider organizations, or providers with multiple sites, the plans will usually conduct a group orientation at one or two sites with several people from the provider organizations attending. The plan usually reviews the following information in an initial orientation:

- products offered in market, including plan designs
- sample covered benefits
- referral authorization procedures
- hospital admissions procedures
- emergency care protocols
- member eligibility verification
- member identification cards
- claims submission and payment policies
- capitation statements and checks (if applicable)
- participating providers, including designated hospitals
- compensation arrangements
- required utilization or quality reports
- covered benefits or "carve-out" programs, if applicable

The MCO continues to train and educate providers and their office staff after the initial orientation, reinforcing compliance with existing plan procedures or introducing new or modified policies. This is done through various methods including telephone calls, provider newsletter, written materials, videos, electronic mail, plan website, and site visits. To meet accreditation standards, many MCOs, particularly HMOs, have developed schedules for the ongoing education of providers. For example, a provider relations representative will make a site visit to each PCP office every quarter to answer questions, review policies and procedures, and address any problems that might exist. High-use specialists, such as obstetricians/gynecologists (OB/GYNs) and general surgeons, might have a site visit from the plan twice a year.

Large provider organizations with full-risk or risk-sharing arrangements with plans usually need to meet more regularly to review clinical and financial performance. Risk contracts often require MCOs and providers to meet quarterly or semi-annually to assess how the group is performing under the contract, particularly if the risk arrangement is new. This gives both parties a chance to compare the actual and expected utilization and costs, and make changes in practice patterns or assumptions if necessary.

In addition to the routine education of providers and staff, MCOs use targeted training and education to address clinical deficiencies and questionable practices or reinforce appropriate treatment protocols. Profiling each provider can expose any number of practices that require plan intervention, like referring a disproportionate number of patients to orthopaedic surgeons for low back pain or performing a high rate of Caesarean deliveries. Based on this referral and utilization information, the plan can target providers for specific education, reinforcing administrative policies or disseminating "best practices" information (i.e., practices that produce the optimal results).

Some MCOs have established formal training programs for network physicians. Very rare, formal education and training programs seek to expand the physician's understanding of managed care, and sometimes to improve the physician's knowledge and skills in specific clinical areas.

HENRY FORD HEALTH SYSTEM'S MANAGED CARE COLLEGE

In 1993, the Henry Ford Health System introduced the Managed Care College, an education program designed to (1) expand the knowledge and skills of physicians practicing in managed care and (2) improve physicians' management of specific medical conditions. PCPs affiliated with the staff-model division of Health Alliance Plan were enrolled in the pilot program. The program consisted of a four- to five-hour class each month, a one-hour study group each week, and occasional seminars. The premise of the program is that both the baseline and condition-specific knowledge will increase the physicians' willingness to follow standardized clinical practices and modify practice behaviors according to guidelines derived from such "best practices," and as a result of the changed provider behavior, the health outcomes of the patient will improve.[13]

INFLUENCING PROVIDER BEHAVIOR

People change their behavior by being educated, persuaded, enticed, punished, required, or otherwise motivated. So it is that MCOs influence physicians, specifically their practice patterns, through various methods of education, rewards, sanctions, and requirements. For example, as a condition of participating in the plan, providers are required to accept the negotiated payment and obtain authorization before admitting patients to the hospital. However, the crucial factor for managed care success—the cost-effective and clinically-sound practice of medicine—cannot be mandated by MCOs. Instead, it is determined by the providers themselves who must be motivated to practice appropriately, both in clinical and economic terms.

While it is generally accepted that rewards are more effective in bringing about change than sanctions are, MCOs have been somewhat slow to adopt this philosophy in their drive to change provider behavior. MCOs are most capable of influencing provider behavior by sharing the valuable information they collect and analyze about physician practice.

Provider Profiling

Comparing the performance of providers against their peers can be an effective tool in changing provider behavior. To assess the performance of participating providers, MCOs collect and analyze cost, utilization, and quality information on physicians, including

- number of hospital admissions
- average length of stay
- number of referrals to specialists, by specialty and by member
- number of diagnostic tests, by specialty and by member
- number of commonly-used procedures within specialty
- numbers and types of prescription drug orders, by drug and by member
- total claims costs
- total claims cost per procedure, per hospitalization, and per member
- number of member complaints or grievances
- percent of members leaving the practice

Provider files enable MCOs to evaluate the performance of these physicians against peers, plan averages, and community or national norms. Depending on how providers are organized within the network, comparisons of physicians can be made within specialties, geographic areas, and medical groups. The plan should consider the severity and mix of patients, the scope of services a physician provides, and the physician's specialty or subspecialty when making comparisons.

For example, through provider profiling, MCOs can identify the average number of laboratory tests PCPs are ordering and for which patients. The number of laboratory tests for each PCP can then be compared to this standard to determine if certain PCPs order more or fewer laboratory tests compared to their peers and why. A comprehensive analysis of provider data can also help the plan identify general deficiencies in treatments. For example, PCPs with higher incidence of asthmatic patients should have a corresponding high rate of prescription drug orders for asthma medications. If they do not, this could tell the MCO that further analysis is warranted.

MCOs gather information on providers from many sources, including

- medical claims or encounters
- patient medical charts
- utilization review/referral systems

- hospital admission logs
- patient satisfaction surveys
- patient health assessments
- input from MCO staff

Primarily, MCOs use provider profiling to help physicians improve the care they give patients. By using actual experience to identify aberrant provider referral and utilization trends, plans can educate physicians about appropriate practice patterns and establish standards and processes of care. It is essential that plans give physicians specific and ongoing feedback so that practice patterns can be modified.

MCOs also use provider profiles to determine performance-based reimbursement arrangements, justify renewal or cancellation of provider contracts, and identify fraudulent billing practices.

Performance-Based Compensation

Some MCOs take providing profiling a step further by tying a portion of the physician's compensation to specific performance. To reward appropriate practice patterns (or discourage costly and clinically-inefficient ones), the MCO adjusts provider compensation based on the ability of providers to meet or exceed certain quality and service standards. Examples of indicators in evaluating provider performance include

- member satisfaction surveys
- rates of member complaints and grievances
- wait time for appointments
- immunization rates
- hospital re-admission rates
- mammography rates

Such quality-based adjustments can be in the form of rewards (i.e., positive motivators) or sanctions (i.e., negative motivators), which may or may not be financial. Rewards give providers something above and beyond what is obligated to them under the basic payment terms of the contract. For example, specialty and hospital bonus pools represent potential rewards for PCPs who would not otherwise receive a portion of hospital or specialty surpluses. Conversely, provider withholds are seen as sanctions since they potentially take away a portion of the compensation the plan allocates to physicians. Examples of how MCOs can reward providers for good performance are lump sum bonuses, increased capitation rates or fee schedules, or awards and special designations. MCOs penalize providers by closing their practices to new members (applicable to PCPs), reducing capitation payments or fee schedules, or increasing the percentage of their compensation that is withheld.

In recent years, MCOs have created specific compensation programs to reward providers, especially PCPs, for improving quality and member satisfaction. For example, Fallon Community Health Plan implemented a bonus program for PCPs to reward high-performing physicians, based largely on member satisfaction measures. The level of bonus a PCP receives depends on how the members perceive the care (i.e., Is the PCP courteous? Does he or she explain medical issues adequately?).[14]

Practice Guidelines

Practice guidelines are generally accepted blueprints for treating specific conditions or patients. For example, it is a widely accepted practice that PCPs or OB/GYNs should perform an annual mammogram on female patients over age 50. Developed by physician organizations, specialty societies, the federal government, and MCOs themselves, practice guidelines are used by plans to educate physicians about appropriate clinical practices. Physicians, however, often view practice guidelines negatively, regarding them as explicit instructions on how to practice medicine rather than recommendations on effective practice patterns. Additionally, the lack of rigorous evidence supporting practice guidelines makes them suspect in the eyes of physicians (see Chapter 7 for a more detailed discussion of practice guidelines).

To assist physicians in managing the care of patients with chronic diseases, plans often give them practice guidelines. For instance, as part of their asthma care management programs, many MCOs disseminate widely-accepted clinical guidelines for the treatment of asthmatic patients to PCPs. Coupled with a profile of each asthma patient showing the use of asthma-related medication and hospitalizations, these practice guidelines help physicians understand how they can improve the care they are presently giving their asthma patients.

CONCLUSION

The relationship an MCO has with its affiliated providers is a critical determinant of the MCO's success. MCOs with acrimonious interactions with providers will ultimately succumb to the side effects of this "bad blood." Unfortunately, the prevailing cost pressures on MCOs and the continued intrusion of MCOs into the practice of medicine create tensions between MCOs and providers. Such discord involves compensation, medical decision making, administrative rules, quality of care, and other issues. If MCO operating margins are further squeezed by employers, they will continue to pressure providers to reduce fees and reduce health care utilization. While aggressive tactics may achieve short-term financial concessions for the MCO, the ill will generated has far-reaching negative repercussions for MCOs, as evidenced by the current provider backlash of managed care. Discontented providers publicly bad-mouth MCOs, undermine member confidence in plans, support anti–managed care legislation, and rebuke the efforts of MCOs to improve the efficiency or quality of care delivered to members.

Anecdotal evidence suggests that some MCOs are adopting a less contentious position toward providers, opting to delegate significant responsibility to provider groups for the management of patient care. Risk-sharing arrangements and disease management programs are indicative of this approach. Some MCOs, such as Pacificare Health Systems, are recognizing that long-term partnerships with provider groups produce enormous gains in network stability, customer satisfaction, quality care, and medical costs. However, the emergence of provider-sponsored health plans presents a conundrum for MCOs, as they watch their participating providers form competing health plans, in many cases based on the lessons from the MCOs themselves. "Friend or foe?" becomes the deciding question. The answer depends entirely on the market and the business philosophies of the MCOs and provider groups. Successful partnerships are based on mutual respect and understanding of each party's contribution to the overall goal of the partnership. Despite the escalating continued strife between MCOs and providers, it is possible for MCOs and provider groups to successfully cooperate in delivering quality care to MCO members.

DISCUSSION QUESTIONS

1. What market and provider characteristics do MCOs consider when analyzing a provider network?
2. Describe the principal sections of a provider contract.
3. Why do MCOs credential physicians before allowing them to join the network?
4. What should an MCO consider when negotiating a sole-source contract with a provider?
5. Describe four types of reimbursement arrangements used by MCOs.
6. Why is capitation a controversial reimbursement method?
7. Identify five reasons why MCOs capitate specialists for specialty care?
8. How can a full-risk capitation arrangement be risky for providers?
9. Describe the two forms of stop loss coverage.
10. By what criteria do MCOs evaluate provider performance?

REFERENCES

1. W. Knight, "Understanding Managed Care Contracting," in *Managed Care Contracting: A Guide for Health Care Professionals* (Gaithersburg, MD: Aspen Publishers, Inc., 1997), 17.
2. W. Knight, "Understanding Managed Care Contracting," 17.
3. W. Knight, "Understanding Managed Care Contracting," 19.
4. W. Knight and L. Sansone, "Ambulatory and Ancillary Care Contracting," in *Managed Care Contracting: A Guide for Health Care Professionals* (Gaithersburg, MD: Aspen Publishers, Inc., 1997), 219.
5. N. Reaven and K. Patterson, "Analyzing Financial Arrangements," in *Managed Care Contracting: A Guide for Health Care Professionals* (Gaithersburg, MD: Aspen Publishers, Inc., 1997), 94.
6. Reaven and Patterson, *Managed Care Contracting: A Guide for Health Care Professionals,* 97.
7. P. Kongstvedt, "Negotiating and Contracting with Hospitals and Institutions," in *The Managed Health Care Handbook,* 3d ed. (Gaithersburg, MD: Aspen Publishers, Inc., 1996), 211.
8. Reaven and Patterson, *Managed Care Contracting: A Guide for Health Care Professionals,* 102.

9. M. Benenson and S. Gutman, "Specialty Care Contracting," in *Managed Care Contracting: A Guide for Health Care Professionals* (Gaithersburg, MD: Aspen Publishers, Inc., 1997), 180–181.

10. Kongstvedt, *The Managed Health Care Handbook,* 184–185.

11. Reaven and Patterson, *Managed Care Contracting: A Guide for Health Care Professionals,* 106.

12. InterStudy Competitive Edge, *HMO Industry Report 7.1* (Bloomington, MN: InterStudy Publications, 1997), 63.

13. J. Wisniewski et al., Promoting More Informed Clinical Decisions through Continuing Medical Education, Practice Guidelines, and Information Systems (Paper presented at Robert Wood Johnson Foundation Chronic Care Initiatives in HMOs, Washington, DC, April 1995).

14. L. Stevens, "Incorporating Satisfaction Measures into Physician Compensation," *Healthplan* 39, no. 1 (January/February 1998).

Appendix 4–A

SAMPLE PRIMARY CARE PHYSICIAN AGREEMENT

This PROFESSIONAL SERVICES AGREEMENT ("Agreement") is made and entered into this _____ day of _____, 19____ by and between _____ ("plan") and _____ ("Professional"), whose specialty is in the field of _____ _____ and having his/her principal place of business at _____.

RECITALS

WHEREAS, Professional intends to enter into agreements with Health Care Service Plans, Hospital Service Plans and Federally Qualified Health Maintenance Organizations ("Plan(s)") which are licensed under the laws of the State of _____ for the provision of medical services to persons enrolled as Members ("Members").

NOW, THEREFORE, in consideration of the mutual covenants and promises contained herein, the parties agree as follows:

ARTICLE I
DEFINITIONS

1.1 "Capitation Fee" means a predetermined monthly fee, to be multiplied by the number of Members assigned to Professional for Covered Services.

1.2 "Co-payment" means those charges for professional services which shall be collected directly by Professional from Member, as payment in addition to the fee paid to Professional by IPA, in accordance with the Member's Evidence of Coverage.

1.3 "Covered Services" means those health care services and supplies that a Member is entitled to receive under a Plan's benefit program and that are described and defined in the Plan's Evidence of Coverage and disclosure forms, subscriber and group contracts and in a Plan's Provider Manual.

1.4   "Emergency" means the sudden onset of a symptom, illness, or injury requiring immediate diagnosis and/or treatment.

1.5   "Evidence of Coverage" means the document issued by a Plan to a Member that describes the Member Covered Services in the Plan.

1.6   "Fee for Service" means Professional will be paid according to a determined payment schedule for all authorized services rendered.

1.7   "Medically Necessary" means medical or surgical treatment that a Member requires as determined by a Participating Provider, in accordance with accepted medical and surgical practices and standards prevailing at the time of treatment and in conformity with the professional and technical standards adopted by the Plan's Utilization Management Committee.

1.8   "Member" means a person who is enrolled in a Plan, also referred to as an Enrollee, including enrolled dependents, and is entitled to receive Covered Services.

1.9   "Non-Covered Services" means those health care services that are not benefits under the Evidence of Coverage.

1.10   "Participating Hospital" means a duly licensed hospital that has entered into an agreement with a Plan to provide Covered Services to Members.

1.11   "Participating Physician" means a physician (duly licensed to practice medicine or osteopathy in accordance with applicable state law) who has entered into an agreement with Plan to provide Covered Services to Members.

1.12   "Participating Provider" means a Participating Physician, Participating Hospital, or other licensed health facility or licensed health professional that has entered into an agreement to provide Covered Services to Members.

1.13   "Referral/Authorization" means the process by which the Participating Physician directs a Member to seek and/or obtain Covered Services from a health professional, a hospital or any other provider of Covered Services.

1.14   "Specialist Physician" means a Participating Physician who is professionally qualified to practice his/her designated specialty and whose agreement with Plan includes responsibility for providing Covered Services in his/her designated specialty.

1.15   "Subscriber" means a person or entity that is responsible for payment to a Plan or person whose employment or other status, except for family dependency, is the basis for eligibility for enrollment in a Plan.

ARTICLE II
SERVICES TO BE PERFORMED BY PROFESSIONAL

2.1   Professional Responsibilities: Professional shall provide Primary Care Physician Covered Services and related administrative services to Plan Members in accordance with applicable legal and professional standards and in compliance with Plan's professional and administrative rules, regulations, requirements, policies and procedure manuals. Failure by Professional to comply with Plan's professional or administrative requirements after reasonable notice and opportunity to comply shall constitute grounds for termination of this Agreement by Plan upon ninety (90) day written notice to providers. Professional agrees to be bound by the Primary Care Physician responsibilities set forth in Exhibit "C." These procedures may be amended from time to time by administrative notice from Plan.

2.2   Covering Physician: If Professional is, for any reason, from time to time, unable to provide Covered Services when and as needed, Professional may secure the services of a qualified covering physician, who shall render such Covered Services otherwise required of Professional; provided, however, that the covering physician so furnished, is a licensed physician capable to provide Covered Services to Members. Professional shall be solely responsible for securing the services of such covering physician and paying said covering physician for those Covered Services provided to Members. Professional shall ensure that the covering physician: (1) looks solely to Professional for compensation; (2) will accept Plan's peer review procedures; (3) will not bill Members for Covered Services under any circumstances; (4) will obtain authorizations as required for Covered Services and hospitalizations, in accordance with the Plan's utilization management program; and (5) will comply with the terms hereof.

2.3   Referral/Authorization: Professional agrees to be bound by the Referral/Authorization procedures as set forth in Exhibits "D" and "E," hereof, and any other procedures adopted by Plan. These procedures may be amended, from time to time, by administrative notice from Plan.

ARTICLE III
REPRESENTATIONS

3.1   Representations by Professional: Professional hereby warrants and represents that Professional is a physician, or professional corporation, duly licensed to practice medicine in the State of _____, and is in good standing with the Medical Board of _____. Professional warrants and represents that Professional is currently and for the duration of this Agreement, shall remain a member in good standing of the medical staff of the Participating Hospital, with appropriate privileges.

ARTICLE IV
CONTRACTING AUTHORITY

4.1   Contracting Authority: Subject to the other terms of this Agreement, and to IPA's general policies regarding third-party contracting payors, Professional hereby delegates to the IPA the authority to bind Professional to contracts with third-party payors, including, but not limited to, Preferred Provider Organizations, and Competitive Medical Plans, and to negotiate on Professional's behalf, regarding such contracts; provided, however, that the Professional compensation terms of such agreements must be more favorable to Professional than the Professional compensation terms set forth in IPA's contracts with Plans.

ARTICLE V
COMPENSATION

5.1   Compensation: Professional agrees to look solely to Plan for any and all remuneration, and agrees not to bill Plan Members for covered services, except where co-payments are required. Payment shall be made in accordance with Exhibit "A" (and/or Exhibit "A/1" when applicable).

5.2   Billing: Professional agrees to comply with the billing procedures set forth in Exhibits "A" and "D." These billing procedures may be amended, from time to time, by administrative notice from Plan.

ARTICLE VI
OBLIGATIONS OF PROFESSIONAL

6.1   Hours: Professional shall make available Professional services to Plan Members during office hours, and shall provide on-call coverage to Members on a twenty-four (24) hour, seven (7) day-a-week basis.

6.2   Malpractice Insurance: Professional shall provide, unless otherwise agreed to by Professional and Plan, at Professional's sole cost and expense, throughout the entire term of this Agreement, a policy of professional malpractice liability insurance with a licensed insurance company, admitted to do business in the State of _____, in an amount of not less than one million dollars ($1,000,000) per claim and three million dollars ($3,000,000) aggregate to cover any loss, liability, or damage alleged to have been committed by Professional, or Professional's agent, servant, or employees.

6.3   License to Practice/Hospital Privileges: If at any time, during the entire term of this Agreement, Professional shall have Professional's license to practice medicine in the State of _____, suspended or Hospital Privileges revoked, impaired, reduced or suspended, this Agreement, at the sole option of Plan, shall terminate immediately and become null and void, and of no further force or effect, except as otherwise provided herein.

6.4   Professional Roster: Professional agrees that Plan may use Professional's name, address, phone number, type of practice, willingness to accept new patients and other marketing information, in the Plan roster of Professional participants. The roster may be inspected by, and is intended to be used by, prospective patients, prospective Plan physicians and others.

6.5   Non-Discrimination: Professional shall not discriminate against any Plan Member, any contract party, prospective contracting party, or person reasonably expected to benefit from any such contract, because of race, color, national origin, ancestry, religion, sex, marital status, or age; and Professional agrees to cooperate with Plans in programs designed to monitor access and quality of care for Plan Members.

ARTICLE VII
MEDICAL RECORDS

7.1   Access to Records: Professional agrees to provide access to an inspection by Plans, the _____ Department of Insurance, the _____ Department of Health, the United States Department of Health and Human Services, and the Controller General of the United States, at all reasonable times and upon demand, to the books, records, and documents of the Professional, relating to the Covered Services provided to Plan Members, and access to the cost thereof, and to the amounts of any payments received from Members or from others, on such Member's behalf. Such records and information shall be open to inspection during normal business hours, and, to the extent feasible, all such records shall be located in the State of _____.

7.2   Standards for Medical Records: Professional shall maintain, with respect to each Plan Member receiving Covered Services hereunder, a single standard medical record. Professional agrees to comply with the standards for medical records referenced in Exhibit "D." These procedures may be amended, from time to time, by administrative notice from Plan.

ARTICLE VIII
TERM AND TERMINATION

8.1   Term and Termination. The effective date of this Agreement shall be the FIRST day of_____, 19__. The initial term of this Agreement shall extend for twelve (12) months following the effective date. This Agreement will automatically be renewed for successive periods of twelve (12) months each, on the same terms and conditions contained herein, unless sooner terminated, pursuant to the terms of this Agreement.

8.2 Termination with Notice: This Agreement may be terminated by Professional by the giving of ninety (90) days' prior written notice, served to Plan by registered or certified mail; provided, however, Plan may, at its sole and absolute discretion, shorten this notice period, upon receipt of written request by Professional, to shorten said notice period. This Agreement may be terminated by Plan by the giving of ninety (90) days' prior written notice served to Professional by registered or certified mail.

8.3 Continuity of Care: Professional agrees that upon termination of this Agreement, Professional will continue to provide Covered Services to Plan Members who retain eligibility under their Subscriber's Contract, or by operation of law, and who are receiving Covered Services from the Professional at the time of termination, until such Covered Services are completed.

ARTICLE IX
UTILIZATION MANAGEMENT AND GRIEVANCE PROTOCOL

9.1 Participation in Quality Assurance and Utilization Management: Professional agrees to participate fully, in formal quality assurance, utilization management, and disciplinary peer review activities, relating to the program conducted by or on behalf of IPA. Such participation includes preparation of reports and documentation, attendance at meetings, conduct of investigations, assessments and such other activities as IPA may prescribe, from time to time, through written rules and procedures. Professional agrees to keep all IPA documents and information (including documents and information related to quality assurance, utilization management and peer review) strictly confidential, and not to disclose such documents or information without IPA's written consent.

9.2 Grievance Resolution: Professional agrees that all disputes or disagreements between Professional and any Plan or Member, shall be resolved in accordance with such grievance resolution process as an applicable Plan may establish, from time to time. Likewise, Professional agrees that all disputes or disagreements between Professional and IPA, relating to this Agreement or to the Plan, shall be resolved according to the grievance process established, in writing, by IPA, from time to time.

ARTICLE X
GENERAL PROVISIONS

10.1   Arbitration: Professional agrees to accept and be bound by the Member's Arbitration Agreement, referenced in Exhibit "B."

10.2   Entire Agreement. This Agreement supersedes any and all agreements, either written or oral, between the parties hereto, with respect to the subject matter contained herein, and contains all of the covenants and agreements between the parties. With the sole exception of IPA's rules, regulations, requirements, policies and procedure manuals relating to Provider Medical and administrative services (as described in Exhibits "A," "A/1," "B," "D," and "E"), this Agreement may not be modified, without a written statement, executed by both parties.

Executed this_____ day of_____, 19_____, at_____
_____, _____.

APPROVED:

NAME OF PLAN   PROFESSIONAL

_____   _____
PROFESSIONAL SIGNATURE   PROFESSIONAL SIGNATURE

_____   _____
PRINT NAME   PRINT NAME

_____   _____
DATE   DATE

CHAPTER 5

Purchasers and Managed Care

Jeanne M. Keller

Nowadays people know the price of everything and the value of nothing.

Oscar Wilde (1854–1900)

"Okay Bob, time is running out! Which plan will you choose for your company? The one behind curtain #1, curtain #2, or curtain #3? . . ."

Learning Objectives

- Understand the role of purchasers in the evolution of managed care.
- Understand the development of different cost containment strategies used by purchasers.
- Understand why and how purchasers are involved in quality measurement and quality improvement.
- Understand the various purchasing strategies used by state and federal government–sponsored health care programs.

Key Terms

Benchmarking—A process used to improve the quality of health care delivered by a managed care organization (MCO). The MCO compares its own performance on specific measures to that of other plans and formulates new goals and strategies to improve its performance.

HEDIS—(Health Plan Employer Data and Information Set). A standardized set of performance measurements collected by MCOs accredited by the National Committee for Quality Assurance (NCQA) that allows employers and consumers to evaluate and compare the performance of MCOs.

Medicaid—A health insurance program jointly funded by the federal government and state governments that provides health care and long-term care coverage for low-income and disabled individuals.

Medicare—A federal program that provides health insurance coverage for aged and disabled Americans.

Purchasing coalition—A group of employers who join together to purchase health insurance coverage in a systematic way and to implement projects to improve the quality of health care in their communities.

Value purchasing—A strategy used by purchasers to select MCOs on the basis of cost and the quality of care and to set performance standards for the MCOs in the areas of cost, quality, and patient satisfaction.

INTRODUCTION

A unique feature of the financing of health insurance in the United States is that many different entities purchase health care benefits on behalf of individuals. In most industrialized nations, the government finances health care for its citizens, but in this country, the government, employers, associations of employers, or labor unions all can purchase health care. Because most health care is purchased for individuals by one of these entities, the requirements placed on health plans are made by the purchasers, not by individual consumers. Therefore, to understand the evolution of managed care in the United States, it is important to understand the changing requirements and demands of the various kinds of purchasers.

The shift of individuals into managed care was stimulated by purchasers' search for better value—that is, improved quality of care at a reasonable price. When health care costs climbed sharply in the 1980s, purchasers responded by developing new strategies for negotiating with their plans. They demanded discounted fees from physicians and hospitals in return for exclusive contracts, thus spawning the preferred provider organization (PPO) model. Purchasers also recognized that the financial risk of managing patient care could be shifted back to (or shared with) health care providers in prepaid health plans, such as health maintenance organizations (HMOs). By imposing this type of risk-sharing arrangement, purchasers forced health care providers to consider costs when caring for patients and gave them financial incentives to keep health care costs manageable.

Throughout the 1980s, purchasers tried a variety of similar strategies to control costs. By providing a fair share of their workforce with health coverage through managed care plans, they had achieved moderate success by the end of the decade. But costs were still increasing at substantial rates—faster than both inflation and wages. Moreover, there was little information available on whether spending more money actually resulted in better health for employees, or conversely, if cutting costs adversely affected the quality of health services. As a result, the next focus for purchasers became the collection and analysis of information. Why were health care costs increasing rapidly? Were the treatments actually producing healthier employees (i.e., what were the outcomes of the treatment provided through the health plan?)? Were consumers satisfied with the care they received?

Today, many purchasers prefer managed care programs because of their cost-effectiveness relative to indemnity insurance. In addition, purchasers increasingly believe that managed care has more potential to improve the quality of health care than traditional insurance programs. Many purchasers also realize that high-quality managed care can produce long-term improvements in employee health status that will ultimately save the employer money. For that reason, they understand that cost containment by itself is a shortsighted policy.[1] Forward-thinking purchasers are moving away from buying health benefit programs on price alone and are selecting a plan based on the plan's combination of price and quality. This strategy, known as "value purchasing," began with private-sector purchasers but is now being used by government purchasers as well.

PRIVATE-SECTOR EMPLOYERS

Brief History of Employer-Sponsored Health Care Plans

Employers began paying for health care coverage in large numbers during World War II. The federal government had imposed wage and price controls on war industries, forcing employers to look for other ways to attract and retain skilled workers. Because limits were not placed on fringe benefits, and because the value of health insurance was not taxed (as are wages), employers and employees welcomed the introduction of health insurance as a workplace benefit. Enrollment in group health insurance plans jumped from 7 million in 1942 to 26 million by the end of World War II.[2]

After the war, continuation of the employer's role in employee health benefits was all but certain when the U.S. Supreme Court ruled (in the *Inland Steel* case) that the new Taft-Hartley Labor Relations Act gave labor unions the right to negotiate health insurance as part of their collective bargaining with employers. As a result of subsequent union negotiations, health insurance plans that had been limited to hospital coverage expanded to include outpatient treatments, prescription drugs, and laboratory tests. The culminating event that bound private-sector employers to health insurance financing occurred in 1959, when the United Steelworkers settled a labor dispute with steel companies that required the companies to pay 100 percent of employee health insurance premiums.[3] From that point, large, private-sector employers felt they had no choice but to provide health insurance benefits to workers.

The Evolution to Managed Care

As described in earlier chapters, employers began to redesign their health benefit programs to take advantage of the HMOs that were emerging in the late 1970s and early 1980s. Typically, the employer was already offering an indemnity plan, either a fully insured plan (i.e., the insurance company assumes the financial risk of providing health care coverage) or a self-insured plan (i.e., the purchaser assumes the financial risk). Because the federal HMO Act required employers to offer their employees an available federally-qualified HMO plan, employers simply added the HMO as an option for employees. Employees were allowed to choose between the indemnity plan and the HMO once each year (called an "open enrollment period"). In the early years, employees were offered little or no incentive to choose HMOs. However, as HMOs became more cost competitive than indemnity plans, employers would require employees to pay a higher contribution for the more expensive indemnity plan.

In markets where HMOs were very efficient and could price their product substantially below indemnity plans, a significant number of employees might join the HMOs. Many employers found that the healthier employees were choosing the HMO, leaving the sickest employees and dependents in the employer's self-insured indemnity plan, with its wider choice of providers and unrestricted access to specialists. As a result, the per employee cost of the indemnity plans rose, as did the premiums, causing even more healthy people to leave the indemnity plan for the less costly HMO. This increased the per employee cost of the indemnity plans again, raising the premium more, causing even more healthy people to leave the indemnity plan for the HMO.

This cycle, once it starts, tends to continue, with fewer and fewer healthy people left in the indemnity plan. The per person cost of the indemnity plan will continue to rise as the HMO (with a higher proportion of healthy people and therefore lower premium rates) attracts the remaining healthy people. Eventually, the indemnity plan faces what is known as a "death spiral," because it can never retain enough healthy people to offset the high claims of the sicker people and keep its premiums affordable. The employer will withdraw the plan, and employees who preferred an indemnity plan, because of its open access to specialty care, will no longer have that plan option.

Consequently, employers would make another change in their health plan strategy: offering more HMOs and phasing out their indemnity plans. This could be done swiftly by eliminating the indemnity plan before the next open enrollment period, or could be achieved over several years with the addition of point-of-service (POS) plans and less restrictive managed care programs as a transition to HMOs.

THE EVOLUTION OF A COMPANY PURCHASING STRATEGY

Bull Information Systems, the American subsidiary of a French computer manufacturer, presents a classic example of the evolution of a purchasing strategy. Bull had been offering workers a self-insured health plan and HMOs as optional choices for employees as required by the HMO Act. As economic pressures on high-tech industries in the late 1980s squeezed the profit margins of technology companies, benefit managers at Bull were expected to reduce the cost of the self-insured health plan. Examining their company's health care experience and that of other companies facing similar situations, the managers at Bull decided to phase out their self-insured plan in favor of staff-model HMOs. Managers responsible for restructuring the company's health program based their decision on two factors. First, staff-model HMOs were less costly than the self-insured indemnity program covering the majority of Bull employees. Second, the company's research found that staff-model MCOs had greater control over service delivery than the more loosely organized HMOs based on the independent practice association (IPA) model.[4] Now, Bull employees nationwide have a choice of several competing HMOs at open enrollment.

The Concern for Quality and Value

As described in Chapter 1, an MCO is fundamentally different from a traditional insurance product. With many MCOs, the purchaser (1) buys protection from the financial obligation of paying for health services (that is, buys insurance), and (2) buys access to health care providers who work for, or are under contract to, the MCO. Because they were now buying "health care," not just health insurance, purchasers began to question the value they received for their money. Was the managed care plan actually improving the health of employees? Were the employees satisfied? Did they have adequate access to the providers? What was the quality of the providers' care? To ensure that the plans addressed these important questions, employers like Bull Information Systems began specifying performance standards and network accessibility requirements for interested MCOs. Such standards were included in the formal request for proposal (RFP) process employers used to select MCOs. Exhibit 5–1 shows an example of information about MCO networks employers often request in the RFP.

> **Exercise: You are the person responsible for purchasing health insurance for a company with 250 employees. Make a list of the 10 most important things you would like to know about an MCO before signing a contract for coverage. Now make a list of what you think your employees would like to know. Compare the lists and discuss why they are/are not different.**

Exhibit 5–1 Sample Questions Contained in a Typical RFP

- How often do you allow plan participants to change primary care providers (PCPs), other than during open enrollments?
- Please provide the following information on all network providers:
  - Is this provider accepting new patients?
  - Is this provider board certified?
- What is the total number of PCPs with open practices available to our employees? What percentage is board certified?
- What is the total number of specialists in your network? What percentage is board certified?
- What incentives are provided to staff providers beyond base compensation? If so, are these incentives based on productivity? quality? other?
- What percentage of your PCPs are capitated? What percentage of medical groups are capitated?

This new "value purchasing" approach had a basic appeal to private-sector businesses, according to the National Business Coalition on Health:

> Not mysterious at all, value-based health care purchasing parallels a process that businesses everywhere use—every day. Just like purchasing any other goods or services, the purchaser needs to be able to specify what it wants, to select the supplier(s) best able to meet those specifications, to spell out mutual responsibilities, to ensure that performance of the supplier consistently meets or exceeds expectations, and to improve or terminate that relationship over time.[5]

The shift from purchasing traditional health insurance to purchasing managed care programs has significantly changed the employer's role in administering health benefit programs. Under managed care, employers' concerns extend beyond the insurer's solvency and claims payment accuracy to encompass the quality of health delivered and the access to needed health services. Corporate benefits managers need new information and skills, as their negotiations with MCOs begin to establish performance standards for medical practice, provider credentialing, and network adequacy. However, few employers want to micro-manage the daily operations of MCOs. By setting specific performance standards for the MCO in the contract and by reviewing periodic reports to evaluate the plan's performance, the purchaser can engage in a long-term partnership with the plan that encourages continuous improvement of quality and consumer satisfaction.

HEDIS

The Origins of HEDIS

As an outgrowth of the quality improvement strategy, representatives from several employers and MCOs in the Northeast began discussing the possibility of developing a standard set of measurements that would allow employers and consumers to evaluate and compare plans. The project, known as HEDIS, began as an independent, voluntary effort spearheaded by business and managed care executives. From the employers' perspective, HEDIS offered the promise of a standard set of quality measures that could be used to evaluate and compare all plans. For MCOs, HEDIS provided an opportunity to truly differentiate managed care from indemnity insurance plans (where quality of medical care is never measured), and allowed plans to compete with each other based on reliable and comparable data measures. Additionally, the standardization of HEDIS data reporting would free MCOs from having to respond to the myriad data requests from employers and their consultants.

The group released the first set of guidelines, known as HEDIS 2.0, in 1993. The guidelines spelled out the kinds of information MCOs should collect and report to purchasers, including

- clinical quality (Are children adequately immunized? Are women receiving mammograms? What is the complication rate for surgery?)
- access to care (How many primary care doctors participate in the plan's network?)
- patient satisfaction (Would patients recommend the plan to friends/family?)
- membership (What are the demographics of plan enrollment—age? gender? location?)
- utilization (How many coronary bypasses were performed? How many Caesarean sections?)
- organizational and financial information (What are the plan's financial reserves?)

Very soon, the large employers participating in the HEDIS planning group, such as Digital, Xerox, and Bull Information Systems, began requiring HEDIS information from all their MCOs as a condition of contracting. These isolated efforts quickly gained the attention of employers and MCOs around the country. As the HEDIS measures gained credibility and were adopted by major MCOs, the HEDIS development process was formalized through sponsorship by the NCQA, an independent agency that accredits MCOs. Today over 300 MCOs report HEDIS data to purchasers.

National Benchmarking

As more was learned about quality of health care, HEDIS performance standards were revised. Version 2.5, for example, was developed specifically to report on the government-sponsored health programs, Medicaid and Medicare. Soon, however, it became clear that all purchasers and MCOs wanted a way to reconcile the numerous quality measurements and reporting efforts. A single set of measures would simplify reporting, provide all purchasers (even those less experienced) with "state of the art" reports, and enable plan-to-plan comparisons. MCOs could compare themselves against local, regional, and national standards in order to set their own improvement goals—a quality improvement exercise known as "benchmarking" (see Chapter 7 for more information on report cards).

HEDIS® 3.0 MEASURES

The latest round of revisions, HEDIS 3.0, is used by MCOs to report performance for 1997 and beyond. As envisioned by NCQA, HEDIS 3.0 significantly changed the purpose and content of the HEDIS data set. HEDIS 3.0 differs from earlier versions in five key ways:[6]

1. HEDIS 3.0 is more "outcomes" (or results) oriented. For example, plans are required to measure and report on patient health status and functioning. HEDIS 2.0 was criticized because it measured processes of care (e.g., how many women received mammograms?), not the outcomes of care (e.g., how many cancers were discovered and how many women survived?).

2. HEDIS 3.0 measures the full spectrum of health care. Preventive and acute health care measures are specifically addressed, and certain chronic health conditions, such as acquired immune deficiency syndrome (AIDS), breast cancer, heart disease, nicotine addiction, and diabetes, are singled out for in-depth review and reporting. HEDIS 2.0 was criticized for its focus on a predominantly healthy working age population (probably because that's the population of concern to the employers in the early HEDIS working groups). In HEDIS 3.0, attention is given to health concerns of children, adults, and seniors.

3. HEDIS 3.0 combines reporting for both public and private purchasers. HEDIS started as a private-sector initiative but is also now used by state and federal government purchasers. With both

private and public reporting, comparisons across different populations can occur to see if the health status or health care received varies depending on the purchaser involved.

4. HEDIS 3.0 covers a broad range of health care issues. In the ongoing development of HEDIS, the different stakeholders have identified their own areas of interest. Subsequently, HEDIS 3.0 has broadened its scope to include clinical quality and satisfaction measures, as well as detailed information on access, cost, and specific areas of clinical care such as mental health and substance abuse.

5. HEDIS® 3.0 has a built-in process for continuous refinement of the data set. A "testing set" of measures will be evaluated for possible inclusion in the next release.

Source: Adapted with permission from the National Committee for Quality Assurance, Book I—HEDIS® 3.0, *Understanding and Enhancing Performance Management*, pp. 5–6, © 1997 by NCQA. HEDIS® is a registered trademark of the National Committee for Quality Assurance.

Comparisons of MCOs are now available from NCQA and are updated every year from new, annual HEDIS reports. The customized comparative reports, which are drawn from NCQA's database called Quality Compass, allow purchasers to compare specific MCOs, all MCOs in a region, or all MCOs nationwide. The collaboration of MCOs and purchasers in the ongoing development of HEDIS has contributed significantly to the improvement of plan quality, by directing MCOs to specific areas of concern for consumers and purchasers. However, use of HEDIS to compare and choose plans is still limited to a handful of large employers and coalitions who have adopted HEDIS in their contracting process with MCOs. While HEDIS has standardized quality reporting for MCOs, it is still a very expensive process, requiring assignment of permanent staff, training of providers, and retooling of existing data systems to adapt to the changing HEDIS requirements. Providers and consumers who do not support managed care criticize HEDIS, arguing that the quality indicators fail to account for the impact managed care has on the doctor–patient relationship. Others who support managed care also criticize HEDIS for selecting one measure (for example, rate of mammography) rather than assessing how a plan performs on an entire episode of care (for example, survival rates for breast cancer).

HEDIS faces the same problem as any system attempting to measure quality: whoever defines the measures is also, by extension, defining quality. HEDIS will probably continue to be limited in its use and impact because of the lack of consensus among purchasers, providers, consumers, and regulators on what constitutes quality in manage care (see Chapter 7 for more information on HEDIS).

Accreditation

Because MCOs are responsible for providing an array of health care services, it was important for employers to evaluate the performance of MCOs in more areas than could be measured by HEDIS. Employers' desire for an independent source of information about the quality of HMOs prompted the development of the NCQA as an independent organization accrediting HMOs. In collaboration with plans, purchasers, researchers, and consumers, NCQA develops standards that measure the structure and function of HMOs and their quality improvement programs (see Chapter 7 for a detailed discussion on accreditation).

Small Employers as Purchasers

Lacking the staff time and financial resources to examine the array of health insurance options and develop purchasing strategies, small firms (generally characterized as employers with fewer than 50 employees) did not quickly contract with MCOs to provide health benefits. Because of the greater financial risks of self-insurance, small firms buy fully-insured products and have limited or no experience in customizing benefit plans or negotiating premium rates with MCOs. As a result, small employers rarely offer employees a choice of plans. Historically, small employers have opted to select one indemnity plan that was easy to understand and offered broad provider choice to employees.

The business practice of MCOs also limited the participation of small employers in the managed care revolution. Because one high medical claim in a small group can consume the total premium the plan collects for the group, small employers are more risky to insure. Additionally, many MCOs did not market actively to small businesses because the administrative cost of marketing, relative to the potential size of the premium, was not cost-effective.

The success of MCOs in containing the rate of cost increases prompted many small firms to be interested in managed care. In the early 1990s, many small businesses began demanding and offering managed care plans, just as their large company counterparts had done a decade earlier. By 1995, more than two-thirds of small employers offered a managed care plan, up from only 27 percent just two years earlier. Figure 5–1 shows the dramatic shift in type of coverage for small businesses over that brief period.

Small employers still differ from large employers in their approach to health care purchasing, however. Without the negotiating leverage afforded to a group with many employees, small employers rarely engage in value purchasing (except when small employers band together in purchasing alliances, as described below). Figure 5–2 shows the extent to which large and small employers have adopted quality- and value-purchasing strategies.

EMPLOYER COALITIONS

Searching for better strategies to negotiate favorable terms with MCOs, employers began sharing information about MCOs in the late 1980s. At first, such collaborations were as simple as sharing a copy of an RFP or teaching a colleague how to use HEDIS information. Eventually, in many parts of the country, formal associations of employers were created to jointly negotiate contracts with local MCOs. These associations, called "alliances," "purchasing coalitions," and "purchasing cooperatives," were a natural outgrowth of the value purchasing and other quality promotion activities of private-sector employers. The formation of purchasing coalitions also allowed small employers to purchase health benefits with similar economies of scale as large employers and to offer their employees multiple managed care options. Today, there are over 100 employer coalitions in the United States with local, regional, statewide, or multi-state membership.

Why Employers Form Purchasing Coalitions

Generally, coalitions are formed to increase the purchasing power of individual employers in a given marketplace. The coalition may encom-

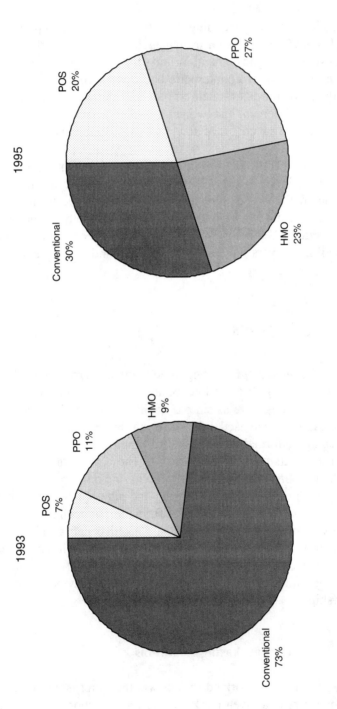

Figure 5–1 Types of Health Insurance Coverage among Insured Workers in Small Firms, 1993 and 1995. Courtesy of Henry J. Kaiser Family Foundation, Washington, D.C.

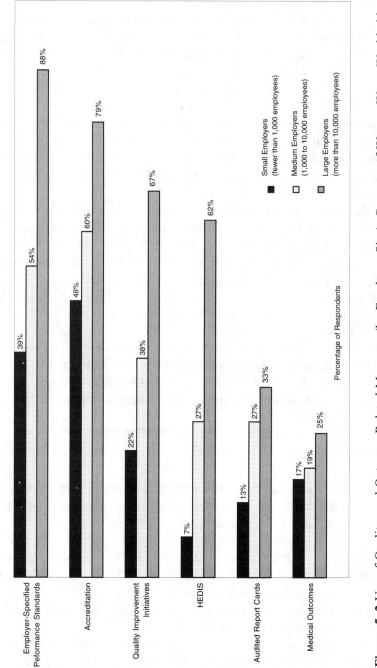

Figure 5-2 Use of Quality- and Outcome-Related Measures (by Employer Size). Courtesy of Watson Wyatt Worldwide, 1997, Bethesda, Maryland.

pass a city, metropolitan area, region, state, or the entire nation. The coalition's founders are usually large employers that believe they are capable of negotiating more favorable terms with MCOs collectively than on their own. As a result, they band together with other employers to maximize their collective bargaining position relative to MCOs.

Employers also create coalitions to set new quality standards in their contracts with MCOs. These include increasing immunization rates, reducing unnecessary hospitalizations, and pressing for better diagnosis and treatment of chronic diseases. While some nationwide employers, such as Bull and Digital, have been able to do this on their own, smaller employers, and even large regional employers, have found more success with MCOs as a group.

Gaining economies of scale in the administration of health programs is a final reason employers join together in alliances. By sharing the cost and staff time of preparing and reviewing RFPs, negotiating with plans, gathering and analyzing data, enrolling plan members, and monitoring the health program, employers can reduce their administrative costs. Because health plan purchasing has been a complex process, many employers find that they can buy expertise not available among their own personnel by pooling resources through a coalition.

> **Exercise: Role-play a meeting where the president of a small business purchasing coalition attempts to recruit a business colleague to join the coalition.**

What Coalitions Do

A recent study of the most advanced and successful purchasing coalitions revealed that employers participating in coalitions carry out at least four of the following five approaches:[7]

1. Employer coalitions contract for health care in a way that incorporates the elements of "value"(i.e., a combination of cost and quality). For example, coalitions may require plans to increase the number of board-certified providers in their networks. This may be more expensive, but it improves the quality of care.
2. Employer coalitions take part in projects designed to improve the quality of health care services. Contracts may include targeted im-

provements in HEDIS measures, such as screening tests for diabetes or immunization rates.

3. Employer coalitions acquire and use information about provider health care costs and provider performance. Some coalitions even publish consumer satisfaction reports on the Internet.

4. Employers in coalitions redesign their plans using financial incentives to encourage and reward desired practices by providers and employees. When employees are willing to use an MCO with a narrow network, they may have lower co-payment requirements or be eligible for coverage of additional services.

5. Employer coalitions encourage employees to become more informed and effective health care consumers. Coalitions publish consumer education magazines, sponsor Internet sites, and produce health plan report cards to help employees choose the most suitable plan at open enrollment.

The strategies of employer coalitions are not fundamentally different from those implemented by individual private-sector employers. The key distinction is that employers joining together in an association are consolidating their purchasing power and pooling their knowledge, expertise, and resources. By working as one organization instead of individual employers, coalitions can impose more requirements on health care providers, negotiate better rates with plans, and optimize administration. Because of the financial power created by mergers of MCOs and the creation of regional health care systems, and because of the complexity of offering multiple managed care plans, coalition participation has become an attractive option for many employers.

Types of Employer Coalitions

The activities a coalition chooses to pursue must reflect the market of its member companies in order for the coalition to be successful.[8] Depending on the characteristics of the market, the coalition may contract directly with health care providers to create its own managed care network, negotiate contracts with multiple MCOs, or negotiate exclusively with HMOs. They may purchase a full range of health services, or target a specific health benefit. The activities of the successful purchasing coali-

tion match the collective needs of the employers who are its founders and
potential members.

Comprehensive Purchasing Coalitions

Generally located in urban areas and composed of the major employers
in the region, purchasing coalitions negotiate with MCOs for the full range
of health care services. Approximately one in four coalitions in the United
States is a comprehensive purchasing coalition.[9] Some comprehensive
coalitions include both large and small employers. The different contracting approaches include the following:

Contracting with a single MCO. A competitive bidding process selects
one managed care plan with which all member employers contract for their
health benefits.

Contracting with multiple, competing health plans. Coalitions also use
a competitive process to select multiple plans that meet the coalition's
requirements. Each employer (or employee) then chooses any of the
qualifying plans.

Contracting with multiple, non-competing plans. This strategy is typical
of coalitions covering a large geographic area. Managed care plans are
designated as the sole plan in a particular region.

Direct contracting. Coalitions using this approach create their own
managed care networks by contracting with physicians, hospitals, and
other providers directly. Self-insured employers in the coalition enjoy the
provider fee discounts and quality of care guarantees that are part of the
contracts negotiated by the coalition. In creating networks, the coalition
does not become a health plan, but merely maintains a master contract with
all network providers.

Single Health Service Purchasing Coalitions

Single health service coalitions are often located in smaller cities and
rural markets where the scarcity of physicians, hospitals, and MCOs
effectively limits the scope of health services coalitions can negotiate
through a competitive bidding process. The services most frequently
purchased by these smaller coalitions are managed pharmacy benefits and
managed mental health services.

Coalitions in urban areas with many hospitals, but little managed care
penetration, have also used this strategy to selectively contract with

hospitals. In this instance, the coalition uses its combined purchasing power to reduce the over-utilization and excessive costs in hospitals, as managed care has done for purchasers in other markets. Because only one type of health service is collectively purchased, individual employers still make their own arrangements for the remaining health care benefits.

Quality Improvement Coalitions

Some purchasers do not want to purchase health benefits together, but want to collectively develop performance requirements in their managed care contracts or want to collaborate with the MCOs to improve the quality of care and customer service.

Quality improvement initiatives are pursued in partnership with MCOs, hospitals, and physicians. Because the coalitions comprise the major employers in a region (i.e., the principal customers of the MCOs) providers are easily persuaded to participate in such efforts. The coalition will usually initiate the process by presenting providers with data on aberrant or questionable health care utilization (e.g., unusually high post-surgical infection rates, hospital stays, or Caesarean rates). The coalition and the providers form a committee, usually known as a "quality institute," or "quality improvement council," to examine the issue and make recommendations on how to improve care. Continued pressure from the coalition in the form of the threat of public exposure or the threat of sending patients elsewhere will often result in the provider or MCO implementing the coalition's recommendations. Some of these programs have produced significant results such as the following:

- The Alabama Healthcare Council was able to change the way local hospitals treated patients with pneumonia, increasing the rate of appropriate use of antibiotics and reducing the average length of hospital stays from 7.2 days to 5.4 days.
- Cleveland Health Quality Choice compared local hospitals on a variety of performance standards. As a result of publishing the data, the poorly performing hospitals improved so significantly that overall mortality rates in Cleveland declined, average length of stay in hospitals dropped, and patient satisfaction with obstetrical care increased.
- Houston Healthcare Purchasing Organization initiated a quality improvement project after reviewing data on the variations in treatments

provided by Houston hospitals and discovering that complication rates for vaginal deliveries ranged from 9.6 percent to 22 percent. Further investigation revealed that physicians in some hospitals were misdiagnosing the complications only to keep the women in the hospital longer than the purchasing coalition's recommended 24-hour stay and collect more money.

- One of the longest-running coalition efforts on quality improvement was initiated in the late 1980s by the Central Florida Health Care Coalition in Orlando. Employers including Walt Disney World, General Mills, and the City of Orlando convinced the hospitals to install a new data collection and reporting system that analyzed all hospital admissions, evaluated the care received by the patients, and produced hospital-to-hospital comparisons. The coalition members used these reports to encourage the hospitals to reduce unnecessary hospitalizations, tests, and surgeries. Beyond reducing the costs for the coalition members, the effort limited costs for all purchasers in the region and prevented many unneeded hospital treatments. Figure 5–3 compares the average rate of cost increases for employers in the Central Florida Health Care coalition with these employers in the state of Florida.

Many coalitions have also taken a significant role in promoting the use and ongoing improvement of the HEDIS data. The Pacific Business Group on Health, Gateway Purchasing Association, and the Colorado Alliance have all participated in efforts to publicize HEDIS reports, examine whether plans report valid data, and develop more meaningful measures and reporting formats.

Consumer Satisfaction

Because studies of how consumers choose their health plans show that they are more likely to base their decisions on how other consumers feel about the plan,[10] some coalitions have placed increased emphasis on consumer satisfaction.

The results of consumer satisfaction surveys can be used in two ways: (1) MCOs can use the consumer satisfaction information to guide their internal quality improvement programs; and (2) the information can be organized into a "report card" to be used by consumers choosing a plan. Purchasers may combine the consumer survey results with the plan's HEDIS information in a "report card" for employees. This dual use of the

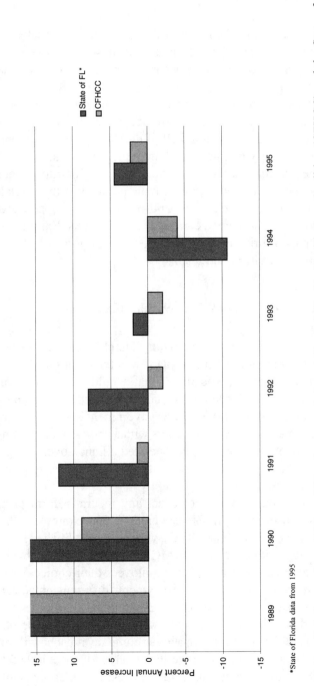

*State of Florida data from 1995

Figure 5–3 Comparison of Rate of Cost Increases between Central Florida Health Care Coalition (CFHCC) and the State of Florida. Courtesy of Central Florida Health Care Coalition.

consumer survey data is an important method used by coalitions to hold plans accountable for quality of care and customer satisfaction.

As research on what information is most useful to consumers emerges, health plan report cards are becoming more widespread. The most evolved report card projects sponsored by coalitions rate several plans on many factors, and many post the results on the Internet for employees and others to view. Figure 5–4 is an example of a comprehensive coalition report card.

The driving force behind all of the quality improvement strategies is a belief that early diagnosis and more effective treatment will reduce costs for purchasers over the long term. Employer coalitions that initiate quality improvement projects often invite public health officials, community organizations, labor groups, and others to participate, giving the health improvement strategy a community-wide focus. Exhibit 5–2 [8,9,10] displays examples of private-sector purchasing coalitions active around the country, their activities, and results.

Government-Sponsored Purchasing Coalitions

A central element of the major federal health care reform proposals in 1994 (including the Clinton plan) was the creation of government-sponsored purchasing associations that would extend the large employer-coalition model to encompass individuals and small employers.[11] As with private-sector coalitions, these government-sponsored "purchasing alliances" would provide consumers with a choice of competing health plans. This model of a government-operated alliance overseeing and managing the purchasing of health benefits from among several private plans is known as "managed competition."[12]

While Congress did not enact any federal reform proposals, several state-sponsored programs were created. One example is the Health Insurance Plan of California (HIPC), which was established in 1993. The HIPC negotiates with many private MCOs to provide affordable health coverage to small businesses and gives employees their choice of health plans and plan design (e.g., size of co-payment, different physician and hospital networks, benefit exclusions).[13] Eligibility for participation in the HIPC is limited to California employers with 3 to 50 full-time employees. Seventy percent of the employees in a given company must be willing to participate in the HIPC, and the employer must agree to pay at least 50 percent of the health insurance premium for the lowest-cost plan available.[14]

Consumer Satisfaction

Overall Quality of Care and Services

	poor/fair	good	very good	excellent
All Plan Response	13%	29%	36%	22%
Plan One	14%	27%	37%	22%
Plan Two	10%	27%	38%	25%
Plan Three	14%	30%	37%	20%

Thoroughness of Treatment

All Plan Response	13%	27%	35%	26%
Plan One	14%	25%	35%	26%
Plan Two	10%	24%	36%	30%
Plan Three	13%	27%	38%	22%

Ease of Making Appointments by Phone

All Plan Response	16%	25%	33%	27%
Plan One	17%	21%	33%	30%
Plan Two	16%	27%	31%	26%
Plan Three	17%	26%	32%	26%

Numbers of Doctors You Had to Choose From

All Plan Response	27%	30%	27%	17%
Plan One	29%	31%	24%	16%
Plan Two	19%	28%	29%	24%
Plan Three	23%	32%	29%	16%

Attention Given to What You Had to Say

All Plan Response	14%	26%	34%	27%
Plan One	14%	25%	33%	28%
Plan Two	10%	23%	36%	31%
Plan Three	13%	25%	37%	25%

Figure 5–4 Sample Coalition Report Card

Exhibit 5–2 Examples of Purchasing Coalitions

Name	Location	Members	Activities	Example of Results
Colorado Health Care Purchasing Alliance	Statewide, CO			Pay 30% less for hospital care
Health Care Network of Wisconsin	Seven counties surrounding Milwaukee, WI	Programs for large and small employers	Direct contracting with physicians and hospitals; built own networks; manage care; report data	Save 30% on hospitals, 15% on physicians
The Alliance	Madison, WI			Save 10–13% of all charges
Memphis Business Group on Health	Metropolitan Memphis, TN			Saved $43 million in one year
Buyers Health Care Action Group	Metropolitan Minneapolis, MN	Large, self-insured employers		Saved 11% by reducing unnecessary care
Northwest Indiana Health Alliance	Urban, northwestern IN	Mostly small, fully insured employers	Contracts with competing managed care systems; reports data; quality improvement projects	Provides 9 different plans to small employers
Employers Purchasing Alliance	Tampa, FL	Large employers		Annual increase 0% compared to 6% in market
Gateway Purchasers Association	Metropolitan St. Louis, MO	Large employers		19% reduction in HMO rates in first year (1994); still below market

continues

Exhibit 5–2 continued

Name	Location	Members	Activities	Example of Results
Employers Health Cooperative	Janesville, WI	Small to medium-sized employers	Contracts with single managed care organizations; quality improvement projects	Partnered with HMO or asthma self-care program
Kansas Employers Coalition on Health	Topeka, KS	Large and small employers	Pharmacy program	Paying 30% below market rate for prescriptions
Vermont Employers Health Alliance	Statewide, VT		"carve out"	Employer of 1,200 saved $250,000 per year on prescriptions
Central Florida Health Care Coalition	Orlando, FL	Large employers	Hospital "carve out," report data, quality improvement projects	Reduced Caesarean sections 50%
Health Care Payers Association of N.J.	Statewide, NJ			30% reduction in hospital charges

Source: Data from *Down the Path of Better Returns: Value Based Health Care Purchasing*, p. 12, National Business Coalition on Health; L. Rybowski, *Making the Case for Purchaser Freedom: How Employers are Reforming the Market for Health Care*, pp. 16–19, © 1994, Midwest Business Group on Health; and E. Wicks et al., *Designing Health Purchasing Cooperatives: Federal Policy Issues and Options*, p. 1, © 1994, Institute for Health Policy Solutions.

The HIPC has been successful in offering workers affordable coverage. Recent rate increases for the 28 health plans offered through the HIPC averaged 3.9 percent in 1997, compared to national averages of 4 percent to 10 percent. Moreover, the HIPC members are paying lower rates than in prior years: the average premium for an individual plan in 1997 was $110.97, 12 percent lower than the rate for the same plan in 1993.[15]

LABOR UNIONS

At the same time that the 1949 *Inland Steele* case gave employers a permanent role in the financing of health care, it also cemented the involvement of organized labor in shaping health care purchasing. As discussed earlier, this Supreme Court case determined that under the Taft-Hartley Labor Relations Act (1946), health care plans were a fringe benefit that could be collectively bargained by labor unions.[16] This meant that labor unions could collectively demand from employers the type of insurance, extent of coverage, and premium contribution they desired for their health insurance program.

Some union members receive their health care benefits through an employer-sponsored plan; others receive benefits through a Taft-Hartley Trust—a trust managed jointly by labor and management under strict rules set out in the Taft-Hartley Labor Relations Act. The Trust-sponsored plans are less flexible than the employer-sponsored plans because all workers in the Trust's plan must agree to any proposed changes in the health benefit program.[17] Furthermore, the union negotiators in Trust-sponsored plans typically have incongruous goals. On the one hand, they promote the expansion of health care benefits for their members, yet as the Trust managers, they also work to keep the plan cost-effective and economically sustainable.

Because of labor's historic opposition to managed care, employers with unionized employees were forced to increase deductibles, co-payments, and employee premium sharing of their indemnity plans to offset the increasing costs of such plans. Predictably, unions and their members opposed this approach, as well, and strikes over health benefits occurred. While only 18 percent of strikes in 1986 were because of health care benefits, roughly 78 percent of strikes in 1989 were due to proposed changes in health care benefits.

A HEALTH CARE LABOR DISPUTE

The telecommunications industry was a visible national example of the tension over health costs. Attempts by nearly all the regional telephone companies to shift health care costs to workers during contract negotiations in 1989 triggered a round of strikes by the Communication Workers of America and the International Brotherhood of Electrical Workers. The settlement agreement that Bell Atlantic negotiated allowed the company to establish managed care networks throughout its service area, but 100 percent of the cost of care would be covered by the plan if employees used the network. A joint labor-management task force was also authorized by the settlement to work on implementation of additional managed care strategies to contain rising health care costs.[18]

Historically, when selecting managed care options, unions have preferred PPOs to HMOs because PPOs cover some of the cost of care for employees who choose a physician not affiliated with the network. Unions view the restricted choice of physician as a reduction in benefits similar to coverage exclusion or a cash reduction in employer contribution.[19]

After the failure of national health reform in the mid-1990s, unions turned their effort toward consumer protections from perceived abuses by MCOs. Many existing federal and state legislative initiatives are spearheaded by some of the largest labor unions in the country. In some markets, unions have worked on quality improvement projects with large employers. For example, the United Auto Workers and General Motors have launched a pilot project to collaborate with hospital and physician groups in reducing the administrative costs of MCOs. Unions in Flint, MI, also worked with local hospitals to eliminate 450 unneeded hospital beds, freeing up more money for direct patient care instead of hospital overhead.[20]

STATES AS PURCHASERS

State Employee Health Plans

State governments usually dominate the employer market in their respective state capitals, especially in rural states where they are one of the largest employers. When acting as purchasers, state governments are often caught between the conflicting goals and processes of cost containment and government bidding. Managers of the plan often want to follow the lead of private-sector purchasers in purchasing health care benefits on value; however, the politics of awarding a major state contract and the regulatory requirements of a public bidding process are not always conducive to such "value purchasing" strategies. For example,

- Value purchasing is based on a long-term partnership with an MCO, while states may be required to seek competitive bids every two or three years.
- Value purchasing involves trade-offs between cost and quality. The lowest cost MCO may not be the best value. State governments, on the other hand, may be required to accept the lowest bid even if quality is poor.
- Value purchasing uses objective criteria to award contracts to MCOs with the best performance. State governments may be subject to political decisions in awarding contracts.
- State governments must negotiate health care benefits with large unions, a process that often stifles the implementation of managed care strategies and locks the state into a benefit plan for the duration of the union contract.

Despite these challenges, some states have forged ahead, implementing purchasing strategies modeled after the private sector. In 1989, both Ohio and Vermont implemented the first managed mental health programs in the country for state employees. California formed the California Public Employee Retirement System (CalPERS), the country's largest purchasing alliance, serving as a model for many purchasing alliances because of its selection of plans, establishment of performance standards, and information provided to consumers. CalPERS experienced premium decreases for several years and has held rates lower than the rest of the highly competitive California market.[21] Utah's Public Employees Health Program (PEHP) contracts with hospital systems for specific services, like obstetrical care, paying a single global fee that covers hospital, physician, and all other costs related to the hospital admission.[22]

Medicaid

What Is Medicaid?

Created in 1965 by Title XIX of the Social Security Act, the Medicaid program is jointly funded by the federal government and state governments to provide health care and long-term care (nursing home) coverage for low-income individuals. When originally conceived, Medicaid operated in tandem with state welfare programs and eligibility was limited to those individuals who also received public assistance, typically children in poor families, head-of-household single parents, and the disabled.

Federal guidelines establish the parameters under which states operate the program. For example, state Medicaid operations must be approved by the Health Care Financing Administration (HCFA), a division of the U.S. Social Security Administration. States choose what benefits to include in the program, set the income threshold for eligibility, and determine the provider fee schedules.[23] The federal-state funding formula is based on the average per capita income of the state, the scope of program the state chooses to implement, and other factors. Because of these variations, the federal government's proportional cost of the program ranges from 50 percent to 80 percent of the total cost of each state's program.[24]

The benefit package of the Medicaid program is comprehensive, covering all in-patient and out-patient hospital care, professional services (including mental health), diagnostic testing (e.g., laboratory and X-ray), prevention and screening services for children and adolescents, and nursing home and home health services. Prescription drugs, prosthetic devices, hearing aids, and services for the mentally retarded are optional benefits states can offer.[25]

The Evolution of Medicaid Managed Care

Medicaid spending sharply increased in the late 1980s and early 1990s. The annual growth rate had jumped to 32 percent in 1991, up from 10 percent in 1980. By 1994, Medicaid had become a $140 billion program, representing 42 percent of the total funds the federal government allocated to the states.

During this same period, however, the number of uninsured persons in the country continued to grow. Because the Medicaid program is only for individuals who fit into an eligible "category," (e.g., low-income children, pregnant women, elderly, blind, and disabled) millions of Americans who could not afford private health insurance (i.e., the "working poor" employed by small firms, the self-employed) also did not have access to the Medicaid program. Because of these eligibility restrictions, Medicaid provides coverage to less than half of the country's low-income population.[26]

Pressure built on the states to expand Medicaid eligibility. However, program costs already were creating fiscal problems. States could see the success of private-sector employers in containing costs by implementing managed care. Both state and federal officials believed that shifting from a fee-for-service program to a managed care model would produce sufficient cost savings to expand Medicaid eligibility to include the working poor.

However, implementation of managed care for Medicaid programs was somewhat restricted by Title XIX, which required that all providers be paid "prevailing reasonable and customary charges," and also required that Medicaid beneficiaries have unrestricted choices of providers.[27] In 1981 and 1982, Congress modified the program to give states more latitude in negotiating with providers. Still, only 3 percent of the Medicaid population was enrolled in a managed care plan by 1983, and the vast majority of this enrollment was concentrated in four states.[28] The growth of managed care was also inhibited by the requirement that states seek federal approval before implementing a Medicaid managed care plan. In response to the growing costs and numbers of uninsured working poor, HCFA simplified this process. By 1996, Medicaid managed care enrollment reached over 13 million, representing one-third of all Medicaid enrollees. Figure 5–5 shows the growth of enrollment in Medicaid managed care plans from 1986 through 1996.

There are two models of Medicaid managed care programs: the primary care case management model (PCCM), and the full-risk HMO model. Federal prohibitions against co-payments, deductibles, and other cost-sharing requirements prevent state Medicaid programs from contracting with PPOs or POS plans that require consumer cost-sharing.

The PCCM model is a fee-for-service program: providers do not assume financial risk through capitation or other payment mechanisms. As with HMOs, Medicaid enrollees must select a primary care case manager (usually a primary care physician or nurse practitioner) who approves and

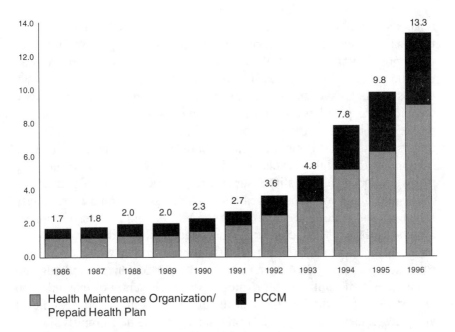

Figure 5–5 Growth in Medicaid Managed Care Enrollment, 1986–1996. Courtesy of the Henry J. Kaiser Family Foundation, Washington, D.C.

coordinates all health care services. Primary care case managers receive a management fee for this activity and fee-for-service payments for care they provide to the enrollees.

The full-risk HMO model is virtually indistinguishable from the HMO model used in the private sector. The state Medicaid agency contracts with an HMO that assumes responsibility for providing the full range of covered benefits for a fixed monthly payment (called a capitation). In some cases, a health insuring organization (HIO) acts as the fiscal intermediary, collecting the capitation from the Medicaid program and then distributing payments to its own network of providers who deliver care. Under both scenarios, the Medicaid agency does not assume the financial risk and does not reimburse providers on a fee-for-service basis.[29]

Managed Care Experience

While the transition to managed care has helped several states expand eligibility for Medicaid to many more low-income children and families,

it has also raised concerns among state officials and low-income representatives about the impact managed care programs have on these disadvan-
taged population. For example, MCOs have little experience marketing,
enrolling, and educating low-income populations. For the most part,
MCOs do not have substantial experience in applying managed care
techniques to populations with multiple and complex health and social
problems. There is particular concern about the potential of MCOs to
underserve this government-supported population. As a result, Medicaid
MCOs tend to be highly regulated and monitored, with each state imposing
its own reporting and quality assurance requirements on their plans.

Despite these concerns, states and HCFA have become increasingly
reliant on the continued participation of MCOs, and as a result, appear
more sensitive to MCO concerns about Medicaid's burdensome requirements. In recent years, HCFA and the states have worked with the managed
care industry and NCQA to rationalize the performance standards and
requirements of public- and private-sector purchasers. For example, the
newest release of the HEDIS data requirements combines the Medicaid
and private-sector employer data sets, standardizing and simplifying data
collection and analysis for MCOs, and allowing for cross-sponsor comparisons of MCOs' performance. Also, the efforts of the Agency for Health
Care Policy and Research (a division of the U.S. Public Health Service) to
develop a standardized managed care consumer satisfaction survey incorporated the needs of private purchasers and Medicaid programs from the
inception of the project. The survey, called the Consumer Assessment of
Health Plan Satisfaction (CAHPS), is being tested on private and public
populations in several states and may be adopted by NCQA as part of the
HEDIS data set.

FEDERAL HEALTH BENEFIT PROGRAMS

The federal government is the major purchaser of health care services in
the country. As the sponsor of health benefit programs for federal employees, military personnel, and the elderly (and co-sponsor of the state-
operated Medicaid programs), the federal government pays for more than
half of the total health care services provided in the United States. Different
agencies within the federal government have responsibility for these
various programs, and each has developed its own rules governing the
benefits and terms of the programs.

The Federal Employees Health Benefit Program

Ten million federal employees, retirees, and their dependents participate in the Federal Employers Health Benefit Program (FEHBP). Authorized by Congress in the Federal Employees Health Benefits Act, FEHBP is administered nationwide by the Office of Personnel Management (OPM), making it the largest single purchaser of health care in the country.

Legislation allows FEHBP to offer a variety of health benefit choices to beneficiaries. As of 1995, OPM had contracted with over 400 comprehensive health plans, most of which were community-rated HMOs.[30] OPM does not engage in a competitive bidding process to select plans for the FEHBP. Each plan must apply for participation in the program annually. The application process requires plans to demonstrate financial stability, adequate provider networks, compliance with OPM's standards, and other basic requirements. Any plan that meets these requirements can participate in the FEHBP.

OPM requires MCOs to offer a minimum set of health benefits (federally-qualified HMOs must offer the benefit package mandated by the HMO Act) and requires plans to offer the same benefit plans they offer their private-sector customers. Enrollees receive extensive information during the annual open enrollment period, including information about available plans, covered benefits, and premium costs. OPM sets its contribution for the health insurance premium at 60 percent of the average premium of the six largest plans participating in FEHBP, leaving the enrollee to pay any additional cost.[31]

CHAMPUS and TriCare

The U.S. government also provides coverage to more than six million beneficiaries in the U.S. military.[32] Unlike the FEHBP, TriCare, the health program for the military, encompasses both the payment and actual delivery of health services to beneficiaries. In addition to paying for health care received by its beneficiaries, the military operates more than 500 treatment facilities around the world, including 127 hospitals.[33] Recent innovations by the U.S. Department of Defense (DOD) in developing managed care programs combined these resources with those in the civilian sector.

Until very recently, the military health program was a fee-for-service insurance plan known as the Civilian Health and Medical Program of the Uniformed Services (CHAMPUS). CHAMPUS was a claims payment program: claims administrators under contract to the military processed and paid the medical claims for health care services delivered to CHAMPUS beneficiaries. These services included most inpatient and outpatient health services, medical supplies, and mental health care. Because of this generous benefit design and medical inflation in the late 1980s, CHAMPUS expenditures doubled between 1985 and 1990.[34] Consequently, DOD initiated several demonstration projects to test the feasibility of implementing various managed care techniques throughout the CHAMPUS system. Many successful features of these demonstrations were incorporated into the reformed program, including

- risk-sharing contracts with private MCOs
- participation of military medical facilities as network providers
- expanded utilization review and quality assurance programs
- a triple-option benefit structure (i.e., PPO, HMO, and fee-for-service plan)

The new program, TriCare, is implemented through 12 health services regions, each managed by the commanding officer of the region's tertiary medical center. Both civilian and military providers and facilities participate in the TriCare regional networks. Participating civilian MCOs, called "managed care support contracts," are selected for each region through a competitive bidding process. Primary care managers coordinate care for individuals.[35] Like the private sector, the DOD has demanded better data from MCOs and has developed new information systems to monitor the performance of plans and the TriCare program itself. By maximizing the use of the military's health care facilities, incorporating competitive risk contracts with civilian MCOs, introducing quality assurance programs, integrating information technology, and designing a triple-option benefit structure, the DOD has fundamentally transformed the military's health services programs.

Medicare

What Is Medicare?

Operated as a nationwide program by HCFA, Medicare provides health insurance for aged and disabled Americans. Medicare Part A covers hospital services and is funded by a payroll tax on private-sector employees and employers. Medicare Part B provides coverage for outpatient services and is financed by a combination of premiums paid by beneficiaries themselves and general federal tax revenues.

Because eligibility for the Medicare program is tied to Social Security eligibility, most people become eligible for Medicare upon turning age 65. Certain individuals who receive Social Security disability payments are eligible for Medicare after a two-year waiting period from the initial date of disability, regardless of age. Enrollment in Medicare Part A is automatic. Although Part B enrollment is voluntary, virtually all those who are eligible enroll.[36] Through Medicare Part A and Part B, over 39 million beneficiaries are provided with a comprehensive range of health care benefits. Because of the increasing number of individuals reaching age 65, costs are projected to grow by over 7 percent each year between 1997 and 2002, compared to 4 to 5 percent annual increases in the private sector. In 1997, the total cost of the Medicare program was $208 billion.

Historically, both Part A and Part B operated as fee-for-service programs with contracted agencies processing claims for health care service provided to beneficiaries. Cost containment programs were implemented by HCFA in the 1980s to encourage providers to be more cost-conscious. Traditionally, hospitals had been paid based on their itemized charges. One of the cost containment strategies implemented by HCFA was the reimbursement of hospital services according to a single fee for the entire episode of hospitalization, based on the diagnosis assigned to the patient. This payment system, called diagnosis-related groups (DRGs), is still the predominant hospital payment method for the Medicare program (see Chapter 4 for a more detailed discussion of DRGs).

Payments to health care professionals under Part B were also modified. Instead of paying the "prevailing, usual, and customary fee" as required in the original legislation, HCFA implemented a fee schedule based on the relative value of the procedures performed. Each medical or surgical procedure is assigned a weight depending on the skill, training, time, and expense of the professional. This system, called Resource-Based Relative Value System (RBRVS), rewards cognitive and diagnostic skills, rather than procedural skills. Consequently, it has increased payments to PCPs and reduced payments to surgeons and other specialists. By implementing RBRVS, HCFA hoped to control costs and encourage greater use of primary care services and less specialty care by changing the financial incentives for practitioners (see Chapter 4 for a more detailed discussion of RBRVS).

The Evolution of Medicare Managed Care

The DRG and RBRVS reimbursement changes were relatively helpful in slowing the growth of health care spending in the Medicare program. However, at the time these changes were implemented, Congress was encouraging HCFA to expand the prevalence of managed care to further control costs. The Tax Equity and Fiscal Responsibility Act (TEFRA) of 1982 established requirements for HMOs to contract with the federal government to serve Medicare beneficiaries. Two types of contracts were envisioned: risk-based and cost-based. Under risk-based contracts, MCOs accept a capitation payment from Medicare to provide both Part A and Part B benefits. With cost-based contracts, MCOs do not accept financial risk and are reimbursed on a fee-for-service basis. Medicare beneficiaries have a choice of remaining in the traditional fee-for-service program or enrolling in a qualifying managed care plan.

MCOs operating under risk-based contracts have been more successful in attracting enrollees than those with cost-based contracts: 88 percent of the five million Medicare managed care members are enrolled in a risk-based managed care plan.[37] The high proportion of enrollment in risk plans is directly attributable to the capitation rules applied to them. The capitation paid for the risk contracts is established at 95 percent of what Medicare estimates it would pay for those enrollees under a fee-for-service system. If the managed care plan is able to deliver all required services for less than the capitation rate, it must return the surplus money to HCFA or provide benefits not typically covered under Medicare. Not surprisingly, most MCOs have chosen to provide additional benefits, such as prescription drugs, vision, dental care, and medical equipment, and have eliminated patient deductibles and co-payments, which are a standard element of Part A and Part B. These added benefits improved the attractiveness of risk-based HMOs. The pace of Medicare managed care enrollment has accelerated throughout the decade. From 1994 to 1997, Medicare enrollment in MCOs increased 50 percent.[38] Figure 5–6 shows the growth in Medicare managed care enrollment and the proportions enrolled in risk contracts versus cost contracts.

Managed Care Experience

One reason for the success of MCOs in Medicare risk contracts is believed to be their ability to attract a disproportionate number of healthy

Millions of Medicare Beneficiaries

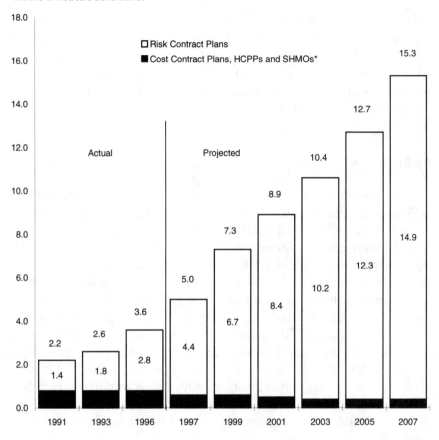

*Health care pre-payment plans and social health maintenance organizations

Figure 5–6 Medicare Managed Care Enrollment, 1991–2007. Courtesy of the Henry J. Kaiser Family Foundation, Washington, D.C.

enrollees, which makes the MCO's actual costs lower than their payment from Medicare.[39] As in the private sector, relatively healthy individuals are the first to join managed care plans, particularly HMOs. The challenge for HMOs is to continue providing quality care and maintaining customer satisfaction when providing care to more of the chronically ill. Studies on the performance of Medicare managed care plans in treating chronically ill patients show different results. For example, one study found that HMO members with cancer were diagnosed at an earlier stage in the disease than were Medicare fee-for-service enrollees. However, other studies show poorer outcomes for patients in HMOs and lower levels of customer satisfaction among the chronically ill enrolled in managed care plans.[40] A major study conducted in 1996 for HCFA found that overall satisfaction with the HMOs was high, and HMO plan members were only slightly less positive about recommending their MCO to someone with serious or chronic health problems. Figure 5–7 summarizes findings of that survey.

Retirees, Medicare, and Managed Care

Not all employers provide health insurance to their retirees. For those who do, however, changes in financial accounting standards (known as Federal Accounting Standard 106) implemented in the early 1990s required employers to estimate and report the future cost of retiree health benefits as a current liability. For many large employers—particularly those in older industries—the substantial future cost of providing retiree health coverage had a significant and immediate impact on their financial reports. It was estimated at the time of implementation that FAS 106 would reduce the book value of the largest industrial companies in the country by as much as 7.8 percent over the next decade.[41] In 1992, AT&T reported that adopting FAS 106 reduced net income that year as much as $7.5 billion. This new accounting requirement, in combination with health care cost inflation, has forced employers to find alternate ways to minimize the cost of retiree health plans or phase out retiree health insurance coverage altogether.

Frequently, employers have removed retirees from the company health plan once the retiree became eligible for Medicare. To supplement the Medicare coverage, the employer usually purchased a Medicare supplement policy for the retiree to cover the cost of required co-payments and deductibles, and to include a few additional benefits, such as prescription drugs. While Medicare would pay for most of the hospital costs, these supplemental plans covered most of the outpatient costs, providing no incentive for an employer to implement managed care programs for its retirees.

The new Medicare managed care programs transfer the financial risks and gains of managing care for retirees from the employer to Medicare and the contracted Medicare HMO. The employer pays the fixed Medicare managed care premium (if any), which usually costs less than what the

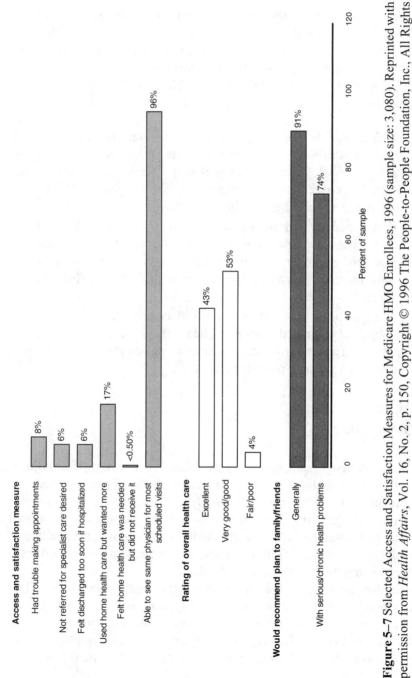

Figure 5–7 Selected Access and Satisfaction Measures for Medicare HMO Enrollees, 1996 (sample size: 3,080). Reprinted with permission from *Health Affairs*, Vol. 16, No. 2, p. 150, Copyright © 1996 The People-to-People Foundation, Inc., All Rights Reserved.

employer would pay to supplement the Medicare fee-for-service plan. All of the cost of the retiree's health care is covered through the Medicare HMO. It may even be possible, according to some analysts, to reduce the employer liability under FAS 106 using this mechanism.[42]

Employers choosing to enroll retirees in Medicare HMOs face potential problems.

- If the union or employment contract promised the employees that retiree health benefits would be the same as those for active employees, the employer must ensure that the Medicare HMO provides sufficient coverage. The employer may have to purchase "riders" to add pharmacy or other benefits, for example.
- If managed care enrollment for retirees is voluntary (that is, if the retiree chooses between an MCO and the employer's self-insured plan), the employer faces the risk that the employer-sponsored plan could retain the less healthy retirees while the Medicare HMO attracts the healthy elderly.
- The quality of care and customer satisfaction record of the MCOs should be examined before Medicare managed care is offered to retirees. The employer may consider using selected MCOs, such as those with superior performance records.

CONCLUSION

There are many challenges purchasers face in maintaining their influential role in the evolution of managed care. First is the increasing legislative and regulatory activity at the state and federal level spurred by consumer and provider concerns about managed care. As government assumes a greater role in setting performance standards and defining the package of health benefits available through managed care, purchasers' involvement in negotiating these parameters will subside.

Another challenge is the recent upswing in health care costs. While many purchasers are truly dedicated to the concepts of value purchasing and quality improvement, cost may always be the determining factor in selecting health plans. This is particularly true for smaller employers, who are able to exert less pressure on plans to reduce health care premiums.

A clear trend in corporate America toward "out-sourcing" personnel functions can also be a threat to direct purchaser involvement. As companies downsize, they often hire an outside personnel management company to handle such functions as employee benefit design and management. With a contractor responsible for establishing employee benefits within a fixed budget, the employer no longer directly makes health care purchasing decisions. Under this arrangement, short-term cost is the paramount concern.

Engaging employees in the quest for value and quality has met with limited success. For many employees and labor groups, the switch from indemnity plans to managed care is seen as merely a cost-driven transaction. When employees are financially insulated from their choice of MCO or provider, they are not compelled to take any action beyond participating in the annual open enrollment.

DISCUSSION QUESTIONS

1. What were the key events that led to employers being the principal sponsors of health insurance for employed Americans? Discuss the positive and the negative impacts of plan sponsorship from an employer's perspective.
2. Why are employers more concerned about quality of health care when they purchase a managed care product than when they purchase traditional insurance?
3. What is HEDIS, and what are the benefits of HEDIS from the perspective of purchasers and health plans?
4. Why are small employers not able to use the same purchasing strategies as large employers?
5. List and explain four reasons why an employer may join a health care purchasing coalition.
6. What is a health plan report card, and why might a consumer find it useful?
7. Discuss the differences between the Medicaid program and the Medicare program in regards to eligibility, administration, and financing.
8. What factors led to the introduction of managed care to Medicaid? To Medicare?
9. Discuss the differences between the FEHBP and the TriCare program in regards to eligibility, administration, and health plan choices.

10. What is the difference between purchasing a health plan based on cost, and purchasing a health plan based on value? Why is this an important distinction for health plans to recognize?

REFERENCES

1. National Business Coalition on Health, *Down the Path of Better Returns: Value-Based Health Care Purchasing* (Washington, DC: 1997), 3.

2. J. Califano, Jr., *America's Health Care Revolution: Who Lives? Who Dies? Who Pays?* (New York: Random House, Inc., 1986), 44.

3. Califano, *America's Health Care Revolution: Who Lives? Who Dies? Who Pays?* 44.

4. J. Maxwell and J. Snow, "You don't have to be the biggest to get the best deals," *Business and Health*, April, 1997, 31.

5. National Business Coalition on Health, *Down the Path of Better Returns: Value-Based Health Care Purchasing*, 1.

6. NCQA, *HEDIS 3.0: Understanding and Enhancing Performance Measurement* (Washington, DC, 1997), 5–6.

7. J. Meyer et al., *Employer Coalition Initiatives in Health Care Purchasing*, Vol. I. (Washington, DC: Economic and Social Research Institute, 1996), 3.

8. National Business Coalition on Health, *Down the Path of Better Returns: Value-Based Health Care Purchasing*, 12.

9. L. Rybowski, *Making the Case for Purchaser Freedom: How Employers Are Reforming the Market for Health Care* (Chicago: Midwest Business Group on Health, 1994), 16–19.

10. S. Edgman-Levitan et al., "What Information Do Consumers Want and Need?" *Health Affairs 15*, no. 4 (Winter, 1996): 44–45.

11. E. Wicks et al., *Designing Health Purchasing Cooperatives: Federal Policy Issues and Options* (Washington, DC: Institute for Health Policy Solutions, 1994), 1.

12. Wicks et al., *Designing Health Purchasing Cooperatives: Federal Policy Issues and Options*, 1–2.

13. Health Insurance Plan of California, *The HIPC Employee Brochure and Application* (Sacramento, CA: 1997), 2 ff.

14. T. Buchmueller, "Managed Competition in California's Small-Group Insurance Market," *Health Affairs 16*, no. 2 (March/April, 1997): 219.

15. "Plans in California HIPC Keep Premium Increases to 3.9 Percent," *Managed Care Week*, 14 April, 1997, 3.

16. Califano, *America's Health Care Revolution: Who Lives? Who Dies? Who Pays?* 44.

17. H. Siegelbaum, "The Union Experience with Health Maintenance Organizations and Preferred Provider Organizations" (panel discussion, Committee on Medicine in Society of the New York Academy of Medicine, 14 and 15 May, 1986).

18. J. Geisel, "Employers, Unions Join To Attack Health Costs," *Business Insurance*, 2 April, 1990, 60.

19. Siegelbaum, "The Union Experience with Health Maintenance Organizations and Preferred Provider Organizations."

20. G. Church, "Backlash against MCOs," *Time*, 14 April, 1997, 35.

21. Rybowski, *Making the Case for Purchaser Freedom: How Employers Are Reforming the Market for Health Care*, 6.

22. National Business Coalition on Health, *Health Care Data and Quality: Where the Rubber Meets the Road* (Washington, DC: 1996), 25.

23. J. Ingelhart, "The American Health Care System: Medicaid," *The New England Journal of Medicine 328*, no. 12 (25 March, 1993): 896.

24. The Kaiser Commission on the Future of Medicaid, *Medicaid Facts: The Medicaid Program at a Glance* (Washington, DC: April, 1997), 1.

25. The Kaiser Commission on the Future of Medicaid, *Medicaid Facts: The Medicaid Program at a Glance*, 1.

26. The Kaiser Commission on the Future of Medicaid, *Medicaid Facts: The Medicaid Program at a Glance*, 1.

27. Califano, *America's Health Care Revolution: Who Lives? Who Dies? Who Pays?* 52.

28. The Kaiser Commission on the Future of Medicaid, *Medicaid Facts: Medicaid and Managed Care* (Washington, DC: June, 1997), 1.

29. The Kaiser Commission on the Future of Medicaid, *Medicaid Facts: The Medicaid Program at a Glance*, 1.

30. J. Michaels and C. Rinn, "The Federal Employees Health Benefit Program and Managed Care," in *The Managed Health Care Handbook,* 3d ed. (Gaithersburg, MD: Aspen Publishers, Inc., 1996), 703.

31. Michaels and Rinn, "The Federal Employees Health Benefit Program and Managed Care," 704.

32. J. Boyer and L. Sobel, "CHAMPUS and the Department of Defense Managed Care Programs," in *The Managed Health Care Handbook,* 3d ed. (Gaithersburg, MD: Aspen Publishers, Inc., 1996), 779.

33. Boyer and Sobel, "CHAMPUS and the Department of Defense Managed Care Programs," 779.

34. Boyer and Sobel, "CHAMPUS and the Department of Defense Managed Care Programs," 781.

35. Boyer and Sobel, "CHAMPUS and the Department of Defense Managed Care Programs," 785.

36. The Kaiser Medicare Policy Project, *The Medicare Program: Medicare at a Glance*, (Washington, DC: April, 1997), 1.

37. The Kaiser Medicare Policy Project, *The Medicare Program: Managed Care*, 1.

38. L. Nelson et al., "Access to Care in Medicare HMOs, 1996," *Health Affairs 16*, no. 2 (March/April 1997): 148.

39. T. Gajda, "How Employers Can Use HMOs' Medicare Programs," *Managing Employee Benefits 3*, Vol. 4 (Fall, 1995), 78.

40. The Kaiser Medicare Policy Project, *The Medicare Program: Medicaid and Managed Care,* 2.

41. A. Starchild, "The Investor's Library," (1995), published on the Internet at http://www.cyberhaven.com/investors/newaccounting.html.

42. Gajda, "How Employers Can Use HMOs' Medicare Programs," 77.

CHAPTER 6

Utilization Management

Physics does not change the nature of the world it studies, and no science of behavior can change the essential nature of man, even though both sciences yield technologies with a vast power to manipulate their subject matters.

Burrhes Frederic Skinner (1904–1990)

"Mommy . . . is that bandage medically necessary?"

Learning Objectives

- Understand why managed care organizations (MCOs) manage the use of health care resources among their members.
- Understand the criteria MCOs use in determining the appropriateness of medical treatment.
- Understand the various components of utilization management.
- Understand the criticisms of utilization management programs.

Key Terms

Length of stay—The number of days a patient is in the hospital for each admission. Counted from the day of admission to the day of discharge.

Medically necessary—The determining criteria by which MCOs decide if proposed or rendered treatments or services should be authorized or reimbursed. Care that is medically necessary is deemed by medical experts to be warranted based on the medical condition and history of the patient.

Pre-certification—The process that MCOs use to authorize hospital admissions or other health care services, such as diagnostic testing. Using medical review, MCOs evaluate whether the patient's condition warrants the proposed treatment or service and determine the most appropriate site of care.

Utilization management—The process of assessing the necessity, appropriateness, and efficacy of health care either before, during, or after services are rendered.

INTRODUCTION

Utilization management (also known as medical management or clinical management) is the process of monitoring and managing the use of health care services. In the late 1970s and early 1980s, numerous published studies began to demonstrate that a significant portion of the health care delivered in this country was not necessary. Unnecessary care is care that is not expected to benefit patients or that could be detrimental to the health of patients. The provision of needless care impacts both health care quality and costs. Clearly, providing medical treatment that is inappropriate or harmful to patients is an indicator of poor quality. Unnecessary care also means nonessential costs: if the use of needless care is minimized, health care costs will decrease. The magnitude of the problem prompted MCOs and health insurers to initiate programs to monitor or control the use of health care services as both a cost containment mechanism and a quality control tool.

MCOs manage the utilization of health care resources through prospective, concurrent, and retrospective review—that is, before, during, and after a procedure or service is rendered. Most health care services are reviewed to determine their appropriateness, including hospital admissions, outpatient diagnostic procedures, and office visits by specialists. The goal of utilization management is to eliminate or minimize the provision of unnecessary care and promote the use of appropriate care. As with any managed care feature, the use of utilization management techniques varies by type of plan (i.e., health maintenance organizations [HMOs] vs. preferred provider organizations [PPOs]) and among similarly structured plans (i.e., all point-of-service [POS] plans do not employ the same utilization management programs).

REVIEW CRITERIA

"Is the proposed treatment medically necessary?" This is the question underlying an MCO's decision to authorize or deny medical treatment. To arrive at this conclusion, MCOs apply medical criteria (also called guidelines or protocols) to each case reviewed. Review criteria can assist an MCO in determining if the proposed treatment is justified and expected to benefit the patient. For example, criteria can identify the symptoms that would warrant a hospitalization for certain medical conditions. Guidelines are often supplemented with medical standards developed by specialty medical societies, local medical associations, and plan medical advisory boards.

Many MCOs use the Healthcare Management Guidelines™ developed by Milliman & Robertson, Inc., an international health care consulting and actuarial firm, as the basis for their medical management decisions. These widely accepted guidelines are developed by medical and risk management experts based on clinical research, and are updated to accommodate the growing body of knowledge on medical practice. Milliman & Robertson publishes guidelines on inpatient, specialty, primary, pharmacy, and ambulatory care. The kinds of criteria used by MCOs include the following:

Length of stay guidelines. By evaluating large databases on hospital admissions, medical experts have been able to develop reasonable expectations of how long patients would require hospitalization. An average length of stay could be developed for diagnoses based on the patient's principal diagnosis and other conditions. These length of stay guidelines are usually adjusted based on community standards and advances in treatments.

Severity of illness criteria. These criteria evaluate the need for hospitalization based on the patient's medical condition. By gathering information on the patient's medical condition, the MCO can ascertain the severity of illness (i.e., how sick is the patient?) and the appropriate level of care (i.e., does the patient need to be admitted to the intensive care unit?).[1]

Appropriateness protocols. The collection and analysis of information on treatments and their related outcomes has led to the development of appropriateness protocols—explicit ways of caring for patients based on clinical evidence and expert medical opinion. Successful appropriateness protocol systems incorporate an extensive review of the clinical literature from multiple medical databases and the evaluation of the data by nationally-known experts in the field.[2] Such clinically-based information enables the plan to determine if the patient will likely benefit from the proposed treatment based on the patient's demographics, clinical condition, and other characteristics (see Chapter 7 for more information on appropriateness criteria).

The application of review criteria in determining the appropriateness of care is highly controversial. Many MCOs believe that making criteria available to physicians will encourage them to "game the system," e.g., deceptively alter the patient's medical condition to conform to the guidelines; therefore, they refuse to publish the criteria on which they make decisions to authorize care. Others, including physicians, argue that the secrecy of review criteria thwarts the advancement of sound medical practice and hampers the accountability of the MCO. Because physicians and consumer groups have been advocating for the public disclosure of the review criteria, some states are passing laws requiring MCOs to release the medical criteria on which they base payment and coverage decisions.

REFERRAL AUTHORIZATION

To monitor the use of specialty and ancillary care, some MCOs require authorized referrals to specialists and ancillary care providers. MCOs that restrict access to specialty care (e.g., HMOs, POS plans) need a process for authorizing and tracking member referrals to specialists and ancillary care providers. Depending on the structure of the plan and the product, referrals to specialists are authorized by the member's primary care physician (PCP) or the MCO itself. For example, some gatekeeper plans will give the PCP responsibility for coordinating referrals to the specialist, but not authorizing them. In these instances, the PCP will make a request to the plan for a member to see a specialist and the plan will authorize the service if it deems the referral to be medically necessary. Other plans delegate the authority to authorize visits for specialty care to the PCP directly. Plans that contract with medical groups, independent practice associations (IPAs), physician–hospital organizations (PHOs), etc., on a risk basis will usually transfer the responsibility for authorizing referrals to the group. The purpose of referral management is to manage the cost and quality of specialty and ancillary services.

MCOs establish parameters for the number of visits and time period in which the specialty care services should occur—generally one or two visits per referral, although this may vary by service. For example, some plans will allow six visits to a physical therapist under the initial referral. In addition to establishing a mechanism for the authorization of initial referrals, MCOs develop a process for referral extensions and specialty referrals. Depending on the service requested or the provider requesting, MCOs may allow the initial referral to be extended to permit subsequent visits or additional services, or they may require the creation of a new referral.

To restrain costly specialty care, most MCOs prohibit the specialist from making secondary referrals, i.e., referring the patient to another specialist for consultation.[3] If the specialist thinks other services are necessary, the patient must receive a referral from his or her PCP first, often generating another PCP visit. Managed care critics see little value with administrative rules like these, arguing that such policies actually generate, rather than eradicate, unnecessary health care services and thus needlessly contribute to higher health care costs and hassles for members and providers. Since the PCP is responsible for tracking all the care a member receives, while the specialist is knowledgeable about only a specific component of the member's care, MCOs contend that the PCP is best suited to make determinations about the member's care.

A manual authorization process requires the PCP to generate a paper referral, sending a copy to the specialist, the MCO, and the member, and retaining one for his or her files. The plan manually enters the referral into the utilization system so that it can be matched with the claim for proper payment. The specialist is instructed not to render the service unless he or she receives the referral or it accompanies the member. More plans are developing capabilities to transmit referral information electronically. Using an electronic authorization system, the PCP can verify the member's eligibility and benefit coverage and notify the MCO of the specialty referral via computer or telephone. The authorization information is downloaded or automatically entered into the plan database, allowing specialists to electronically access the system to verify member eligibility and referral authorizations. The electronic exchange of referral information reduces administrative expenses, improves workflow, and eliminates the hassles of paper exchanges (i.e., lost referrals, wait time for referrals).

> **Exercise: You are a medical director of an MCO and are reviewing a request by a participating PCP to refer a 29-year-old male patient to an orthopaedist. What information do you look for on the referral request, and what questions do you ask in order to decide whether to grant the referral?**

PRE-CERTIFICATION

One of the earliest and most enduring forms of utilization management, hospital pre-certification, aims to reduce the frequency of hospitalizations by shortening the length of hospital stays or substituting other types of care. By pre-certifying hospital care and other high-cost services, MCOs hope to curb health care utilization, thereby reducing expenditures. MCOs measure and monitor the frequency of inpatient care by calculating bed days per 1,000 members. Exhibit 6–1 illustrates how MCOs calculate bed days per 1,000. Most MCOs require elective hospital services to be pre-authorized—or pre-certified—before the procedure occurs in order to

- determine the medical appropriateness of the procedure
- establish an initial length of stay
- identify potential admissions for intensive case management
- ascertain whether an alternative treatment or setting is more appropriate
- verify member eligibility and benefit coverage

Depending on the plan and product, either the PCP, admitting physician, hospital, or member has the obligation for pre-certifying procedures. For example, many self-insured benefit plans require members to contact the plan before scheduling elective surgery, while HMOs generally require the hospital or admitting physician to perform pre-certifying procedures. Authorizations can be granted by the plan directly, a designated utilization review agency, or a provider group under a full-risk arrangement. Using inpatient and surgical care guidelines developed by Milliman & Robertson,

---

Exhibit 6–1 Example of Bed Days for the Month to Date (MTD)

Assume:	Total gross hospital bed days in MTD = 300
	Plan membership = 12,000
	Days in MTD = 21
Step 1:	Gross days MTD = 300 ÷ (21 ÷ 365)
	= 300 ÷ 0.0575
	= 5,217.4
Step 2:	Days per 1,000 in MTD = 5,217.4 ÷ (12,000 ÷ 1,000)
	= 5,217.4 ÷ 12
	= 435

Therefore, the days per 1,000 for the MTD equals 435.

Source: Reprinted from P. Kongstvedt, Managing Basic Medical–Surgical Utilization, in *The Managed Care Handbook*, 3rd ed., P. Kongstvedt, ed., p. 259, © 1996, Aspen Publishers, Inc.

Inc., or other organizations, nurse case managers will assess whether the case meets the criteria for admission and may determine the length of stay or scope of the requested procedure. When the member's condition requires an immediate admission to the hospital, it is not possible or prudent for the physician or member to obtain permission from the MCO first. In these cases, the MCO usually requires that the PCP, hospital, or member notify the plan within 24 hours or the next business day.

Some medical conditions can be treated just as effectively, if not more effectively, in a less intensive setting. For instance, when the member's condition does not warrant an admission to the hospital, the pre-certification process can identify suitable alternatives to hospital care, such as outpatient dialysis or subacute care. Moreover, many conditions require fewer and less intense medical resources after the initial acute treatment phase—surgeries, for example. The recovery period for many post-surgical patients can occur at home or in hospital step-down units.

Originally used solely for hospitalizations, the pre-certification process today encompasses many services performed on an outpatient basis, including ambulatory surgical procedures, home care services, durable medical equipment, laboratory services, imaging services, and high-cost drugs. This reflects the dramatic shift from inpatient to outpatient care that has occurred over the last decade, particularly with surgical procedures. In fact, as a condition of reimbursement, some MCOs will require that defined surgical procedures, such as rhinoplasty, endoscopies, and cardiac catheterization, be performed on an outpatient basis (often called mandatory outpatient surgery review).

CONCURRENT REVIEW

During the patient's hospital stay, the MCO will assess the progress of care and determine the appropriateness of the continued hospitalization. Concurrent review (also called continued stay review) looks at the treatment and setting: Is the treatment still useful and necessary? Is the hospital still the most suitable setting? Nurse case managers review the patient's medical chart and talk with clinicians about the treatment and patient's progress. This can be done on site or telephonically. MCOs with sufficient resources and aggressive utilization management efforts will conduct on-site reviews. For example, PPOs almost always review medical cases telephonically. The physical presence of a utilization management nurse in reviewing hospital care benefits MCOs because nurse managers can

- gather the most up-to-date information on the patient's condition and prescribed treatments
- detect physician practice patterns that negatively impact utilization and costs
- uncover quality of care issues in hospital or physician care
- identify social or personal circumstances of patients that affect pending discharge and continuation of care[4]

A principal component of concurrent review is discharge planning, the process of planning and coordinating the continuation of patient care upon discharge from the hospital. An effective discharge planning effort begins as soon as the patient is admitted to the hospital. In conjunction with the treating physician, the patient, and the patient's family, the nurse case manager will assess the expected duration of the patient's hospital stay, as well as the patient's unique medical needs, living situation, and support network. While the need for hospital treatment may end, patients often require continued care at a different level and in an alternative setting. For example, a patient leaving the hospital after a major accident may need outpatient rehabilitation services or speech therapy, or a post-surgical elderly patient may need follow-up care in a skilled nursing facility. The nurse manager plays a critical role in communicating information about the pending discharge with the patient and patient's family.

CASE MANAGEMENT

Case management is the ongoing management and planning of care for complex, chronic, protracted, or high-cost medical problems. Major surgery, trauma, premature births, high-risk obstetrics, cancer, acquired immune deficiency syndrome (AIDS), and stroke are examples of medical conditions and events that are often subject to case management. The purpose of case management is to maximize a member's benefits to provide the most appropriate care in a cost-effective manner. Case management services are typically provided by the MCO or an independent utilization review or case management company.

The nurse case manager works with the patient, family, PCP, admitting physician, hospital staff, and other health care professionals to ensure that the patient receives the most appropriate treatment in the right setting. It is an individual approach to managing care. The nurse case manager assesses the specific medical, financial, personal, social, and psychological needs of the patient and family to determine the range of services the patient might require and identifies the medical and social resources available to the patient. In addition to coordinating the provision of services, the case manager functions as the liaison between the patient/family and the myriad of health care professionals treating the patient and gives the family information and support.

In arranging for the most appropriate care for patients, the case manager considers the benefits covered under the member's plan and the availability of community resources, such as support groups and non-profit health organizations. Often the case manager determines that the member's situation warrants the extension of covered benefits or an exception to pay for non-covered services. For example, for an elderly patient lacking an adequate family support system, it may be more beneficial to authorize home care visits beyond those allowed under her plan than to arrange for care in a skilled nursing facility. Table 6–1 compares conventional case management to disease management.

RETROSPECTIVE REVIEW OF EMERGENCY CARE

Since MCOs usually have explicit policies for covering emergency treatment, most MCOs retrospectively review claims for emergency care to decide if the member's medical condition warranted a visit to the emergency department or an urgent care center. Generally, MCOs will not pay for emergency treatment unless the symptoms motivating the visit were severe, occurred suddenly and unexpectedly, or would have resulted in loss of limb or life if immediate care was not sought,[5] or if the emergency department visit was authorized by the MCO or the member's PCP. Claims for emergency care services that do not meet these conditions are denied.

Sometimes a member will get injured or become sick while temporarily outside of the service area and will seek emergency services at non-participating hospitals. If truly an emergency, the MCO will reimburse the hospital, but only for those services necessary to treat the member before he or she can be transferred to a participating hospital. Emergency visits at

Table 6–1 Comparison of Conventional Case Management and Disease Management

	Case Management	*Disease Management*
Goal	Reduce per case cost, improve episodic care	Reduce per disease cost, improve patient outcomes
Emphasis	Appropriate treatment of illness, use of alternative settings	Improved management of chronic care, prevention and eduction for patients, families, and physicians
Scope	Patient often has multiple diseases	Patient is initially evaluated for a single disease
Review	Periodic concurrent review	Prospective and concurrent review
Guidelines	Generic, externally imposed	Customized to diagnosis, internally designed
Caregivers	Generalists, nurses	Specialists, multidisciplinary team
Data sources	Primarily inpatient (tracks length of stay, profit margin per confinement, mortality)	All points of service (tracks annual episode of care cost, medication compliance, functional status)
Integration	Isolated medical management	Integrated medical management
Risk	Lacks ability to bear financial risk	Increased ability to bear financial risk

Source: Adapted from D.W. Plocher, Disease Management. in *The Managed Health Care Handbook*, 3rd ed., P.R. Kongstvedt, ed., p. 321, © 1996, Aspen Publishers, Inc.

out-of-area hospitals that result in admissions can be problematic for MCOs. To reduce hospital costs and monitor the continued care of the member, the MCO will attempt to move the member to a participating hospital under the care of a participating physician as soon the member is physically able to be transferred. Such aggressive tactics are often viewed by patients, hospital administrators, and physicians as callous attempts by MCOs to save money to the detriment of patient care.

DENIALS AND APPEALS

In some instances, the decision by an MCO to deny coverage for treatment will be challenged by physicians or members. As discussed in other chapters, federal and state regulations require MCOs to establish a process for physicians and members to appeal benefit coverage and medical management decisions. Many denials of treatment involve experimental treatment of life-threatening medical conditions. Since the patient is likely to die without such treatment (despite the fact that he or she may die anyway), denials of such care make headline news. At least one plan is dealing with this issue head on by submitting any denials of investigative treatments to an independent organization for an external review.[6]

MEDICAL TECHNOLOGY ASSESSMENT

An element of managing the use of health care resources is determining whether to pay for new technologies, which are often far more expensive than existing courses of treatments. Using objective, third-party expert panels, many MCOs will evaluate the safety and efficacy of emerging medical technologies, including diagnostic procedures, surgical interventions, and drug therapies. The goal of technology assessment is to determine if new technologies improve the health of patients. Such evaluations give MCOs scientific information to establish practice guidelines, justify benefit coverage decisions, support utilization management programs, and target quality improvement initiatives.

CONCLUSION

Utilization management techniques are a major reason for the intense dislike of managed care. They are often seen by members as obstacles to needed care rather than genuine attempts to ensure that the member receives appropriate medical treatment. Health care practitioners resent the skepticism about their professional judgment and medical decision-making abilities that are seemingly inherent in utilization management programs. However, a recent study indicates that MCOs ultimately approve the majority of care physicians propose.[7] Do these findings support the notion that utilization management techniques are needless administrative burdens for physicians, or are they evidence that utilization management controls have been effective in influencing physician practice patterns? One can reasonably argue either position.

Practice guidelines, outcomes research, and other quality initiatives are beginning to replace utilization management techniques. The advancement of medical knowledge is allowing physicians, researchers, and MCOs to create guidelines or algorithms for the optimal treatment of certain conditions, rather than review the appropriateness of such care on a case-by-case basis. As this knowledge expands and physicians begin to use this clinically-based information more broadly, the need for MCOs to question every treatment decision a physician makes will subside.

DISCUSSION QUESTIONS

1. Why do MCOs manage the use of health care resources?
2. What types of criteria do MCOs use in evaluating the appropriateness of medical treatment?
3. Why is the use of medical criteria controversial?
4. What are the three general types of medical reviews an MCO conducts?
5. Give an example of how an MCO prospectively reviews medical care.
6. Why do MCOs require hospital admissions to be certified?
7. Describe what a nurse case manager does when conducting concurrent review.
8. What types of medical conditions are often subjected to case management?
9. Under what circumstances would an MCO deny a claim for emergency treatment?
10. Why do health care practitioners resent utilization management programs?

REFERENCES

1. B. Chaiken, "Evolution of Utilization Review Criteria: Appropriateness Protocols and Managed Care," *Managed Care Medicine*, May/June 1996, 17.
2. Chaiken, *Managed Care Medicine*, 17.

3. P. Kongstvedt, ed., *The Managed Health Care Handbook,* 3d ed. (Gaithersburg, MD: Aspen Publishers, Inc., 1996), 255.

4. Kongstvedt, ed., *The Managed Health Care Handbook,* 264.

5. W. Knight and L. Sansone, "Ambulatory and Ancillary Care Contracting," in *Managed Care Contracting: A Guide for Health Care Professionals* (Gaithersburg, MD: Aspen Publishers, Inc., 1997), 214.

6. W. Guglielmo, "Curbing HMO Treatment Denials: Is a Trend Taking Hold?" *Medical Economics*, 25 August, 1997, 99.

7. D. Remler, "What Do Manage Care Plans Do To Affect Care? Results from a Survey of Physicians," *Inquiry 34*, Fall, 1997, 196–200.

CHAPTER 7

Quality of Care

Quality is in the eye of the beholder.

Elizabeth A. McGlynn (1997)

"One hand clapping? . . . Piece of cake. I'm having trouble with that 'quality of care' thing though."

Learning Objectives

- Understand the principal ways in which the various participants in the health care system define quality health care.
- Understand the importance and challenges of measuring quality.
- Understand the various criteria on which quality is measured.
- Understand the strategies managed care organizations (MCOs) use to measure, monitor, and improve the quality of care delivered to their members.

Key Terms

Disease management—The systematic approach to improving care by identifying patients with (or at risk for developing) specific diseases, implementing processes to better treat and manage care, and measuring the results of such interventions.

Outcomes data—Information that shows the results of specific medical treatments or processes (e.g., mortality statistics on patients who undergo heart bypass surgery).

Patient satisfaction surveys—Questionnaires that attempt to determine how satisfied members are with their managed care plan or primary care physician.

Performance measurement—A standardized process of assessing an MCO's ability to deliver high-quality care and maintain high levels of customer satisfaction.

Quality assurance—The activities MCOs use to assure regulators, purchasers, consumers, providers, and the public that the care delivered by affiliated providers under the guidelines of the plan meets basic standards of quality.

INTRODUCTION

How health care delivered in managed care arrangements differs from care delivered in a traditional health insurance system has been an area of concern since the introduction of prepaid medicine in the early 1900s and a topic of study in recent years. Do the principal features of managed care, i.e., discounted fees, restricted access to specialty care, and focus on preventive care, impact the quality of health care patients receive? And if so, how? Many critics of managed care contend that patients in managed care settings receive lower quality of care than those in fee-for-service programs. These critics argue that the reimbursement methods and administrative rules of MCOs inhibit timely access to specialty care and encourage under-utilization of needed health care. That managed care focuses on primary and preventive care and verifies the credentials of its participating providers demonstrates its superiority in delivering better care than traditional insurance programs, counter proponents of managed care. Empirical evidence exists to support each argument, fueling the ongoing debate on quality.

Theoretically, in taking responsibility for providing (or arranging for the provision of) medical care to members, MCOs also shoulder the burden for how that care is delivered, just as providers do. However, only recently have plans truly focused on influencing the quality of care their members receive, largely prompted by employers and other purchasers demanding evidence that MCOs provide value. After successfully demonstrating the ability to reign in rising health care costs, MCOs were asked to prove that such cost containment successes did not come at the expense of quality. Today, MCOs must show that they actually improve the quality of care their members receive.

Oversight of providers has been the traditional method MCOs used to ensure quality. However, as MCOs assume the extended role of care manager, their scope has broadened to include initiatives to improve the quality of health care their members receive through affiliated providers. But to improve quality, it must first be defined. And therein lies the difficulty. Exactly what is quality health care? The answer is as imprecise and evolving as medical science itself. The continuous efforts to better understand what constitutes quality health care is a burgeoning area of study, pursued by medical practitioners, researchers, health care managers, purchasers, and consumers independently and collaboratively. In their broadest terms, discussions about quality of health care focus on the overuse, underuse, and misuse of medical care.[1]

Overuse. A procedure is provided even though there is no apparent benefit to the patient or the risks are greater than the expected benefit. This is known as providing unnecessary or inappropriate care. Numerous studies have shown that a significant amount of surgical procedures, including hysterectomies and certain heart procedures, have been provided inappropriately. MCOs reduce or eliminate the overuse of unnecessary or inappropriate care through utilization management techniques, like case management and pre-certification, and by implementing practice guidelines and best practices.

Underuse. A service is not provided that has been demonstrated to benefit patients. Examples of the failure to provide necessary care include not performing scheduled mammograms, detecting clinical depression, or administering beta blockers for patients suffering from heart attacks.[2] MCOs attempt to increase the delivery of necessary or appropriate care by identifying underusers and encouraging them to seek treatment; for example, annual exams and cancer screenings. Plans also notify physicians of particular members due for important preventive care services and send them preventive care guidelines.

Misuse. Appropriate service is provided poorly so that the patient does not benefit as might be expected. Complications from surgical procedures and medications are two principal examples of misuse of health care services.[3] The use of on-line drug utilization review programs can substantially reduce the risk of adverse effects from overmedication. To minimize surgical complications, some plans direct their complex surgical procedures to specific institutions that perform a high volume of the procedures with good patient outcomes.

DEFINITIONS OF AND PERSPECTIVES ON QUALITY

The current definitions of quality by recognized medical experts or institutions are useful starting points in a discussion about quality care in MCOs. Avedis Donabedian, widely acknowledged to be an authority on the theory and management of quality care, defines quality care as "that kind of care which is expected to maximize an inclusive measure of patient welfare, after one has taken account of the balance of expected gains and losses that attend the process of care in all its parts."[4]

The American Medical Association defines quality health care as that "which consistently contributes to the improvement or maintenance of quality and/or duration of life."[5]

The Institute of Medicine defines it as the "degree to which health services for individuals and populations increase the likelihood of desired health outcomes and are consistent with current professional knowledge."[6]

Common elements of these or other quality definitions include the following:

Improved health status. A fundamental consideration of quality care is that it improves a patient's health, e.g., the patient lives longer as a result of the surgery. Clinical outcomes studies link various treatments to specific outcomes and guide practitioners in pursuing treatments that yield the best results. However, the scarcity of outcomes studies forces practitioners to rely on other methods of determining quality.

Patient satisfaction. How patients regard their care is a critical aspect of quality, but difficulties in obtaining and assigning value to reliable patient measures have, until recently, hindered their incorporation into accepted standards of quality. New techniques that enable researchers to more accurately assess patient perspectives,[7] the recognition of the importance of patient values and preferences, and the unavailability of outcomes data have made patient satisfaction an increasing determinant of MCO quality.

Professional opinion. Traditionally, the most valued consideration of quality was the opinion of the clinician as to the technical aspects of the care provided. Technical quality of care incorporates the appropriateness of care provided (i.e., did the physician make the right decision about which treatment to provide?) and skill with which care was provided (i.e., did the physician possess the clinical competence and judgment to perform the treatment?).[8]

Perspectives on quality vary according to the individual or entity involved in the health care system: clinicians, purchasers, consumers, MCOs, regulators, and others. In today's dynamic environment, useful definitions of quality as they pertain to managed care need to incorporate the evolving perspectives and values of all participants.

Patient

While lacking the knowledge to evaluate the technical aspects of quality, patients are well suited to ascertain how they feel, physically and mentally, about the care they receive. A determinant of high-quality care from a patient perspective is how the care addresses his or her individual needs.[9] The "miracle of medicine" (i.e., the belief that modern medicine can cure any sickness) unrealistically elevates patient expectations of medical care. Despite the questionable reliability of self-reported satisfaction scores, patient satisfaction will continue to be an integral part of quality measurement.

Focus groups and studies show that patients have different perspectives on quality measures than experts. For example, a recent study showed that consumers believe that friends and family are more reliable sources of information on the quality of their plan than quality experts or official agencies, including independent or government agencies, doctors, employers, and plans. Sixty-nine percent of the respondents said that friends and family were a good source of information about the quality of their plan. Conversely, only 36 percent of respondents said that employers, who have taken the lead in disseminating quality information, are reliable sources of information.[10]

Purchasers

In their attempts to obtain value for their health care premium dollars, purchasers have assumed a significant role in measuring health care quality in recent years. Purchasers use quality measures to rank and compare the performance of MCOs and affiliated providers. This focus on comparative quality measures has spawned the development of standardized measures (Health Plan Employer Data and Information Set [HEDIS]) that can be compared across plans in the form of report cards. These measures reflect purchasers' value for organizational performance[11] and processes of care. As purchasers shift their emphasis from cost consciousness to quality improvement, they are giving greater importance to population-based quality measures (i.e., how well does a plan immunize its pediatric population?), rather than utilization measures (i.e., how many outpatient surgeries per 1,000 members did the plan perform?).

MCOs

Like purchasers, MCOs also value population-based quality measures.[12] While traditionally some MCOs have emphasized the need to reduce the use of unnecessary procedures, more MCOs are implementing population health management programs (or disease management programs) to measure and monitor their ability to improve patient care among specific disease categories. Early detection and prevention are critical elements in managing the entire health of populations. As such, MCOs will increasingly be measured on their success in encouraging non-users to seek needed health care. Of great importance to MCOs is the ability to demonstrate organizational processes that foster patients' unencumbered access to appropriate medical care. As such, the availability of providers becomes important and is measured by the percentage of closed primary care physician (PCP) practices, wait time in physicians' offices, and number of specialists in the network.

Providers

Accustomed to relying on their own clinical judgment about what constitutes quality, physicians are now being asked to incorporate the varied perspectives of others into their traditional concepts of quality medical practice, which have been confined to the narrow scope of technical quality.[13] Increasingly, the performance of physicians is being evaluated by how well their practice patterns conform to certain national or community standards, often defined by MCOs. However sensible practice guidelines may seem to the non-clinician, they are often viewed by physicians as "cookbook medicine" that is not responsive to individual patient needs.[14]

Exercise: Describe your perspective on quality health care from the following vantage points:

a. consumer
b. specialist
c. MCO executive
d. plan manager

QUALITY MANAGED CARE: AN OXYMORON?

Cultural biases about consuming goods and services impact the perceptions people have about the quality of care in a managed care environment.

First is the notion that "you get what you pay for." Equating price and quality means that if a product has a lower price relative to a competitive product, it must be a product of inferior quality, not a better value. As the less expensive health benefit option, managed care is often viewed as the least quality-oriented plan. In many markets, discounted arrangements with providers and hospitals are a euphemism for low-quality providers or high-quality providers being forced to provide minimal care. Second is the idea that "more is better." The American consumer ethic suggests that the greater the quantity or choices of products we have, the better off we are. In managed care, this creed translates into the desire for more providers, more product choices, and more health care. Offering people fewer choices (i.e., network of providers, limits on medical coverage), managed care is not seen as a selective product, but as an inferior, and less desirable, one.

Medical research on the impact that access to care has on the quality of care intensifies people's suspicions about the ability of managed care to deliver quality care. Research shows that patients with limited access to care have inferior health status. That managed care restricts or monitors access to specialty care suggests to some that, by definition, it reduces the quality of care it offers members. Barriers to care can be structural (i.e., availability of providers, refusal to cover specific treatments) or procedural (i.e., referrals to specialists, pre-certification process). They are often measured by the time patients must wait in the doctor's waiting room, or before scheduling an appointment to see a specialist. To be recognized as an organization in sincere pursuit of quality improvement, an MCO must overcome the inherent biases people have about managed care.

MEASURING QUALITY

What Are We Measuring?

Current thinking on quality assessment is based on Avedis Donabedian's conceptual model of three aspects of care: structure, process, and outcome.[15] This model suggests that information should be collected and measured on all three components of care.

Structure. Structural information is the characteristic of the provider or MCO,[16] such as a plan's ownership, size, and provider selection criteria, and a physician's specialty, board certification status, and medical training. From this information, conclusions can be made about the plan's or provider's ability to deliver quality care. Regulatory agencies and accrediting bodies frequently rely on structural information to assess quality.

Process. Processes of care relate to how the practitioner or MCO provides (or facilitates) care to patients (i.e., what was done?). This includes the type and frequency of treatments or tests, such as the rate of mammograms and the percentage of pregnant women receiving prenatal care, and the processes plans have in place for improving care, such as member outreach programs. Because of the unavailability of outcomes data, many national quality measurement sets, as well as specific employer or coalition report cards, emphasize process of care indicators.

Outcomes. Data on outcomes tell us about the patient's health status as a result of the treatment or procedure. Hospital re-admission rates and mortality rates are traditional measures of patient outcomes. Today, the results of medical care are viewed more broadly than the biological status of patients historically used by physicians (e.g., improved symptoms, lower cholesterol levels). The definition of health status has been widened to include the patient's physical, emotional, and social functioning[17] (e.g., how soon does the patient return to work, and how does he or she feel as a result of the treatment?). The direct and indirect economic consequences of a procedure are also evaluated. How cost-effective is the procedure? Did it result in fewer hospitalizations or office visits?

Process versus Outcomes Information

There is considerable debate about the relative merits of process and outcomes measurements. Some argue that data on how the care was delivered (i.e., the process of care) do not tell us the result of the treatment,[18] and are therefore an incomplete measure of quality. For example, the fact that a plan routinely screens its female members for breast cancer does not mean it is successful at reducing the death rates attributable to breast cancer among its population. Those critical of outcomes measures argue that patient characteristics, rather than skill and judgment of the physician, are more influential in determining outcomes and that such measures cannot be adequately adjusted for the type of patient or severity of the illness.[19,20] Others suggest that reporting on traditional outcomes measures for some chronic diseases signifies a failure in the treatment of the disease, and that measures that reflect how care is managed would be more useful. For example, hospitalization rates for asthmatic patients indicate the extent to which the care was not managed well.[21] More useful measures might include the percentage of patients that were counseled on the use of peak flow meters or received prescriptions for inhaled corticosteriods, interventions that help patients control their asthma. Clearly, evaluating both the treatment and the outcomes of the treatment is critical in conducting a complete assessment of quality. Figure 7–1 depicts a model of evaluating treatments and their results.

The value of data outcomes depends on the type of individual or organization reviewing the information. For example, providers might be more interested in clinical outcomes measures, whereas patients might be

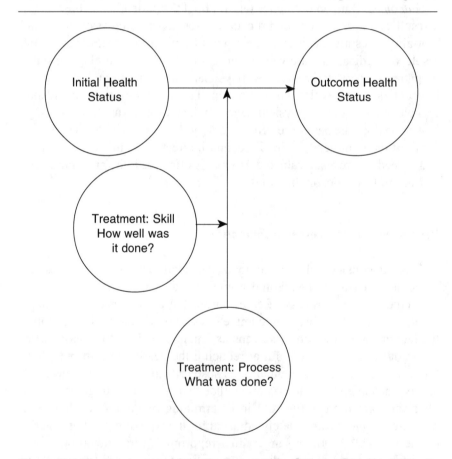

Figure 7–1 The Treatment and the Treatment Effect. *Source:* Reprinted from P. Hebert, Treatment, in *Understanding Health Care Outcomes Research*, R. Kane, ed., p. 95, © 1997, Aspen Publishers, Inc.

more concerned with humanistic results, such as quality of life.[22] An intended purpose of publishing outcomes data is to distinguish providers with "good" outcomes from those with "poor" outcomes so that plans, purchasers, and consumers can select providers accordingly. However, the publication of outcomes data does not always have this effect, as is the case in Pennsylvania, where the release of hospital mortality rates has not swayed consumers to avoid hospitals and providers with poor outcomes.[23] Moreover, surveys of consumers show that they are likely to rely on alternate sources of information about the quality of providers, such as feedback from family and friends, rather than published quality data.[24] Other surveys of consumers show that they lack sufficient information on which to make informed decisions about provider and plan selection.[25]

CASE STUDY: TYPE I DIABETES

Comparing process and outcomes measures for the treatment of Type I diabetes gives us a sense of the relative merits and deficiencies of these measures.

Process measurement: Annual dilated ophthalmoscopy to detect diabetic retinopathy.

Outcomes measurement: Rates of blindness among Type I diabetics.

Some clinicians regard a yearly exam for all Type I diabetics as excessive and a waste of resources to monitor diabetics who are not at risk for developing diabetic retinopathy. That an MCO screens X percentage of Type I diabetic members every year tells us nothing about the health status of those members who develop diabetic retinopathy. An alternative measure is to determine the rates of blindness among Type I diabetics, one possible outcome of diabetic retinopathy.[26] This would indicate how the plan was managing the care of Type I diabetic patients.

Exercise: You are the director of quality at an MCO. You are permitted to use only one type of measurement for evaluating the quality of care your members receive—process of care or outcomes of

> **care measures. Choose one, explaining how this will yield the best evidence of quality for the MCO.**

How Are We Measuring It?

Just as there are varying definitions of quality, there are different ways to evaluate quality. Criteria on which to assess quality are based on scientific research, such as clinical efficacy and effectiveness studies (i.e., evidence-based medicine) and the professional opinions of clinicians (i.e., consensus-based medicine). Because they were developed primarily for research studies, existing quality-of-care criteria are not particularly relevant in determining the level of quality in the day-to-day practice of medicine and must be updated to incorporate the rapid advance in medical treatments.[27] Quality can be assessed using implicit (i.e., no existing or previous standards about quality) or explicit (i.e., existing or previous standards about quality) criteria. There are five different methods a reviewer might use in evaluating quality.[28]

1. Was the process of care adequate? (implicit)
2. Was the outcome of care acceptable, i.e., could better care have improved the patient outcome? (implicit)
3. Was the overall quality of care acceptable? (implicit)
4. Were the processes of care that should have been performed for the specific condition and patient actually performed? (explicit)
5. Did the results of care conform with the expected outcome based on a scientific model? (explicit)

Appropriateness Criteria

Appropriateness criteria identify the patients who will benefit most from the medical intervention given the associated risks.[29] Is the treatment appropriate for that particular patient, i.e., age, sex, medical history, symptoms, and severity of condition? Appropriateness criteria have been developed for procedures with disparate professional opinions on their effectiveness or with questionable outcomes, such as hysterectomy. Used in the context of MCOs, appropriateness criteria are often used to minimize over-utilization of unnecessary care. For example, if a hysterectomy is recommended for a member, the plan will ascertain if the treatment is suitable for the patient, e.g., would she likely benefit from the procedure?[30] MCOs also use appropriateness criteria to ensure that more necessary care is provided to members, particularly preventive care screenings and tests that can detect diseases at early stages. Some plans send care guidelines based on appropriateness criteria to affiliated physicians as part of their disease management programs. Such guidelines remind physicians to perform the recommended screenings and tests for applicable patients.

Outcomes Data

Outcomes research is the population-based study of certain treatments and their related outcomes. Research demonstrates that wide variations in treatments produce different outcomes. The goal of outcomes research is to determine which treatments yield the most favorable results. The assumption is that by measuring the related outcomes of specific treatments, optimal care can be achieved.[31] Outcomes research is a valuable tool in measuring and improving quality. The availability of outcomes data facilitates the following:

Assessment of quality. By comparing the outcomes of each provider, facility, or plan against the average of the group or expected norms, providers with lower-than-expected results can be identified.

Clinical decision making by providers. Providers can pursue therapies and procedures that are proven to produce the best results.

Continued improvement in care. Outcomes management or continuous quality improvement (CQI) is the application of outcomes research to practice.[32] Treatments that yield the best outcomes can be identified and implemented. The results of these interventions can be further analyzed and measured, thus facilitating the continuous improvement of care.

Conducting outcomes research requires a common set of measures, the uniform collection and coding of outcomes data, and the linking of outcomes data to process and structure.[33] Unfortunately, the challenges of defining suitable quality indicators and collecting data hinder broad-based outcomes studies. Outcomes research begins with the establishment of goals (i.e., the desired outcome of the treatment) followed by a determination of what is to be measured and how it will be measured. A quality indicator establishes the specific parameters for measurement. Exhibit 7–1 illustrates the process for developing an outcome indicator.

To make meaningful comparisons and assumptions about quality performance, outcomes data must be adjusted for the severity of illness and mix of patients. Unlike clinical trials, outcomes studies do not randomly assign patients to different providers or alternative treatments. Since outcomes studies are based on the actual practices of physicians, neither

Exhibit 7–1 Developing an Outcome Indicator

Goal?
>   Survival

What will be measured?
>   Patient mortality

When?
>   Some possible answers:
>>   48 hours after admission to hospital
>>   Upon discharge from facility
>>   30 days after admission
>>   60 days after discharge
>>   6 months after admission
>>   5 years after treatment

How will data be collected?
>   Some possible answers:
>>   Medical record
>>   Hospital discharge statement
>>   Death certificate in courthouse
>>   Application for survivor's benefits
>>   Attempt to contact patient by phone
>>   Insurance records

Indicator?
>   Patient alive 30 days after admission to hospital or clinic,
>   as determined by follow-up call from physician's office.

Source: Reprinted from *Outcome-Based Measurement of Quality*, Supplement 2, p. 2:3, © 1992, Aspen Publishers, Inc.

the random selection of patients or the withdrawal of appropriate treatments can occur. To account for the fact that some physicians might have a sicker population of patients, outcomes data must be adjusted. Despite their importance in measuring and improving quality, reliable risk-adjusted outcomes are scarce. MCOs are beginning to collaborate with purchasers, federal agencies, research organizations, and academic medical centers in conducting research that will generate such essential data.

Patient Satisfaction

A widely used measure of MCO quality is the members' satisfaction with the plan. According to the American Association of Health Plans

(AAHP), 99.5 percent of health maintenance organizations (HMOs) and 80.6 percent of preferred provider organizations (PPOs) conduct member satisfaction surveys. Despite their prevalence, there is considerable debate about the ability of satisfaction surveys to actually assess quality. One reason is that satisfaction surveys tend to focus on service, rather than quality, indicators. For example, was the member service representative knowledgeable and courteous during the member's last interaction with the plan, and how long did the member wait in the PCP's waiting area at the last visit? How satisfied a member is with a plan often has no relationship to how well the plan's affiliated providers deliver care to the members. Studies have shown that MCOs with high ranks on patient satisfaction scored low on quality measures and vice versa.[34]

Patient satisfaction surveys that ask members questions about their interactions with affiliated providers can frequently help MCOs identify perceived or actual deficiencies in care. Occasionally, member responses will suggest potential quality of care issues with specific providers. For example, a member might comment on the uncleanliness of a participating hospital or the lack of follow-up care by a physician.

In addition, surveys that ask patients to rate how a particular treatment or service affected their health are very important in disease management and other CQI efforts. A patient's perception of how a specific treatment impacted his or her health and functional status is a vital component of determining if the desired health outcome was achieved as a result of the treatment. For example, if a patient reports that he or she can walk more easily and comfortably after back surgery, this is one indicator of the quality of the back surgery.

Performance Measurement

Though not widely used yet, standard measures of quality and service indicators allow for the comparison between two or more plans (or providers), and comparisons across time (i.e., longitudinal comparisons) within a given MCO or provider group. National organizations like the National Committee for Quality Assurance (NCQA) and, most recently, the Foundation for Accountability (FACCT) are developing standard measures for MCO and provider performance. Employers and business coalitions like GTE, General Motors, and the Pacific Business Group on Health, have also developed health plan performance measures that complement or expand on existing national standards. Based on standard measures, MCOs' data are submitted to these entities, which in turn publish the information in the form of report cards. Such report cards compare the performance of MCOs against local, regional, or national norms and among competing plans.

Existing performance measures pose many difficulties for those attempting to measure plan performance. First, their focus on the process of care, not the outcome of care, leaves many unanswered questions about the ability of MCOs to deliver quality care. Whether plans actually improve the care delivered to their members cannot be assessed with current performance measures. Second, because the information is reported by the MCOs themselves, the reliability and accuracy of the data are questionable. For example, if MCOs are not reporting data in the same manner, it is not possible to make meaningful comparisons of quality.

HEDIS Measures

Developed by a broad-based committee of the NCQA, a not-for-profit organization focused on MCO quality, HEDIS is a set of standardized measures used to compare the performance of MCOs in various clinical, administrative, and financial areas. Initially released in 1995, HEDIS measures have been updated to reflect evolving improvements in quality measurements. The most widely used tool for evaluating MCO performance, HEDIS measures are used by purchasers and consumers to rank and compare performance of MCOs. They are also used by MCOs to develop benchmarks from which to measure continued improvements in performance. The data set includes structure, process, and outcomes measures; however, most measures focus on the structure and process of care—the extent to which the plan partners with public health organizations or immunizes older adults, for example.

In reviewing possible indicators to include in the standardized data set, NCQA's broad-based committee, the Committee on Performance Measurement, considers each measure's relevance, scientific soundness, and feasibility.

Relevant. Measures need to be relevant to purchasers and consumers in comparing MCOs. Do purchasers and consumers value the measures? Do the measures pertain to treatments known to significantly affect health outcomes? Will the measures be used to make health care decisions?

Scientifically sound. Measures that are scientifically sound are reliable (i.e., the measure produces the same results when repeated with the same populations and settings), valid (i.e., the measure reflects what is actually happening), and adjustable (i.e., the measure considers other factors besides quality).

Feasible. Measures need to be achievable for MCOs. Do the measures permit the plans to collect data in a way that is cost-effective? Preserves patient confidentiality? Produces meaningful comparisons? Do the measures cover a broad range of services?[35]

The most recent measurement set, HEDIS 3.0, attempt to improve the methods and scope of MCO assessment. For example, new measures are included that assess the ability of plans to improve the functional well-being of their members and care for their chronically ill members. In recognition of the need for continuous improvement, the HEDIS 3.0 data set incorporates emerging measures so plans can prepare for their eventual implementation. HEDIS 3.0 measures are organized into eight performance categories.

1. *Effectiveness of care*. How well is the care delivered by the plan producing appropriate clinical results? Is the plan addressing both members who are healthy and members who are sick? Examples of measures include the use of beta blocker treatment after a heart attack and childhood immunization status.
2. *Access/availability of care*. Can members assess care in a responsive, timely, and accessible manner? Examples of measures include the availability of PCPs and the availability of obstetrical/prenatal care providers.
3. *Satisfaction with the experience of care*. Is the plan satisfying the health needs of its members? Examples of measures include member satisfaction with choice of physician and referrals to specialists.
4. *MCO stability*. Is the plan financially solvent and is the provider network stable? Examples of measures include provider turnover rates and total membership.
5. *Use of services*. How well does the plan use its resources, i.e., what services are being delivered and how often? Examples of measures include Caesarean section rate and readmission rate for chemical dependency.
6. *Cost of care*. How well does the plan perform financially? Examples of measures include annual premium rate trends and the incidence of high-cost hospital cases.
7. *Informed health care choices*. How well does the plan involve members in the active management of their own health care? Examples of measures include language translation services.

8. *MCO descriptive information.* What are the operating characteristics of the plan? Examples of measures include re-credentialing programs and preventive care and health promotion activities.[36]

Foundation for Accountability Measures

Comprising primarily purchasers and consumer groups, FACCT is a non-profit organization whose mission is to develop consumer-focused quality measures. FACCT organizes quality measures developed by NCQA, the Agency for Health Care Policy and Research, and other groups and identifies areas where new measures are needed. Unlike these groups, FACCT does not collect and report quality data but develops recommended measurement sets. Believing that existing quality measures do not necessarily provide evidence of quality in a way that consumers want or need, FACCT attempts to enhance the usefulness of quality measures by

- organizing measures into five basic categories based on how consumers think of care: The Basics, Staying Healthy, Getting Better, Living with Illness, and Changing Needs[37]
- evaluating existing quality measures for their usefulness to consumers and applicability to one of the five categories
- developing new consumer-oriented measures in areas where no useful measures exist

To date, FACCT has created measurement sets for adult asthma, breast cancer, diabetes, health risks, health status, and major depression disorder. Table 7–1 identifies the FACCT measurement set for breast cancer care. Additional measurement sets are being assembled for coronary artery disease, pediatrics, end of life care, alcohol misuse and dependency, and human immunodeficiency virus (HIV) and acquired immune deficiency syndrome (AIDS).

Data Collection

The principal methods for collecting quality data are through medical charts or claims, each with their own deficiencies and benefits. Computerized information systems have enabled MCOs to collect and examine claims and encounter data across an entire population, greatly improving

Table 7–1 Breast Cancer Measurement Set

Measure	Performance Value	Instrument/Data Source
Steps to Good Care		
Mammography	*Proportion* of women age 52–69 who have had a mammogram within a two-year period	Doctor's billing or claims records (NCQA's HEDIS 3.0 Breast Screening measure used)
Early stage detection	*Proportion* of patients whose breast cancer was detected at Stage 0 or Stage I	Patient records from cancer registry
Informed about radiation treatment options	*Proportion* of Stage I and Stage II patients who indicate that they had completed three to six adequate information about their radiation treatment options before deciding about treatment	One question in patient satisfaction survey completed three to six months after diagnosis
Breast-conserving surgery	*Proportion* of Stage I and Stage II patients who undergo breast-conserving surgery	Patient records from cancer registry or claims records
Radiation therapy following breast-conserving surgery	*Proportion* of breast-conserving surgery patients who receive radiation treatment after breast-conserving surgery	Patient records from cancer registry or claims records
Experience and Satisfaction		
Patient satisfaction with care	*Mean* score for patients' level of satisfaction with breast cancer care including the technical quality, interpersonal and communication skills of their cancer doctor, their involvement in treatment decisions and the timeliness of getting information and services	Thirty-two-item patient satisfaction survey completed three to six months after diagnosis

continues

Table 7-1 continued

Measure	Performance Value	Instrument/Data Source
Results		
Experience of disease	*Mean* score for patients on CARES-SF survey, which assesses patients' quality of life and experience in living with breast cancer	Fifty-nine-item CARES-SF patient survey completed 12–15 months after diagnosis
Five-year disease-free survival (cancer treatment center measure)	*Probability* of disease-free survival for a group of patients, Stages I–IV, who were diagnosed during prior five years	Patient records from cancer registry

Source: FACCT—The Foundation for Accountability, FACCT Breast Cancer Measures—Breast Cancer Measurement Specifications–version 1.0, October 1997.

the efficiency of measuring quality. While data from a large claims database produce more meaningful results, claims and encounter data are often unreliable because of the errors that occur in coding diagnoses and procedures.[38] Moreover, they lack clinical information useful in assessing quality. A medical claim will identify the principal diagnosis and the specific procedures performed but will not reveal characteristics of the patient (e.g., patient's weight or medical history), how care was delivered (e.g., did physician note patient's weight fluctuations in the chart), or the result of the laboratory test (e.g., high or low cholesterol level)—important indicators of quality. This information is typically found in a review of the patient's medical record. While most clinically useful, actual medical records are administratively challenging to review. Unless the plan has computerized patient records, data from medical charts must be extracted manually, a costly and laborious process. In addition, data from medical charts are compromised by the small sample size that this method generates.

ENSURING QUALITY

MCO quality assurance programs intend to convince purchasers, consumers, regulators, and others that the plan and its affiliate providers meet basic standards for providing or arranging for health care. They include external validation processes and internal plan initiatives. Current quality assurance activities focus on the structural components of care. For example, state regulation requires that plans have a member grievance process (external process), and, through its provider contracts, an MCO will require its participating providers to cooperate with the plan's quality assurance programs (internal process). For some plans, traditional quality assurance programs have been supplanted by quality improvement initiatives. The vast majority of MCOs, particularly PPOs and point-of-service (POS) plans, still rely on rudimentary programs to ensure quality.

State and Federal Regulation

To obtain a business license, MCOs must meet basic state requirements on quality, which vary widely by state. Plans providing care to Medicare, Medicaid, and other government program beneficiaries must meet federal quality requirements, as well. These can include geographic access standards for provider availability, an external auditing process, and quality-data reporting. Recent state legislative activity has increased the regulation of MCOs in the area of quality (see Chapter 8). For example, anti–managed care laws attempt to preserve quality by ensuring patient access to particular providers or facilities and mandating hospital length of stays for specific admissions.[39]

Private Accreditation

MCOs seek external accreditation from private accrediting bodies to demonstrate that they meet certain industry quality standards. Accrediting organizations include the NCQA, the Joint Commission on Accreditation of Healthcare Organizations, and the American Accreditation Health Care Commission–Utilization Review Accrediting Commission. Accreditation is viewed as an accepted "seal of approval" and is customarily required by many purchasers. At present, more than half of the MCOs in the country have sought accreditation from NCQA. To obtain accreditation, a plan must meet or exceed standards in quality, service, and financial areas. After an extensive review of information and an on-site visit, the accrediting body determines whether to deny or grant the plan accreditation.

Provider Contracting and Profiling

Selecting health care professionals who meet or exceed high standards of practice is often the first step in a plan's quality assurance program. A plan's credentialing program distinguishes providers who satisfy specific quality criteria from those whose credentials or practices are questionable. This is done by verifying that physicians maintain the necessary credentials, such as a current medical license and proper board certification status. In addition, MCOs review random patient medical charts to demonstrate that the physician practices within accepted medical standards. For instance, chart reviews indicate if tests and procedures that should have been performed are actually performed, if the physician conducted a complete medical history during the initial consultation, and if the results of laboratory tests are properly documented.

Plans hold providers accountable for delivering quality care by contractually requiring them to abide by the plan's quality assurance programs, such as following clinical practice guidelines and making medical charts available. By regularly monitoring each provider's performance and comparing it to established norms and the performance of peers, plans can identify provider outliers who can be targeted for additional education, discipline, or eventual termination (see Chapter 4).

IMPROVING QUALITY

The emphasis of MCO quality activities is evolving from quality assurance to quality improvement. The independent agencies that assess MCO quality are increasingly requiring MCOs to include outcomes measures as proof of quality when seeking accreditation or submitting quality data. Consequently, improving the quality of care for members has become a central mission for some MCOs, primarily HMOs with significant membership.

Total Quality Improvement

Combining clinical epidemiology methods and quality management techniques from industrial companies, MCOs are working to improve quality through total quality improvement (TQI), sometimes referred to as CQI or total quality management (TQM) initiatives. While such initiatives can be implemented for both clinical and service issues, this chapter will concentrate on quality improvement efforts. The goal of TQI is to improve existing outcomes.

The basis elements of TQI are *assessment, intervention,* and *measurement.* Figure 7–2 shows a CQI process.

Assessment

Identification is the first step in a TQI program. Plans must identify the process or outcome of care that needs improvement, for example, the high incidence of cardiovascular disease among its population or a low childhood immunization rate. Identifying the incidence of disease, existing patterns of care, and patients with risk factors or specific diseases is achieved through the collection and analysis of various data including

- medical claims data
- patient medical records
- hospital admission records
- utilization data
- laboratory and pharmacy data
- personal health assessments

By understanding the prevalence of certain diseases among its population, as well as individual patients who might have the disease or be at risk for developing the disease, MCOs can design targeted quality improvement initiatives.

Intervention

Recommendations for specific interventions are based on the member and provider information that was gathered; a review of pertinent clinical research, including available outcomes data; the expert opinions of specialists and other health care professionals; and suggestions from MCO staff. Interventions aid or change the process of care so that patient outcomes will improve. These might include

- dissemination of established practice guidelines
- development of clinical protocols

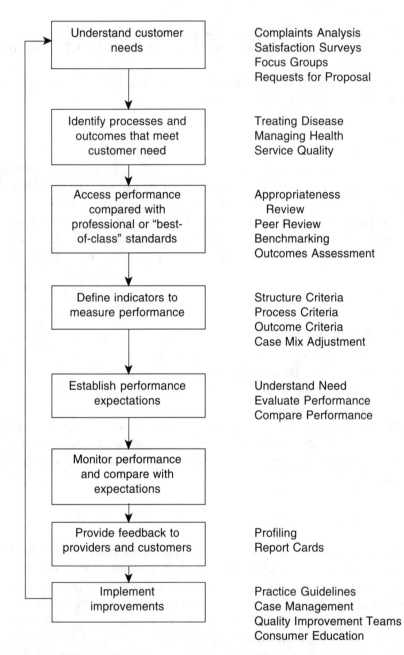

Figure 7–2 CQI Process Summary. *Source:* Reprinted from P.B. Siren and G.L. Laffel, Quality Management in Managed Care, in *The Managed Health Care Handbook*, 3rd ed., P.R. Kongstvedt, ed., p. 423, © 1996, Aspen Publishers, Inc.

- physician educational program
- comprehensive member/family education program
- change in reimbursement policy
- formation of multi-disciplinary care management teams
- designation of specialists as the principal care manager
- enhanced referral guidelines

Practice guidelines.   MCOs can identify the clinical practices that are most effective in improving the process and outcomes of care for specific patients or diseases by profiling providers, analyzing utilization and cost trends, and consulting with affiliated physicians. Practice guidelines give practitioners specific recommendations for optimal care—for example, female patients over the age of 50 should have a mammogram performed each year. Plans develop their own practice guidelines and use guidelines established by specialty societies and research organizations. According to the AAHP, over 85 percent of HMOs promoted the use of practice guidelines among network providers in 1995. As discussed in Chapter 4, practice guidelines are not regarded favorably by physicians. They are seen as attempts to replace the judgment and expertise of physicians with a generic and inflexible approach to treating patients. Practice guidelines developed in conjunction with physicians or by physician specialty societies are more effective in influencing physician practice patterns.

SUCCESSFULLY USING PRACTICE GUIDELINES

An HMO in Georgia has been successful in using clinical practice guidelines in improving the care of its diabetic patients. After reviewing the medical records and claims data for its members with diabetes, the HMO found that many PCPs were not ordering a simple blood test that monitors the average blood sugar levels of diabetics. Since monitoring blood sugar levels is an important component of managing this chronic illness, the plan realized that PCPs needed some additional education on the treatment of diabetes. The HMO formed a physician advisory panel on diabetes comprising local physicians specializing in the care of diabetic patients. The advisory panel reviewed and modified practice guidelines developed by the American Diabetes Association, and the plan subsequently published and distributed those guidelines to participating PCPs.

Clinical protocols.   Based on practice guidelines, clinical protocols (also called clinical paths, critical pathways, and algorithms) represent the timing and coordination of treatments for specific diseases that produce the best outcomes. Clinical paths can be developed for complete episodes of care that would encompass a range of health care services or for defined procedures, such as hospital admissions or ambulatory surgeries.[40]

Measurement

To measure the success of the intervention, the plan needs to determine the goal of the intervention and the appropriate indicator for measurement. Plans want to know how the interventions affect the process and outcome of care—for example, did more female patients receive mammograms? Were fewer asthmatic patients hospitalized? Did patients suffering from back pain report decreased symptoms? The various ways to measure interventions are discussed earlier in the chapter. They include measures of processes of care, outcomes of care, and patient satisfaction with care.

Disease Management

The prevailing application of TQI to MCO operations is disease management (also known as outcomes management, disease state management). Disease management is the "... systematic, population-based approach to identifying persons at risk, intervening with specific programs of care, and measuring clinical and other outcomes."[41] The goal is to find the best way to treat patients with a specific illness to reduce costs and improve patient health outcomes.

Disease management is the comprehensive treatment of a disease across the continuum of care, including prevention, early detection/diagnosis, acute treatment, and management.

Diseases that are expensive, chronic, complex, and likely to have large variations in practice patterns are typically targeted for intensive management. These include pediatric and adolescent asthma, diabetes, congestive heart failure, high-risk pregnancy, and breast cancer. To best manage these complex diseases, MCOs use multi-disciplinary teams of practitioners, including PCPs, specialists, plan staff, health educators, case managers, nutritionists, and home care providers.

The goals of these programs are to

- reduce the incidence of disease through targeted preventive care efforts
- detect members at risk for developing the disease
- minimize the medical complications associated with the disease
- improve the health and functional status of patients with the disease

The basic structure of disease management is the same as that of TQI: identification, intervention, and measurement. Plans employ a variety of strategies to improve the care of chronic disease, ranging from educating patients to conducting clinical trials. Table 7–2 gives examples of disease management components.

As an information-driven process, disease management depends on the collection and analysis of data. Using computer and information technology to gather and examine information on members from a variety of internal sources—including medical and pharmacy claims, referrals, hospitalizations, and personal health assessments—MCOs can

- recognize the incidence of chronic diseases among their populations
- identify specific patients with diseases or risk factors for developing diseases
- understand physician practices related to these chronic diseases
- assess the health status, habits, and behavior of members

To develop specific interventions, the MCO will gather and analyze member information, review clinical literature, evaluate practice variations, solicit expert opinions, and examine existing guidelines. Using this information, plans will develop appropriate educational programs and clinical interventions to assist both physicians and patients in managing the disease. Since managing chronic disease requires input of patients, families, and physicians, most disease management programs incorporate

Table 7-2 Examples of Components of Disease Management Programs

Component	Identification	Implementation	Measurement (Outcomes)
Health risk assessment	✔		
Chart audit protocols	✔	✔	✔
Database analysis	✔	✔	✔
Psychometrics (such as quality of life)	✔		✔
Satisfaction indices	✔		✔
Practice surveys	✔		✔
Health fairs	✔	✔	
Clinical guidelines		✔	
Clinical pathways		✔	
Centers of excellence		✔	
Clinical trials		✔	✔
Effectiveness studies		✔	✔
Economic analyses		✔	✔
Professional education		✔	
Patient education		✔	
Automated telephone systems		✔	
Compliance programs	✔	✔	✔

Source: Reprinted with permission from Epstein and Sherwood, Outcomes Research to Disease Management: A Guide for the Perplexed, *Anals of Internal Medicine*, Vol. 124, pp. 832–837, © 1996, American College of Physicians.

both physician and patient education. Member education includes written health education materials, videos, interactive shared-decision software programs, reminders for preventive health screenings, scheduled calls from nurse case managers, and nurse-staffed telephone hotlines. Plans educate providers about the most appropriate treatments by disseminating outcomes data, practice guidelines, clinical protocols, or best practices. Figure 7–3 outlines the percentage of plans using selected components of disease management programs.

Intuitively, managing care comprehensively makes sense, particularly for patients with medical conditions requiring multiple health care services. But there are many obstacles to the large-scale implementation of disease management programs by MCOs. First, the process of managing patients with particular diseases requires a commitment of financial resources many plans are unable or unwilling to make. Because many consumers and employers are quick to switch health plans based on price

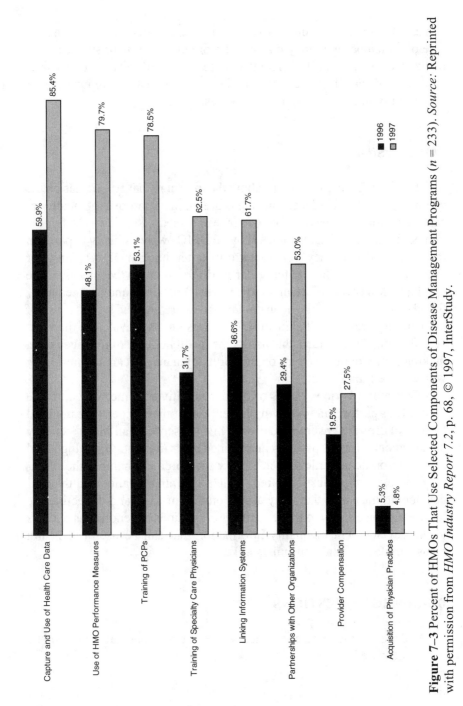

Figure 7–3 Percent of HMOs That Use Selected Components of Disease Management Programs (*n* = 233). *Source:* Reprinted with permission from *HMO Industry Report* 7.2, p. 68, © 1997, InterStudy.

alone, MCOs are reluctant to invest the time and money in managing the care of a member who may disenroll before the benefits of such care are realized. Conversely, MCOs fear that more chronically-ill (i.e., expensive) patients will enroll in their plan if they develop a good reputation for successfully managing particular diseases.[42]

CONCLUSION

What does the research tell us about the impact managed care has on the quality of health care? Does managed care, in fact, improve the quality of care its members receive? The evidence is mixed. A review of a limited number of quality of care studies showed HMOs were as likely to perform more poorly than as they were to perform better than non-HMO plans. For example, one study showed that elderly HMO patients in the intensive care unit had a lower risk of dying than non-HMO patients, and another study found that newborns in the neonatal intensive care unit had a greater risk of dying if they were enrolled in an HMO.[43] Despite its prevalence, there are very few empirical studies that assess the quality of care of managed care, making firm pronouncements on the ability of managed care to improve or worsen care impossible.

MCOs are in various stages of quality initiatives: some fully embrace their role as partners in improving patient care; others expend the minimal amount of effort in ensuring quality. While the scope of an MCO's quality management efforts is partially determined by its motivation, the logistical and philosophical challenges in quality measurement hamper the initiatives of even the most inspired MCO. Defining quality health care, developing measures that truly assess quality of care, and collecting the information necessary to make such determinations are enormous barriers to the development of quality information that can be useful to health plans, employers, and consumers alike.

DISCUSSION QUESTIONS

1. Describe the three components of care that experts agree should be measured.

2. Describe three elements present in most definitions of quality.
3. Why is the care provided by managed care programs seen as inferior to the care provided by traditional insurance programs?
4. What are the challenges and benefits of using outcomes data in evaluating quality?
5. Why are patient satisfaction surveys important to MCOs?
6. How do HEDIS and FACCT measures compare? How are these performance measures used?
7. Compare the advantages and disadvantages of using medical charts and medical claims for collecting quality data.
8. Describe the three elements of TQI.
9. How do clinical protocols differ from practice guidelines?
10. Why do MCOs develop disease management programs?

REFERENCES

1. M. Chassin, "Assessing Strategies for Quality Improvement," *Health Affairs 16*, no. 3 (May/June, 1996): 151.

2. Chassin, *Health Affairs*, 152.

3. Chassin, *Health Affairs*, 153.

4. A. Donabedian, *The Definition of Quality and Approaches to Its Assessment: Explorations in Quality Assessment and Monitoring,* vol. 1, (Ann Arbor, MI: Health Administration Press, 1980).

5. American Medical Association, Council of Medical Service, Quality of Care, *Journal of the American Medical Association 256* (1986), 1032–1034.

6. K. Lohr, M. Donaldson, et al. "Medicare: A Strategy for Quality Assurance," Quality of Care in a Changing Health Care Environment, *Quality Review Bulletin 18* (1992): 120–126.

7. D. Blumenthal, "Quality of Care: What Is It?" *The New England Journal of Medicine 335*, no. 12 (1996): 892.

8. Blumenthal, *The New England Journal of Medicine*, 892.

9. E. McGlynn, "Six Challenges in Measuring the Quality of Health Care," *Health Affairs 16*, no. 3 (May/June, 1996): 9.

10. Kaiser Family Foundation and the Agency for Health Care Policy and Research, *Americans as Health Care Consumers: The Role of Quality Information* (Washington, DC) October, 1996.

11. Blumenthal, *The New England Journal of Medicine*, 893.

12. Blumenthal, *The New England Journal of Medicine*, 893.

13. E. McGlynn, *Health Affairs*, 10.

14. McGlynn, *Health Affairs*, 10.

15. K. Lohr, "How Do We Measure Quality," *Health Affairs 16*, no. 3 (May/June 1996): 24.

16. R. Brook, E. McGlynn, and P. Clearly, "Measuring Quality of Care," *The New England Journal of Medicine 335*, no. 12 (1996): 966.

17. McGlynn, *Health Affairs*, 10.

18. Brook, McGlynn, and Clearly, *The New England Journal of Medicine*, 966.

19. Brook, McGlynn, and Clearly, *The New England Journal of Medicine*, 966.

20. M. Kassberg and P. Wynn, "What Quality Measurements Miss," *Managed Care*, March 1996, 23.

21. Kassberg and Wynn, *Managed Care*, 36.

22. R. Epstein, MD and L. Sherwood, MD, "From Outcomes Research to Disease Management: A Guide for the Perplexed," *Annals of Internal Medicine American College of Physicians 124*, no. 9 (May, 1996): 833.

23. Kassberg and Wynn, *Managed Care*, 23.

24. S. Robinson and M. Brodie, "Understanding the Quality Challenge for Health Consumers: The Kaiser/AHCPR Survey," *Journal on Quality Improvement 23*, The Joint Commission on Accreditation of Health Care Organizations, no. 5 (1996): 239.

25. A. Enthoven and C. Vorhaus, "A Vision of Quality in Health Care Delivery," *Health Affairs* 16, no. 3 (May/June 1996): 50.

26. Kassberg and Wynn, *Managed Care*, 26.

27. McGlynn, *Health Affairs*, 14.

28. Brook, McGlynn, and Clearly, *The New England Journal of Medicine*, 966.

29. McGlynn, *Health Affairs*, 14.

30. P. Siren and G. Laffel, "Quality Management in Managed Care," *The Managed Health Care Handbook,* 3d ed. (Gaithersburg, MD: Aspen Publishers, Inc., 1996), 405.

31. Epstein and Sherwood, *Annals of Internal Medicine*, 835.

32. Epstein and Sherwood, *Annals of Internal Medicine*, 835.

33. Epstein and Sherwood, *Annals of Internal Medicine*, 835.

34. E. Spragins, "The Numbers Racket," *Newsweek*, 5 May, 1996, 66.

35. McGlynn, *Health Affairs*, 16.

36. Http://www.ncqa.org/hedis/30exsum.htm, pp. 1–6 and http://www.ncqa.org/news/heismeas.htm, pp. 1–4.

37. *Accountability Action,* Vol. 2, Issue 1, Fall 1996. FACCT, 5.

38. M. Dresser, L. Feingold, S. Rosenkranz, and K. Coltin, "Clinical Quality Measurement: Comparing Chart Review and Automated Methodologies," *Medical Care 35*, no. 6 (1997): 540.

39. A. Gosfield, "Who Is Holding Whom Accountable for Quality?" *Health Affairs 16*, no. 3 (May/June, 1996): 30.

40. R. Coffey, J. Richards, S. Wintermeyer-Pingel, and S. LeRoy, "Critical Paths: Linking Outcomes for Patients, Clinicians, and Payers," in *The Managed Health Care Handbook,* 3d ed., 302.

41. Epstein and Sherwood, *Annals of Internal Medicine*, 832–836.

42. R. Miller and H. Luft, "Does Managed Care Lead to Better or Worse Quality of Care?" *Health Affairs 16*, no. 5 (September/October, 1996): 20.

43. Miller and Luft, *Health Affairs*, 14–16.

SUGGESTED READING

Kane, R. *Understanding Health Care Outcomes Research* (Gaithersburg, MD: Aspen Publishers, 1996).

CHAPTER 8

Regulatory and Legal Issues

Jeanne M. Keller

Scarcely any political question arises in the United States that is not resolved, sooner or later, into a judicial question.

Alexis de Tocqueville (1805–1859)

"Don't worry! I'm doing this for your own good!"

Source: Drawings copyright © 1998, Donovan Andrews.

Learning Objectives

- Understand the federal and state framework for regulation of managed care plans.
- Understand emerging legislative and regulatory trends related to managed care organizations (MCOs).
- Understand the liability issues facing MCOs in their relationships with providers and consumers.
- Understand the legal framework for addressing fraudulent and false health care claims.

Key Terms

Anti-trust—Laws and court decisions establishing the authority of state and federal governments to intervene when business practices have the affect of interfering with free and competitive markets.

ERISA—The Employee Retirement Income Security Act. A federal law that establishes requirements for employer-sponsored benefit plans and has been interpreted to preempt state regulation of self-insured health plans.

Kickback—A cash bonus or other financial reward paid to a provider in return for referring a patient to another provider or facility for treatment.

McCarren-Ferguson Act—A federal law that grants to states the authority and responsibility for regulating the business of insurance.

INTRODUCTION

The rapid evolution of MCOs presents new challenges for the state and federal regulation of these entities. For decades, government agencies fulfilled their consumer protection role of monitoring health insurance programs that rarely changed. Today, however, previously competing health care providers and institutions are merging, and new corporations consolidating the financing and delivery of health care have emerged. In the midst of this constantly changing landscape, government still maintains its responsibility for protecting consumer interests, maintaining fair competition, and ensuring the financial integrity of MCOs.[1] However, the rapid restructuring of the health care industry has required federal and state governments to assume a broader role in monitoring the actual delivery of health care provided to individuals.

THE REGULATORY FRAMEWORK

While the regulation of managed care has typically been a state responsibility, the expansion of managed care into federal health benefit programs has broadened the federal government's influence over MCOs. The court system has also contributed to the body of law that governs the operation of MCOs. Regulation of MCOs is a complex web of government oversight by various state and federal agencies governing MCOs (depending on the organizational structure of the MCO and to what entities health coverage is sold).

Federal Responsibilities

McCarren-Ferguson Act

Passed by Congress in 1945, the McCarren-Ferguson Act gave states the exclusive right to regulate health insurance plans. As such, there is no single federal agency responsible for overseeing the health insurance industry. However, various federal agencies are involved in health plan regulation and administration, depending on the health benefit program; for instance, the U.S. Department of Defense regulates the military health program, and the Health Care Financing Administration (HCFA) oversees the Medicare program. (See Chapter 5 for information on federal government programs.) Each of the 50 states is given authority to establish its own regulatory schemes, even though most MCOs operate nationwide or in multiple states.

While McCarren-Ferguson does not designate a federal agency to regulate health insurers, Congress itself maintains the Constitutional authority to pass laws that override state legislation and establish nationwide industry standards, which it increasingly appears to be doing (see "Benefit Mandates" and "Consumer Rights").

ERISA

ERISA was passed by Congress in 1974 to protect employee health benefit programs by giving fiduciary (i.e., legal) responsibilities to the employers who manage such programs and establishing penalties for mismanagement of employee pension funds and other benefit plans. Because of decisions by Congress and the courts, ERISA effectively establishes federal jurisdiction over self-insured, employer-sponsored health benefit plans and preempts (i.e., overrides) regulations that states may impose on insured health plans under McCarren-Ferguson. For example, while a state law may require insured MCOs to maintain certain cash reserves to pay claims, no such requirements may be imposed on self-insured, employer-sponsored plans. ERISA protects the self-insured plan (and any managed care plan under contract to the self-insured employer plan) from state regulations. There are exceptions to ERISA. ERISA's preemption does not apply to any group health plan for state and local government employees, churches, or church-affiliated organizations, or to any health insurance policies or plans issued to individuals.

It is estimated that 40 percent of employees with employer-sponsored coverage are in ERISA-qualified self-insured plans.[2] Whether managed care or fee-for-service, an employer health benefit plan is considered self-insured (self-funded) when the employer does not transfer the financial risk of the health plan onto an insurer by purchasing an insurance contract. Even self-insured plans that have stop-loss insurance (which reimburses the plan for claims in excess of some dollar threshold) are not considered insurance plans because the employee covered by the plan does not have a claim against that stop-loss insurance program. Also, stop-loss thresholds are generally quite high—often as high as $150,000 for an individual claim, and over $1 million for the plan's annual expenditure, which subjects the employer's health plan to substantial financial risk (i.e., self-funding) before any "insurance" mechanism is triggered.

To qualify as a plan protected by ERISA (and thereby exempt from state regulatory oversight), there are certain requirements that must be fulfilled by plan administrators.[3]

1. Plan administrators must file various reports with the Department of Labor or the Internal Revenue Service.
2. The plan and its rules of operation must be described in detail in a Summary Plan Description that must be distributed to plan beneficiaries (i.e., employees and retirees) and filed with the Department of Labor.
3. The plan administrator is given the duty of a fiduciary, which means that all decisions concerning the plan must be made solely in the interests of the plan's beneficiaries (not the administrator's interests), and only for the purpose of providing benefits to participants.
4. Plan fiduciaries must administer the plan in accordance with the summary and exercise the care, skill, and diligence that a prudent person would in such a position.

The federal courts have broadly interpreted the ERISA preemption to prohibit any state law or regulation that "relates to" employee benefit plans. Therefore, while laws or regulations may impose detailed legal requirements on MCOs conducting "the business of insurance," self-insured MCOs (as long as they meet ERISA's minimal reporting and fund-management requirements) are not affected. Consequently, self-insured plans may offer any level of benefits to employees and change those benefits relatively easily. Since state laws do not govern self-insured MCOs, employees enrolled in a self-funded plan must file a federal lawsuit under ERISA if they believe they were unfairly denied benefits or otherwise treated unjustly. The courts have also extended the ERISA preemption to other state laws, such as breach-of-contract claims and state medical malpractice laws.

TWO IMPORTANT ERISA LAWSUITS

The McGann case[4] (1991) involved an employee's challenge of a Texas employer that imposed a $5,000 annual limit on the pharmaceutical coverage provided under its self-insured plan after it learned that the employee had developed AIDS. The federal court upheld the employer's right to change the benefits covered by the self-insured plan's in mid-year without advance notice. The national news coverage of the ruling highlighted for state and federal lawmakers the impact of ERISA on individuals covered by self-insured plans.

A 1995 Supreme Court ruling, the Travelers case,[5] upheld a New York state law requiring all MCOs, including ERISA plans, to pay a state tax on hospital services (the tax funded programs for the uninsured in New York). Travelers, an insurance company that also administers plans for self-insured employers, argued that the tax "related to" the employee benefit plans, which were protected by ERISA. However, the court ruled that the tax had a beneficial public purpose and did not constitute regulation of "the business of insurance." As a result of this ruling, more states have taxed hospitals and MCOs to fund state welfare programs.[6]

Defenders of ERISA believe there are several advantages to a national regulatory mechanism for a self-insured health plan. Many large employers conduct business in several states. One justification for the federal oversight of self-insured plans is that without the ERISA preemption, their employee benefit plans would be subject to 50 different sets of rules and requirements. By qualifying their plans under ERISA, these employers enjoy the simplicity of uniform plan requirements nationwide.

ERISA's preemption also gives self-insured employers flexibility in managing their employee benefit plans. It is widely believed that ERISA enables self-insured plans to develop innovative, cost-effective strategies and that innovation is stifled when state regulators impose rigid rules standardizing all plans.[7]

A major criticism of ERISA is that it eliminates state regulatory oversight of self-insured plans without substituting a correspondingly detailed federal regulatory system. For example, ERISA does not establish minimum benefits, grievance and appeals rights, or financial reserve requirements. The lack of a systematic regulation of ERISA plans (known as "the ERISA vacuum")[8] has led to numerous attempts by states to find loopholes and by Congress to impose nationwide standards (see "Benefit Mandates" below).

The Health Maintenance Organization (HMO) Act

As described in Chapter 1, the HMO Act of 1973 spurred the growth of HMOs through grant programs for HMO development and requirements that employers offer a qualified HMO to employees. Just as McCarren-Ferguson transfers health insurance regulation to the states, the HMO Act explicitly gives states responsibility for overseeing HMOs. The Act encouraged states to pass their own laws setting up licensing procedures for HMOs, and by 1986, nearly every state had adopted HMO oversight laws.

State Responsibilities

Through the McCarren-Ferguson Act and the HMO Act, states have exclusive powers to regulate MCOs. Because of the interplay among McCarren-Ferguson, the HMO Act, and ERISA, a state may not directly regulate or impose requirements on some employer health benefit plans. However, it can indirectly affect employer plans through its power to regulate the insurance contract between the employer and the health plan.[9] For example, states cannot require employers to provide health insurance as a benefit to their employees, or set standards for the content of the benefit plan. On the other hand, states can order insurance companies and MCOs to include certain benefits in all products sold or to include particular health care practitioners in their provider networks. In other words, states can regulate what MCOs can sell, and thus indirectly, what purchasers can buy for their employees. Often, more than one state agency has jurisdiction over the operations of an MCO, usually the department of insurance and the department of health. States may have separate laws governing the operations of the different types of MCOs. For example, most states have laws specific to HMOs, while the oversight of preferred provider organizations (PPOs) may fall under the state insurance laws. State laws and regulations govern many aspects of plan operations, including

- quality assurance
- utilization review
- solvency
- benefits
- marketing
- access to health care services
- provider contracting
- rating
- grievances and appeals

- organizational structure
- reporting
- confidentiality[10]

Health Plan Licensure

Depending on their organizational structure, MCOs must receive a license from each state in which they do business. However, not all states require PPOs to be licensed. In most states, the insurance or commerce department grants this privilege. While the requirements for receiving a license to sell health insurance vary greatly by state, they are designed to ensure that

- the company's managers and investors are reputable and trustworthy
- the company is financially sound and will be able to pay medical claims
- the company's operations are sound
- the company can fulfill its contractual obligations to provide health care services to purchasers and consumers

Because of the controls that MCOs impose on providers and consumers, insurance regulators have increasingly assumed a significant role in overseeing the delivery of health care, an activity that did not exist under a traditional insurance system.[11] Before managed care, regulators mediated disputes about insurance policy coverage or prompt payment of claims; now they are drawn into disputes between consumers and MCOs about the medical necessity of certain treatments or appropriate lengths of hospital stays.[12] As such, states may require MCOs to meet certain quality standards relating to

- adequacy of provider networks
- requirements for the grievance and appeals procedures available to consumers
- adequacy of the plan's quality assurance programs
- terms of the provider contracts
- types of guidelines to be used in the utilization review process
- qualifications of the managerial and medical leadership

Only recently have states attempted to regulate the quality of medical care provided through MCOs. This responsibility can be assigned to the insurance regulators or the state health departments. Of 46 states surveyed, one-half of them involved their health departments in regulating the quality assurance activities of MCOs, including standards for provider credentialing, member and physician grievance procedures, and medical practice standards used by the plan's quality assurance committee.[13]

Benefit Mandates

Even before the prevalence of managed care, states passed laws mandating health insurers to include particular benefits in their insurance plans. During the past 20 years, more than 1,100 state laws have been enacted requiring MCOs to cover certain services in all health insurance contracts. Benefit mandates expand coverage in different ways.[14]

- requiring a specific type of treatment to be included (e.g., bone marrow transplants for breast cancer)
- requiring that the services of a particular provider be covered (e.g., all chiropractors)
- expanding the category of people a plan must insure (e.g., same-sex couples or part-time employees)
- specifying terms and conditions of coverage (e.g., that the payments for mental and physical health services be the same, often called "mental health parity")

The cumulative cost of multiple benefit mandates is high. A study of the Blue Cross and Blue Shield plans in 13 states found that premiums rose between 5 percent and 15 percent in 1992 due to mandated benefits.[15] Besides objecting to the cost, MCOs object to benefit mandates because they override the medical judgment of the providers. Benefit mandates also create an atmosphere of entitlement (i.e., patients feel entitled to receive particular treatments or to be seen by certain types of providers, even if it is medically inappropriate or unnecessary). MCOs argue that benefit mandates conflict with their goal of delivering appropriate care based on proper diagnosis, clinical effectiveness research, and high-quality provider networks. Generally, consumers and providers support the passage of state mandate laws, while plans and purchasers oppose them. Among consumers, the lead proponents for mandates are generally people who themselves, or through a family member, have discovered that their plan does not cover a particular treatment or procedure, or that their favorite provider is not a part of a managed care plan's network. By forcing the plan (and all insurers) to pay for the desired treatment, the mandate ensures that the consumer's particular health problem or provider will be covered under the plan. Among providers, the support for mandates is driven by the same concern: the treatments in which they specialize (e.g., chiropractic care or bone marrow transplants) are not covered, or they find the managed care plan's network standards too restrictive.

AN EXAMPLE OF A BENEFIT MANDATE

An excellent example of the dispute over benefit mandates was the passage of a federal mandate relating to maternity care. Despite expert medical testimony on the cost-effective and beneficial alternatives to hospitalization for post-maternity care (for example, home visits by nurses), Congress amended ERISA in 1996 to establish a national benefit requirement for maternity care. This amendment specified that all employee benefit plans (including insured and self-insured plans) cover, at a minimum, a 48-hour hospital stay for vaginal deliveries, and a 72-hour hospital stay for Caesarean section births. This legislation became known as the "drive-by delivery" bill, a derisive name given to a common managed care practice of limiting reimbursement for vaginal deliveries to a 24-hour hospital stay.

Complying with individual state mandates is challenging for MCOs that operate in multiple states. States vary in the scope and terms of their benefit mandates, so that an MCO with operations in 10 states may have 10 different policies for health coverage. Even similar-sounding mandates may change slightly from state to state. Exhibit 8–1 displays the various types of state legislation affecting MCOs. Exhibit 8–2 displays a comparison of the variety of mandates implemented by states for obstetrical and gynecological (OB/GYN) services.

Exercise: Imagine that several individuals have been invited to testify at a congressional committee considering legislation to mandate that health plans cover bone marrow transplants. Role-play the debate that would ensue among an employer, a consumer, a health plan administrator, a specialist, and the congressperson sponsoring the legislation.

Exhibit 8–1 Examples of State Regulation of Managed Care

Type of Regulation	State
Comprehensive rules prescribing access standards, disclosures, grievances and appeals (consumers and providers), credentialing requirements, contents of benefit plan, quality assurance program, utilization review standards	Vermont New York Minnesota
Extensive requirements about information plans must provide to consumers	Rhode Island
HMOs must also offer point-of-service (POS) plans, so that employees have a choice of HMO or POS (requirements vary slightly among states by employer size, whether in group or individual market, etc.)	District of Columbia and 23 states including Idaho, Oregon, New York, Georgia, Minnesota, Montana, and Virginia
Independent review of utilization review decisions	Vermont Rhode Island New Jersey Tennessee
Ombudsman program to assist consumers with complaints	Florida
Regulation of mergers and acquisitions of health care organizations (managed care plans and/or hospitals)	Massachusetts Vermont California Rhode Island New Hampshire

Anti–Managed Care Legislation

Patients and providers are increasingly objecting to the restrictions on care imposed by MCOs, such as the requirement to see a primary care physician (PCP) before seeing a specialist. In response to such complaints, state legislatures have passed laws dictating how MCOs select their networks and structure their referral process. The most prominent of these mandates is the "any willing provider" (AWP) laws, so called because they require managed care plans and insurers to accept in the network any provider willing to sign a contract (and meet plan requirements). A

Exhibit 8–2 Comparison of State Mandates Regarding OB/GYN Services

State	What Is Required by Mandate
Florida	OB/GYNs can serve as PCPs if they are so designated by the HMO. Does not mandate self-referral to OB/GYNs for specialty services.
Alabama	OB/GYNs can serve as PCPs if willing and able to meet the criteria of the HMO. Mandates self-referral to OB/GYNs.
Georgia	OB/GYNs cannot serve as PCPs, but self-referral to OB/GYNs for specialty services is mandated.
Oregon	OB/GYNs can serve as PCPs, and mandated self-referral is limited to only two visits per year.

fundamental tenet of managed care is selecting the optimal number of qualified providers necessary to provide access to care for the covered population. Thus, AWP legislation requires MCOs to operate as indemnity insurance plans, paying any provider for care delivered.

Another example of anti–managed care legislation is "patient freedom of choice" laws that require plans to cover health care services rendered by any provider, even those not in the network. "Self-referral" laws allow patients to refer themselves directly to specialists, overriding a plan's requirement to see a PCP (i.e., gatekeeper) first. There are also laws that designate specialists (such as OB/GYNs) as PCPs and require MCOs to allow them to fulfill the gatekeeper function. Obviously, this kind of legislation completely eradicates many essential managed care techniques by allowing patients full coverage to see virtually any licensed provider.

If any provider must be included in the managed care network, or a patient is covered when visiting any provider, the MCO loses the leverage to direct a sufficient volume of patients to providers to justify discounted provider fees. Moreover, even though the MCO is held responsible for the quality of care provided under the plan, this legislation makes it impossible for the plans to control the quality of the providers treating patients, since non-network providers are rendering care to members. This can have significant legal consequences for the plan.

Anti–managed care legislation is often passed by states in response to consumer or provider objections to managed care. Plaintiffs' attorneys (the attorneys who specialize in representing consumers in lawsuits) are also instrumental in promoting such legislation. While plaintiffs' attorneys have traditionally sided with consumers against physicians, they have recently joined physicians and consumers in legal disputes against MCOs, particularly in the area of extending malpractice liability to MCOs (see "Liability Issues" below).

Consumer Rights

States also may establish requirements for the kinds of information plans must provide to members and participating providers. Some of the consumer information is required to ensure that members are fully informed of their rights and responsibilities and that they have adequate instructions to navigate the often confusing rules of a managed care system. States are also requiring plans to provide members with information on quality, such as satisfaction levels of other plan members, utilization statistics, and HEDIS data on plan performance.

Examples of information states may require MCOs to disclose include

- the plan's financial arrangements with contracted providers, including how capitation rates and bonuses are set, or whether such bonuses are paid
- the plan's clinical criteria used in making medical treatment decisions and information on how these criteria are developed and updated
- the number and type of grievances filed against the plan by members or affiliated physicians, and how the grievances were resolved (that is, in favor of the member or in favor of the plan)

Another area of consumer rights receiving increasing attention from state regulators is the grievance and appeals procedures available to members and providers. Many states are imposing explicit requirements on MCOs for these processes, such as

- establishing the time frame in which appeals must be heard, who will hear them, and what must be included in the plan's written decision
- establishing an external appeals process that can overrule the decisions made by the plan's affiliated providers and medical directors
- giving providers the right to appeal a plan's decision to terminate a provider contract even if the contract includes a provision that the plan can terminate the provider "without cause"

Frequently, multiple consumer protection and anti–managed care provisions are combined into a single proposal, often known as a "Consumer Bill of Rights" (or in the case of the proposal sponsored by the American Medical Association [AMA], the "Patient Protection Act"). There are ongoing efforts to pass a "Patient Protection Act" at the federal level and a presidential commission was formed to make recommendations to Congress on a "Consumer Bill of Rights." Areas included in most of the proposals are

- information disclosures
- state consumer assistance programs
- network adequacy requirements
- direct access to specialists under certain conditions
- a definition of what constitutes a medical emergency
- a requirement that plans pay for out-of-network care in emergencies
- requirements for grievance and appeals processes

Rates and Forms

State regulators also approve the health insurance premiums ("rates") MCOs intend to charge customers. Some states require approval of actual premiums, while others require approval of the formula to be used to calculate the premiums. In approving rates, insurance regulators must strike a balance between protecting consumers from excessive rates, containing rising health care costs, and ensuring that insurers remain solvent (that is, ensuring that plans do not become bankrupt because of insufficient premiums).

Insurance regulators also approve the "forms" (i.e., written materials) MCOs use to market and communicate their products and services. Traditionally, this approval process has focused on the subscriber agreements (i.e., contracts between plan and purchaser). However, regulators are beginning to scrutinize the brochures, notices, handbooks, and other materials provided to members, as well as the plan contract with providers.

Certificate of Need

Certificate of Need (CON) is a regulatory process developed by the federal government in the 1970s to control hospital construction and spending on high-technology equipment. While the federal government withdrew support for the program in 1988, some states re-authorized or extended the program. Because some MCOs, particularly staff-model HMOs, spend money on buildings and equipment, states with active CON programs may require MCOs to obtain a CON (in addition to a license) to conduct business in the state.

Requirements for obtaining a CON vary by state. For example, many states do not require reviews of physician office buildings but would require a CON for the construction of a new hospital wing. There is usually a spending threshold that triggers the requirement for a review. CON programs may be under the jurisdiction of the state insurance or health department. Approximately 25 states require HMOs to apply for a CON.[16]

Licensing of Facilities and Providers

States also license health care facilities to ensure that they meet applicable health and safety codes. This function is usually under the jurisdiction of the health department. To the extent that MCOs own, operate, or employ health care facilities and providers, they may need to comply with these requirements, as well.

States also have authority to establish requirements that individual providers must meet in order to see patients. State legislatures define the background and educational requirements, internships, examinations, continuing education, and other standards that an individual must demonstrate in order to be licensed to practice medicine. The requirements of the law may be carried out by a state health department for health care professions, but some states combine all professional licensing (ranging from cosmetology to medicine) in a commerce department or the secretary of state's office.

Anti-Trust Issues

At the turn of the century, railroad, steel, and other companies formed huge monopolies in the United States. To prevent the concentration of economic power in a few corporations, Congress passed laws establishing rules of fair competition among businesses (known as "anti-trust" laws). The underlying philosophy of anti-trust legislation is to create an open and competitive market to ensure lower prices, better quality, and more choices for consumers.

A specific health care unit of the Federal Trade Commission (FTC) is the primary enforcer of federal anti-trust laws. State attorneys general can also prosecute individuals or companies for anti-trust activities, and individuals who believe their right to compete in a market has been limited or restrained may file a legal action against a competitor.

The Sherman and Clayton Anti-Trust Acts

The two key federal laws regulating competition are the Sherman Anti-Trust Act and the Clayton Act. The Sherman Act prohibits contracts between parties "in restraint of trade," that is, contracts that interfere with another entity's ability to conduct its business competitively or contracts limiting competition that could be beneficial to consumers. The Act also prohibits individuals and companies from creating monopolies that by nature restrict trade. For example, if two railroad companies agreed that each would take one of two available routes instead of competing for both routes, this would deprive consumers of a choice of railroad companies and would represent collusion "in restraint of trade."

Anti-trust law carries some of the most severe penalties of any federal law, and for that reason, any business considering mergers, consolidations, or acquisitions always conducts a thorough legal examination in advance to ensure compliance with such laws. A corporation violating the Sherman Act can be held liable for a fine of up to $10 million for each violation proved.

The Clayton Act prohibits specific practices that are anti-competitive and interfere with a free market. While the specific activities named in the law are not always violations of the Clayton Act, regulators will examine whether the activities will limit competition. Potential anti-competitive activities include price fixing (agreements made between competitors on the prices they will charge to consumers), contracting between otherwise competing parties that bind parties to exclusive relationships with each other, locking out other competitors, and establishing mergers and acquisitions limiting the number of competitors in a marketplace.

Applicability to Managed Care

Before managed care, anti-trust concerns in health care usually involved challenges among providers. For example, chiropractors filed suit claiming the AMA engaged in a variety of activities to limit chiropractors' access to patients. Physicians who had been denied hospital admitting privileges would sue the medical staff of the hospital for collusion or restraint of trade, arguing that denial of admitting privileges at the hospital denied the physician the ability to practice medicine in that community.

Many of the recent changes in the health care system are drawing the attention of government anti-trust officials. One change is the integration of the financing and delivery of health care under managed care, also known as "vertical integration," because it combines activities from different levels of the industry. The merging of formerly independent and competing providers raises another concern. This is known as "horizontal" integration because it combines activities of similar entities. While such integration enables MCOs to achieve the economic efficiencies and quality control not available in traditional health insurance programs, it creates the potential for anti-competitive activity.[17] Both horizontal and vertical integration create anti-trust concerns about managed care systems because of the potential to monopolize their market area and eliminate competition.

Exhibit 8–3 displays the relevant anti-trust rules that may apply to common managed care activities. These activities are not automatically violations of the law, however, and the enforcement agencies have established detailed instructions on how these activities can be carried out legally.

Current Issues

The growth of managed care is testing new areas of anti-trust law. For example,

- Physicians or other practitioners restrain the ability of MCOs to build marketable networks by actively organizing "boycotts" against the plans and refusing to sign managed care contracts
- In some markets, such as Minneapolis, virtually all the major health care facilities and providers belong to one of three or four large integrated health care systems
- In rural areas, financially troubled non-profit hospitals are purchased by hospital chains, creating a monopoly of the available hospitals in the area
- Physicians and hospitals are forming their own plans to compete with MCOs, while simultaneously participating in the provider networks of these competitor MCOs

Exhibit 8–3 Examples of Anti-Trust Regulations

Managed Care Activity	Relevant Anti-Trust Regulations
Mergers and acquisitions	Anti-trust law considers a monopoly to exist when one person, corporation, or group of people controls a service or a product in a particular geographic area
Selecting physicians or hospitals to be in managed care networks	Anti-trust law considers a contract to restrain trade when the contract interferes with a person carrying out his or her profession. Also, it may be a restraint of trade to deny a person a contract.
PPOs, independent practice associations, and other network providers establishing a fee schedule or prepaid fee health plan	Anti-trust law prohibits sellers of the same product to join together to fix the price that will be paid by the buyers.
HMOs requesting bids from various vendors (pharmacies, medical equipment suppliers, and others) to be their sole provider of supplies, and require their plan members to use those vendors (a losing bidder may lose access to a large part of the market)	Anti-trust law considers a contract to restrain trade when the contract interferes with a person carrying out his or her profession. Also, it may be a restraint of trade to deny a person a contract.

The FTC has responded to recent changes in the health care system by issuing detailed guidelines on how plans and providers can avoid violating anti-trust regulations. In 1993, the FTC and the Department of Justice jointly issued policy statements that identified provider activities that the agencies generally believed would not challenge the anti-trust laws (called "safety zones"). The agencies updated and expanded these policies in 1994 and 1996 to reflect continuing changes in the health care market. By specifying what will and will not be considered a violation of anti-trust law, the policies allow providers and MCOs the flexibility to create new financial and care management relationships.

LIABILITY ISSUES

Traditionally, liability lawsuits against insurance companies intended to force timely payment of a claim, either by the physician, or by the insurance subscriber. MCOs, however, have new liability issues. Managed care plans select providers and facilities to provide care to their members. Those providers who are not selected for participation in a managed care network or whose contracts are terminated may file suit against the MCO to win or regain their "rights" to a managed care contract.

MCOs make determinations about the necessity of medical care that extend beyond whether a claim will be paid or not and may affect whether medical care will be delivered to a patient. This may cause a patient to sue the plan to force payment for the care, or to penalize the plan for denying care that allegedly resulted in long-term harm to the patient. The patient may also sue to hold the MCO liable for poor quality of medical care, if the plan contracted with providers who were not properly qualified or credentialed.

The two major areas of liability for a managed care plan are *provider contracting* and *quality management*.

Provider Contracting

The process of selecting and de-selecting (i.e., terminating provider contracts) providers can expose MCOs to legal challenges from providers who have been excluded from the provider network. In addition to potential anti-trust liability, managed care plans face civil liability if their contracting decisions violate participating providers' contractual rights (also known as "due process" rights).

Decisions to exclude providers from the network (either by not contracting with a provider or by terminating an existing provider's contract) are made for many reasons, including the following:

Ethical considerations. For example, the provider was the subject of a disciplinary action by a court or professional licensing authority or was convicted of a crime.

Qualifications. For example, the provider lost his or her hospital admitting privileges, or does not meet the network's requirements for provider education, training, experience, or other areas.

Quality performance. For example, the provider fails to adhere to the plan's quality guidelines or consistently receives low scores in member satisfaction surveys.

Cost-effectiveness. For example, the provider consistently orders too many unnecessary tests, keeps patients in the hospital too long, or refuses to accept the plan's fee schedule.

Provider contracting and termination activities pose great legal challenges for MCOs; for instance, even when providers are terminated for failure to perform according to the plan's quality guidelines, the MCO must defend the guidelines as reasonable and prove that the provider failed to meet those guidelines. Furthermore, the provider contract must specify the failure to meet guidelines as a condition for termination.

In response to the significant number of legal challenges to provider contracting decisions, some MCOs have included "without cause" termination provisions in their provider contracts giving them the option of terminating provider contracts without a particular reason. Some states have enacted specific laws giving providers the right to appeal an MCO's decision to terminate the contract, while other states permit providers to challenge terminations through the state's general laws governing contracts. Courts have identified the following procedures an MCO must use to legally terminate a provider: (1) a reasonable notice that includes the reason(s) for the termination, and (2) a reasonable opportunity to appeal the decision.[18]

MCOs can minimize the risk of liability by establishing specific procedures for selecting and deselecting providers. These include

- developing a provider recruitment strategy that identifies the number, types (i.e., specialties), and locations of providers needed to serve the plan's membership, and communicating this to all prospective and existing network providers
- developing criteria for participation in (or removal from) the network, including basic credentials, quality standards, compliance with plan procedures, and financial performance, and communicating this to all prospective and existing network providers
- developing clearly delineated procedures for medical decision making, including criteria for payment and coverage decisions (based on medical necessity)

- developing the process by which providers can appeal plan decisions about payment, coverage, and treatment (this should include how the appeal hearing will be conducted and a time frame for completion of the process)[19]

Even with a detailed and fair appeal process, an aggrieved provider can challenge an MCO in court. However, adopting and adhering to a provider appeal procedure can minimize the plan's risk of liability.

Quality of Care

Only recently have MCOs needed to concern themselves with patients' lawsuits relating to quality of care. Historically, health insurers and MCOs have successfully averted malpractice lawsuits, arguing in court that malpractice claims against them are preempted by ERISA, because the plan is neither a health care provider or a health care insurer, but simply an administrator of an employee benefit plan. While this argument has shielded plans in the past, 3 of the 12 U.S. Circuit Courts of Appeals (which have jurisdiction to hear cases on ERISA) have ruled against MCOs in the past two years.[20]

Examples of the kinds of actions taken by an MCO that may expose it to claims of liability for quality of care include

- decisions that care should be received in the outpatient, rather than inpatient, setting
- decisions regarding the number of hospital days that are appropriate
- decisions regarding tests that are appropriate
- decisions regarding whether a recommended treatment is standard medical practice or is experimental

Each of these decisions actually relates to whether the plan will reimburse for the care, and not whether the patient will receive the care. However, patients, providers, and juries do not always agree with that distinction, and they often assert that denial of reimbursement is equal to denial of the medical care itself. These lawsuits attempt to draw a cause-and-effect connection between the denial of reimbursement and any injury to the patient, and ask the courts to hold the MCO liable for medical negligence.

The laws used to assert that a plan is liable for quality of care are often the same medical negligence laws that apply to medical malpractice cases. In such a case, a plan member could allege that injury resulted from wrongful denial of medical care by the MCO, which constitutes medical negligence. Under state medical negligence laws, the plan member could sue the plan for lost wages, other economic damages, attorneys' fees, pain and suffering, and punitive damages, and would expose the MCOs to multi-million dollar judgments for their care management decisions.

A well-known example of this type of case occurred several years ago in California, where a jury awarded $80 million to the estate of a patient in which an HMO would not pay for a bone marrow transplant the MCO judged experimental. The patient received the transplant (paid for by the facility where it was performed) but subsequently died of cancer.[21]

The emergence of specific legislation in several states regarding managed care negligence compounds the liability MCOs already face from general state medical malpractice laws. Texas, for example, enacted legislation that requires MCOs "to exercise ordinary care in making treatment decisions that affect the quality of care" and would "hold the plan accountable for negligent decisions that result in injury." Proposed legislation in Georgia would hold insurers legally responsible for any coverage decision that results in medical care that is below a minimally acceptable level. In both states, the legislation was principally sponsored by the state's medical society.[22]

Another area of liability for quality of care relates back to provider contracting. If a plan member alleges that a network provider gave substandard medical care, or acted in a negligent manner causing the member injury, the MCOs could be brought into the suit for having contracted with that provider. Using the legal theory of "vicarious liability," the injured patient sues the plan for the provider's medical negligence.

> **Exercise: You are the attorney for an MCO that just learned that a fourth malpractice suit has been filed against one of your network physicians and, subsequently, the plan. What could you have done to minimize the possibility of a lawsuit against the plan?**

FRAUD AND ABUSE

What Is Health Care Fraud?

A health care fraud investigation can be initiated because a current or former employee blows the whistle, a customer or competitor makes an allegation, or the insurer uncovers a problem in the process of a routine audit.[23] MCOs may use state and federal laws to prosecute providers or consumers who commit fraud. Statutes also protect purchasers and consumers from fraud that may be perpetrated by MCOs and their affiliated providers. In addition to the traditional fraud, false claims, and anti-kickback statutes, federal prosecutors may also use laws regarding conspiracy, false statements, theft or bribery, or impeding a federal auditor.[24] The U.S. Department of Justice has identified health care fraud against government health programs as a priority for prosecutions in coming years.

The National Health Care Anti-Fraud Association (NHCAA) defines health care fraud as "the intentional deception or misrepresentation that an individual or entity makes when the misrepresentation could result in some unauthorized benefit to the individual, or the entity or to some other third party."[25] Recent studies estimate that of the $1 trillion spent on health care in 1994, approximately $30 million was spent on fraudulent claims.[26]

Fraud in traditional health insurance programs usually involves providers submitting invoices or falsifying records to document services and supplies that were not actually provided to patients. Fraudulent schemes also have included providers referring patients (who did not need subsequent care) to laboratories or other medical facilities in which the provider had a financial interest (a practice known as a "kickback"). Providers have also committed fraud by coding cases as more complicated than they actually were, in order to receive a higher reimbursement. Fraud committed by consumers typically involves a consumer falsely reporting insurance coverage in order to receive care, or filing false medical claims to collect reimbursement.

In managed care, fraud and abuse includes these kinds of examples but also activities that are unique to managed care. For example, a provider may submit false quality reports or patient data in order to conceal poor performance or to boost capitation or bonus payments. A provider may conceal data that would identify underutilization. Providers may attempt to bill patients for charges not paid for by the MCO, a practice that is prohibited by most managed care contracts.[27]

Some MCOs have been accused of abusive practices in marketing and enrollment, such as misrepresenting the quality and availability of services offered by the plan or misrepresenting the provider network endorsements. There have also been allegations of selective marketing to only healthy or high-income people or refusing to contract with providers who treat high-risk patients.[28]

The new business relationships inherent in managed care are challenging the traditional fraud and abuse laws. Two principal laws were established to prevent fraud under fee-for-service medicine.

1. laws that prohibited kickbacks (e.g., mutual arrangements between physicians who refer their respective patients to each other for unneeded consultations and collect a "referral fee")
2. laws that prohibited self-referral (e.g., referring patients for services at a facility, such as a laboratory or surgical center, in which the provider has an ownership interest).

Clearly, these kinds of practices could result in the delivery of many unnecessary services, to the financial gain of the providers involved. However, managed care often involves the integration of providers. Especially in provider-owned MCOs, physicians will be referring their patients to hospitals or other facilities in which they have an ownership or financial interest. Even though the intent and outcome of this integration may be improved efficiency and reduced costs for consumers, traditional "anti-kickback" laws have clearly prohibited the act of referring patients to a facility from which the provider earns revenue. Therefore, the new corporate structures and relationships being formed may place MCOs directly at odds with the traditional anti-fraud statutes.

The Medicare Anti-Kickback Provisions

Incorporated into the Medicare law in 1977, the Medicare anti-kickback provisions made "the knowing and willful solicitation, receipt, offer or payment of remuneration [by health care providers] in return for referrals illegal."[29] The courts broadly interpreted this provision to cover any financial motivation that might affect physician referrals, and to apply even if the services were necessary. Thus, any business relationship among providers designed to ensure a flow of Medicare patients, even if medically necessary and appropriate, could be construed as violating this law.[30]

The Stark Amendment and OBRA 1993

The self-referral prohibition was expanded in 1992 by the Stark Amendment and again in 1993 as part of that year's Omnibus Budget Reconciliation Act (OBRA). Stark prohibits physicians from referring patients to a clinical laboratory in which the provider has an ownership or investment interest or has a compensation arrangement of virtually any type. OBRA 1993 significantly broadened the self-referral prohibition to include referrals to physical and occupational therapy, radiology, and other diagnostic services, durable medical equipment and prosthetic device suppliers, home health services, outpatient pharmaceuticals, and in- and outpatient hospital services.[31]

Safe Harbors

Recognizing that the courts had interpreted the intent of the anti-kickback legislation too restrictively (for example, by ruling out business relationships that could be beneficial), Congress authorized the Department of Health and Human Services (DHHS) to identify appropriate conduct that should be granted exceptions to the law. These exceptions, which protect providers from prosecution, are known as "safe harbors." Examples of safe harbors include personal services and employment contracts (e.g., an employed emergency room physician admits patients to the hospital that employs him or her) and certain managed care arrangements.[32]

False Claims Act

The False Claims Act was enacted in 1863 to permit the government to initiate an investigation of civil or criminal fraud against contractors and others who receive or use government funds. The Act also contains a unique provision called "Qui Tam" (meaning "one who sues for the King as well as for himself") that allows private citizens to file a lawsuit on behalf of the U.S. government and share in any money recovered.

The Qui Tam provision was designed to encourage current or former employees (i.e., "whistle blowers") to identify fraudulent acts of employers by offering employees a share of the money recovered. Although the law was originally intended for military contractors, many actions are being filed in the Medicare program, recovering millions of dollars that had been fraudulently paid to providers.

Health Insurance Portability and Accountability Act

Acknowledging that the fraud and abuse laws needed to better reflect the changing health care system, Congress amended the anti-kickback provisions in 1996 through the Health Insurance Portability and Accountability Act (HIPAA), also known as the Kennedy-Kassebaum Act. HIPAA modified existing fraud and abuse laws in three important ways.

1. It provides a broad exception from anti-kickback provisions for arrangements in which providers assume a significant financial risk for their treatment decisions. For example, if part of a PCP's withhold payment is determined by the number or type of referrals to specialists, then that physician is assuming financial risk for making the referral. Providers could refer to other affiliated providers and facilities without violating the anti-kickback provisions.
2. It requires the Health Care Financing Administration (HCFA) to give advisory opinions on specific arrangements providers intend to make, allowing providers to obtain governmental approval on their arrangements in advance and not be prosecuted later. This allows a case-by-case application of the law to evolving managed care relationships.
3. It requires the HCFA to establish a formal process by which further safe harbors can be developed. Recommendations for new and revised safe harbors will be solicited by HCFA. Recommendations not implemented by HCFA must be reported and justified to Congress annually.[33]

CONCLUSION

Spurred by consumer and provider concerns about the perceived restrictions of MCOs, state and federal governments are increasing their regulation of MCO activities, and courts are weighing in with critical decisions. This expanded judicial and regulatory oversight of MCOs will have enormous implications for how MCOs design and sell products, contract with providers, monitor health care use, deliver specialty services, and establish medical practice guidelines, for example. As MCOs grow in size and complexity, such legal involvement is sure to increase. Additionally, if MCOs fail to deliver on their promise of delivering cost-effective, quality health coverage, consumers and purchasers may lose patience with private-sector solutions and encourage greater government involvement, as we are starting to see in some instances. While government has a legitimate interest in protecting consumers from detrimental corporate practices and ensuring the existence of a fair marketplace, there is a very real possibility that strict regulation could stifle innovations in the delivery and improvement of health care.

DISCUSSION QUESTIONS

1. Explain the significance of the McCarren-Ferguson Act and ERISA in relation to state regulation of MCOs.
2. What is meant by "the ERISA vacuum"?
3. Can states require or prohibit employers from purchasing managed care plans for their employees? Why or why not?
4. Why has the advent of managed care changed the role of state health insurance regulators?
5. Give three examples of a benefit mandate, and explain why purchasers and MCOs object to them.
6. Discuss the impact of AWP laws on a managed care plan.
7. What is the potential conflict between the current trend in health care toward mergers, and the restrictions imposed in anti-trust laws?
8. What agency is responsible for investigating activities for violations of the anti-trust laws, and what has been that agency's response to managed care?

9. Provide an example of an activity an MCO may undertake that could expose it to lawsuits.
10. Give three examples of provider fraud. Are these examples applicable to insurance plans, to managed care plans, or to both?

REFERENCES

1. W. Sage, "Health Law 2000: The Legal System and the Changing Health Care Market," *Health Affairs 15*, no. 3 (Fall, 1996): 10.
2. K. Polzer and P. Butler, "Employee Health Plan Protections under ERISA," *Health Affairs 16*, no. 5 (September/October 1997): 93.
3. J. Saue and G. Doogne, "ERISA and Managed Care," in *The Managed Health Care Handbook*, 3d ed., ed. P. Kongstvedt (Gaithersburg, MD: Aspen Publishers, Inc., 1996), 949–950.
4. *McGann v. H&H Music Company*, 946 F.2d 401(5th Cir. 1991), *cert denied sub nom. Greenberg v. H&H Music Company*, 506 U.S. 981 (1992).
5. *New York State Conference of Blue Cross and Blue Shield Plan v. Travelers Insurance Company*, 115 S. Ct. 1671 (1995).
6. Sage, *Health Affairs*, 12.
7. A. Enthoven and S. Singer, "Markets and Collective Action in Regulating Managed Care," *Health Affairs 16*, no. 6 (November/December, 1997): 30.
8. Sage, *Health Affairs*, 12.
9. Saue and Doogne, *The Managed Health Care Handbook*, 947.
10. *The Regulation of Health Plans: A Report from the American Association of Health Plans*, 3 February, 1998, Washington, DC.
11. J. Musser, interviewed by J. Inglehart, "State Regulation of Managed Care: NAIC President Josephine Musser," *Health Affairs 16*, no. 6 (November/December, 1997): 37.
12. Musser, interviewed by Inglehart, *Health Affairs*, 38.
13. T. Riley, "The Role of States in Accountability for Quality," *Health Affairs 16*, no. 3 (May/June, 1997): 42.
14. Vermont Business Roundtable, *Laws and Consequences: An Examination of Certain Economic, Medical and Policy Implications of Mandated Health Care Benefits* (Burlington, VT: January, 1998), 2.
15. Vermont Business Roundtable, *Laws and Consequences: An Examination of Certain Economic, Medical and Policy Implications of Mandated Health Care Benefits*, 3.
16. G. Carneal, "State Regulation of Managed Care," in *The Managed Health Care Handbook*, 3d ed., ed. P. Kongstvedt (Gaithersburg, MD: Aspen Publishers, 1996), 820.
17. Sage, *Health Affairs*, 15.

18. D. Elden and R. Elden, "Trends in Provider Terminations from Managed Care Plans," *Health Care Innovations 7*, no. 4 (July/August, 1997): 5.

19. W. Miller and J. Miller, "IPA Provider Panel Changes: How to Withstand Legal Challenge," *Tips on Managed Care,* June/July, 1997, 7.

20. "Bills in Five States Would Make HMOs Liable in Patient Lawsuits over Quality of Care," *State Health Watch 4*, no. 3 (March, 1997): 1.

21. *Fox v. Health Net* (Ca. Super. Ct., December, 1993).

22. "Bills in Five States Would Make HMOs Liable in Patient Lawsuits over Quality of Care," *State Health Watch*, 8.

23. The Bauman & Rasor Group, Inc., The Qui Tam Information Center (Internet Website located at http://www.quitam.com, February, 1998).

24. E. McDonough, "What Is Qui Tam?" The Qui Tam Information Center (Internet Website located at http://www.quitam.com, February, 1998).

25. M.N. Coppola, "Identifying and Reducing Health Care Fraud in Managed Care," *Group Practice Journal,* March/April, 1997, 46.

26. Coppola, *Group Practice Journal*, 47.

27. G. Imperato and K. Steward, "Managed Care Plans Are Victims, Perpetrators of Fraud and Abuse," *Managed Care Week*, 3 March, 1997, 1.

28. Imperato and Steward, *Managed Care Week*, 1–2.

29. J. Blumstein, "Rationalizing the Fraud and Abuse Statute," *Health Affairs 15*, no. 4 (Winter, 1996): 127. The cited law is 42 U.S.C., sec. 1320a–1327b.

30. Blumstein, *Health Affairs*, 121.

31. "Physician Self-Referral Prohibition Expanded," *Epstein Becker Report on Health Law*, no. 20 (Fall, 1993): 1.

32. T. Stoltzfus Jost and S. Davies, "The Fraud and Abuse Statute: Rationalizing or Rationalization?" *Health Affairs 15*, no. 4 (Winter, 1996): 129.

33. Blumstein, *Health Affairs*, 126.

SUGGESTED READING

Gosfield, A., "Who Is Holding Whom Accountable for Quality?" *Health Affairs 16*, no. 3 (May/June, 1997).

INDEX

Group model, features of, 24
Group record, 77

H

Health care facilities, 29–31
  managed care networks, types of, 30
Health Care Financing Administration
  (HCFA), 103, 163
Health insurance
  origin of, 5–6
  traditional compared to managed care,
  38–42
Health Insurance Portability and
  Accountability Act, 252–253
Health insuring organization, 165
Health Maintenance Organization (HMO)
  Act of 1973, 2, 8, 139, 232–233
Health maintenance organizations (HMOs)
  competition to, 11
  definition of, 2
  group model, 24
  growth of, 9–10
  history of, 6–11, 139–140
  independent physician association
  (IPA), 24
  network model, 24
  staff model, 23
  types of, 2
HEDIS (Health Plan Employer Data and
  Information Set), 208–210
  benchmarking, 143–146
  measures in, 208–209
  origins of, 142–143
  performance categories, 209–210
  purpose of, 136
  revised version, 144–145
Home Owner's Loan Corporation, 4
Hospital capitation, 112
Hospital contracting, 96–98
  contracting checklist, 97
  quality measures as basis of, 98
  sole-source contracting, 99
  and volume of patients, 96

I

Image/message marketing, 53
Incurred but not reported (IBNR) claims, 80–81
Indemnity plans, 139

Independent practice associations (IPAs),
  features of, 24, 29
Information management, 81–82
  definition of, 46
  electronic data interchange, 82
In-network, point-of-service (POS) plans, 36

J

Joint Commission on the Accreditation of
  Health Care Organizations, 213

K

Kaiser Foundation Health Plans, 9
Kaiser Permanente, origins of, 5
Kennedy-Kassebaum Act, 252–253
Kickback, meaning of, 228

L

Labor unions, 138–139, 160–161
  as purchasers, 160–161
Length of stay
  meaning of, 180
  and utilization management, 182
Letter of intent, 95
Liability issues, 245–249
  provider contracting, 246–247
  quality of care, 247–249
Licensure
  of facilities, 241–242
  of health plan, 234–235
Loos, H. Clifford, 3

M

Managed care
  features of, 22
  growth of, 11–14
  health maintenance organizations (HMOs),
  23–24
  and hospitals, 29–31
  independent practice associations
  (IPAs), 29
  managed care organizations (MCOs), 22–24

ABOUT THE AUTHOR

Wendy Knight is a health care consultant with 11 years of experience in managed care operations, health care communications, and health policy. She is President of Knight Communications and Consulting, a firm that develops market and communication strategies for health plans, pharmaceutical companies, physician groups, hospitals, technology firms, trade associations, and other health care clients.

Much of her professional work has focused on educating physicians, consumers, legislators, and others about managed care and related health care issues. This has involved conducting workshops, seminars, and training sessions; and writing books, training manuals, articles, opinion pieces, and advertorials.

Ms. Knight has worked for various managed care organizations in Southern California and Washington, DC, including Aetna, Prudential, NYLCare, where she was responsible for negotiating provider contracts, managing network operations, and training physicians and health plan staff. Most recently, she served as the acting Executive Director of CIGNA Managed Care Network of New England. In addition, she was the Assistant Director of Managed Care for the Health Insurance Association of America, where she developed and implemented the association's managed care communication activities.

Ms. Knight is the editor of *Managed Care Contracting: A Guide for Health Care Professionals*. Her work has appeared in *Group Practice Journal, Healthplan Magazine, Managing Employee Benefits,* and *Newsweek.* She received a BS in Industrial and Labor Relations from Cornell University.